Corporate Excellence
in the Year 2000

CORPORATE EXCELLENCE IN THE YEAR 2000

A FRAMEWORK FOR SUCCESS

LYNDA KING TAYLOR

CENTURY
BUSINESS

First published in the United Kingdom by Century Ltd
Random House, 20 Vauxhall Bridge Road, London SW1V 2SA

Random House Australia (Pty) Limited
20 Alfred Street, Milsons Point, Sydney
New South Wales 2061, Australia

Random House New Zealand Limited
18 Poland Road, Glenfield
Auckland 10, New Zealand

Random House South Africa (Pty) Limited
PO Box 337, Bergvlei, South Africa

Random House UK Limited Reg. No. 954009

Papers used by Random House UK Limited are natural, recyclable products made from
wood grown in sustainable forests. The manufacturing processes conform to the
environmental regulations of the country of origin.

Companies, institutions and other organizations wishing to make bulk purchases
of any business books published by Random House should contact their local
bookstore or Random House direct: The Special Sales Director
Random House, 20 Vauxhall Bridge Road, London SW1V 2SA
Tel 0171 973 9000, Fax 0171 828 6681

ISBN 0 7126 7522 1

Typeset by SX Composing, Rayleigh, Essex
Printed and bound in Great Britain by
Mackays of Chatham plc, Chatham, Kent

Contents

Foreword
by Sir John Harvey-Jones MBE

It is a brave person who writes a book on corporate excellence in the future, but Lynda King Taylor has never lacked courage. The problem is, as we all know, that corporate excellence is all too often an ephemeral concept. Maintaining a standard of excellence depends vitally upon change and relevance to the fast changing environment in which business has to operate. Perhaps understandably, excellence tends to breed belief in the way things are done today, and our relative competitive success against the best that the rest of the world can produce. However, our success today merely sets the benchmark for everyone else. It is not enough to be in front in the marathon race which business represents for two or three laps. The task that we face is continually to set new and ever more taxing standards so that we remain in front.

It is no accident, therefore, that so many of the firms selected by Lynda have suffered traumas, come back from the brink, or even been woken from a sort of 'Sleeping Beauty' situation, to blossom again under new leadership with higher aspirations. The common ground in all these studies is that of the quality of the leadership of the chief executive. It is ultimately the ambition, insight and style of the chief executive which sets the drum beat for the company. No company will be a world leader unless the chief executive has such an aim firmly in his sights. No degree of excellence today will protect an organization from the need continuously to change and improve, not only its products or services but the ways in which these products and services are made to deliver.

Corporate excellence is all encompassing. It is not enough to have superb product design or fantastic distribution. Corporate excellence demands not only that every aspect of the business is of the highest quality but also that every activity is changing and improving faster than the competition. Nor is it enough to judge the competition by that which exists within our own island. Even though we are still surrounded by the sea the days are long gone when our market was isolated from the rest of the world. We may well be the best in Britain today, but rest assured the front runners in Europe, America or the Far East are buckling up even now to test our standards against theirs. Indeed our only defence lies in taking our products or services into their market and forcing them to react to us.

How do we achieve these standards, and having achieved them how do we hold this highly desirable recognition? The keys, as these case studies show, lie in concepts which appear deceptively simple but in reality are extraordinarily difficult to put into practice. First, we have to listen to our customer. In some cases we may well be capable of delivering products or services they don't even know they want (no-one asked for a Walkman, for instance), but unless we meet a need and adapt to what we hear we have no chance at all.

Second, we have to constantly watch the competition, which may well come from anywhere. Different industries, different countries or different technologies may all attack our business and we can only succeed and prosper if we constantly outperform our competitors and search for excellence in every area of activity. Third, and perhaps most difficult of all, we have to set and increase the rate of change. Even the fastest pace will barely meet the changes in technology, knowledge and world economic trends.

Corporate excellence means getting in front and staying in front. The corporate leaders who achieve this are great men and women. I am lucky to know many of those whose firms are featured in this book and Lynda is fortunate in having achieved their collaboration and involvement.

Every one of us can profit by reading these studies and learning from them. Only open minds and an ambition to be the best will enable us to survive in business by the year 2000. Let us hope our country has more than its share.

Acknowledgements

Achieving corporate excellence is a journey and never a destination, as the organizations in my book will testify. Travelling with them has been an honour and I thank all those executives who have shared with me their boardroom theatre, talent, thoughts, tenacity and time.

I am grateful to all of those mentioned in the book, and to their support staff who managed meetings, mechanics and much more to a standard of service which was a delight to this customer and one of which the chief executive can be proud.

There were many who were both instructive and informative, and I would like to acknowledge in particular Sir John Hoskyns, John Garnett CBE, and also Lord Hanson. At a time when James Hanson had lost his dear friend and business partner of some 40 years, Lord White, he still found the time to talk personally with me and discuss the book. Gordon White was the acknowledged architect of the success of Hanson PLC, and as Lord Hanson says a 'bold, brave and utterly charming latter-day buccaneer'. The inclusion of Hanson PLC in this book is a tribute to such a fine man.

I also want to thank Sir John Harvey-Jones MBE whose inspiration has not only been instrumental in my 'Making it Happen', 'Getting it Together' and 'Managing to Survive' but who found the time to read my manuscript, and to write the foreword when he himself was deluged with his own book deadlines. Thank you for being a rare businessman who makes business – and life - exciting. Oh! how I hope the UK will breed more like you for the millennium and beyond.

There are others involved without whom the successful completion of a manuscript does not happen. First, Linda Mantle and Anne and John Matthews were resilient with research rigours and maintained a sense of humour to the end! Also, Jane Holmes who arranged the Notting Hill Gate team at Adia Alfred Marks; Nicola Davies and John Downie worked beyond the call of duty – they were energetic, enormously exceptional and excellent.

Random House, my publisher of long standing, gave, as ever, their encouragement, enthusiasm and experience, and are without doubt the best in the business in reminding this author of her aims and where the apostrophe goes.

I also want to praise the peace offered to me on the Isle of Mull, and to thank Ken McCulloch whose two hotels, One Devonshire Gardens in Glasgow and Malmaison in Edinburgh gave supreme standards of corporate excellence to this author to plan the project.

Finally, to those wonderful residents of the Royal Forest of Dean who offered me sanity and serenity in a digital age; in particular Margaret and Jack. And to my finest friends who reminded me that a day without laughter is a day wasted.

Lynda King Taylor
1995

ADIA HOLDINGS UK LTD

A leading UK employment services provider, owning a range of recruitment companies specializing in specific market sectors.

Parent Company: Adia SA (Swiss-owned), an international personnel services group.

Turnover (1994)	SFR 3.5 billion
Operating profit	SFR 107 million
Profit before tax	SFR 68.6 million
Employees (full-time)	5,500

Simon Grinstead – Chief Executive Officer

Appointed as CEO of Adia UK in 1992. Previous experience includes

CEO	Bromptom Holdings PLC (UK based)
CEO	Inspectorate International Inspection Services Group (Swiss based)
President	T.A.S. (Italy)
Also:	Investment Banker, Strategic Management Consultant and entrepreneur

Companies in the Adia UK Group:

Adia Alfred Marks Recruitment Consultants supplies office, administrative and light industrial staff, with a network of 125 branches covering the UK. Adia Alfred Marks has the highest spontaneous awareness amongst all leading agencies and has been established for 76 years.

Adia Management Services serve major companies in the UK by bringing together tailored recruitment solutions provided by the Adia group of companies.

Jonathan Wren & Company Ltd is the largest established financial recruitment consultancy in the City of London and Bristol and has been operating since 1968.

Taskforce IT PLC specialize in the provision of contract computing staff nationwide.

Lee Hecht Harrison is one of the world's leading outplacement specialists, providing expertise in career transition management, executive one-on-one and group outplacement, career counselling for senior executives and personal development programmes.

Accountants on Call is part of the highly successful accountancy specialist business owned by Adia in North America and now established in the UK.

Adia Alfred Marks
Simon Grinstead, Chief Executive

Ask anyone who frequently walks down a high street in the UK who Alfred Marks are. They will say a recruitment agency for temporary and permanent secretaries. What few will appreciate is that it is part of Adia SA, an international personnel service corporation which provides total business solutions for companies at local, regional and global levels. Adia delivers one consistent, reliable product – people. Whatever the need for quality services, whether in temporary help, permanent placing, consulting, auditing or out-placement, Adia is recognized as supplying the best employees available, selected and trained by local branch staff who understand their customers' needs.

A sea change is occurring in the nature of the contract between employers and employees. Increasingly, flexibility is sought by companies seeking shelter from unstable economic conditions, rapid technological change and shorter product life-cycles. Adia's worldwide CEO, John Bowmer, says this has led to 'the development of the integrated flexible workforce as a permanent and important part of corporate human resources strategy. Given the disruptions and downsizings within large organizations, many employees are now more loyal to their skill than to their employer. Flexible work suits their need for independence, control and skill development, while providing an opportunity to sample the work environment with a number of different employers. We are ideally positioned to ride this wave and help candidates and clients achieve their objectives.'

Adia in the UK owns several different and successful recruitment companies, the largest of which is Adia Alfred Marks. Adia Alfred Marks is seventy-five years old – the oldest recruitment agency in the UK – and it intends to be around for the millennium. If it is going to achieve that goal it must embrace the concept of flexibility, and offer

11

services to its clients which will help them adjust to the rapid changes in the workplace.

Simon Grinstead, chief executive of Adia UK began his career as an entrepreneur, starting four small businesses while still at university. This experience developed his personal strategy, which has always been to create the very best environment within which the individual or team can flourish. He believes that the number of flexible workers in the UK will increase to about 10 per cent from the current 1 per cent, which will then exponentially increase the size of the marketplace within which Alfred Marks operates.

'We are talking about the integrated flexible workforce, and Alfred Marks having to move from being a very reactive recruitment agency to becoming a pro-active, solutions-driven business which serves the bottom line needs of our customers. We are not selling people any more, we are selling productivity. Selling productivity means helping customers with their manpower planning in such a way that they can address changes that happen in the marketplace.'

For Simon Grinstead these changes are driven by numerous pressures. 'There is the international pressure of competitors entering into marketplaces and suddenly becoming a presence. We have seen that in the car industry and many more. There are changes in technology, and some companies leap-frogging others. In the Fortune 500 companies more than 50 per cent that were listed in 1980 are not on the list in 1990, with smaller companies coming through, taking over where the larger companies with the largest resources in the world no longer have any command of the market share. That is what the "nano-second" nineties mean for the customer. Internally, we used to have a product life-cycle turnover time – that is, a concept of an idea moving through to implementation – on average nine months. Now it means bringing what used to be nine months down to nine days, nine days down to nine hours, nine hours down to nine minutes. Being able to react or be pro-active in changing things, much faster than it has ever happened before.'

In the 1980s, in its field, Alfred Marks was the clear leader and had a strong market position. It had leveraged on its reputation and experience and was making money hand over fist. Simon Grinstead says the company was complacent in many respects and when the recession hit at the end of the eighties the company was totally unprepared. 'The people who had worked for Alfred Marks had built up a tradition of keeping people on a long-standing basis. It had been so successful that no expense was spared in any area of the company. The strategy of being on the high street, with the associated high costs of being there, turned out to be a millstone around its neck when the recession dug in. What we are talking about today, and what we are selling to our customers towards 2000, is a hard-learnt lesson about needing to be flexible.'

Alfred Marks certainly was not flexible in the eighties, and had to change radically. The Marks family continued to dominate the business and ran it until about 1981, when Bernard Marks retired. He was the last Marks to manage the business and left it on a sound footing at the time. The company went from strength to strength for the years following, and because it was the market leader, was able to command the highest margins in the market. What transpired after that period was what Simon Grinstead calls the 'nano-second nineties'. 'All the rules of the game changed. Customers became far more discerning in their requests, far more demanding in terms of the service required, far more exacting in their requirements of the staff we provided. The supply and demand relationship changed: the number of orders placed by customers dropped, and the number of people available in the market shot up when we entered recession. The abnormal profits available in the eighties were no longer there.'

Alfred Marks sold out to Adia in 1976/77. Starting in Switzerland in 1957, Adia had grown from a one-man show. It moved next into Belgium and, through an acquisitions strategy, throughout continental Europe. It had grown in the USA, and in the early eighties launched in Japan. Adia was and is an acquisitive company with international ambitions. Today it is operating in thirty countries, and wants to expand quite dramatically in new markets such as China, Taiwan, South America and Eastern Europe.

When recession hit, the key realization was that the Alfred Marks business had to mature in terms of professionalism. Being an agency was not good enough any more. It had to identify what its core competences were, and how it was going to meet and exceed its customers' needs and expectations. Says Simon Grinstead, 'That led to the belief that we would become acknowledged experts in managing our clients' recruitment campaigns. We had to become sophisticated in the assessment, testing, selection, motivation, and to an extent, training, of people, and match that with our clients' requirements. We had to become acknowledged experts in a new area which nobody had ever thought about. If someone is working as a contractor in a company on a set time assignment, where do their loyalties lie, and how do we continuously keep them motivated? For instance, we had to resolve such problems as obtaining a mortgage for those working on contract, which previously had only been given by the banks to full-time employees.'

Simon Grinstead has five templates of strategy, which have always stood him in good stead in thinking through the direction his organization travels. They are very simple. Which products? To which clients? At what price? Through which distribution channels or networks? How do you organize yourself to deliver that?

Take the first one, 'which product?' or in this case 'which service?' 'We were an agency providing, on a fairly *ad hoc* basis, an individual, or group of people, to a client in the hope that they would somehow match, but we were not too particular about the exact matching of the person. Our services have now moved from being an agency to an added value service, where we need to pro-actively understand our clients' needs better, almost better than the clients themselves. What kind of people are they looking for? At what cost? What kind of fit is it? For the future, we need to select people in a much more professional way. We need to know that when we send an individual to the customer we are sending somebody who will be a representative for our business, for our company.'

Simon Grinstead says, 'In the eighties we were providing CVs, now we are providing skills matches. We were providing a body, today we are providing someone who will hit the deck running on our customer's site, and be able to address their productivity. That is the product re-definition we have gone through, the end result being that we are selling not bodies, but productivity. That is producing the service in the first template of our strategy.'

Simon Grinstead's second template is, 'to which clients?' Every company has its way of segmenting customers. Alfred Marks has decided it wants to work with the type of clients who can see it through any future recession.

Alfred Marks has also organized itself for specialization within a client's organization structure. 'If they have an accountancy section, we have accountancy specialists to deliver it to them. If there is an IT section, we have an IT business person for them, someone who specializes exclusively in that. We can service their needs with a higher degree of accuracy than we ever could before when we were purely generalist. It is a move from the traditional and mainstream, to a far more specialist type of business.'

Simon Grinstead believes that is a clear trend. 'It is how we differentiate ourselves from our competitors, because today, many competitors have been extremely successful. A lot were more successful through the recession than Alfred Marks and the Adia UK Group, but we still see many of them carrying out the strategies that were formed in the eighties, and they are just continuing with the same old direction. Today's clients get a far higher added value service from us. We have organized ourselves to work on a partnership basis with our customers, everything from a different sales and account management technique, which was never really a concept in the industry before, through to computer systems which allow us to integrate and communicate with the customer.'

His next three templates address the need for change to maintain a competitive advantage. The fact is, margins have been decreasing in the industry over the past five years. Alfred Marks's challenge is to deliver ever higher quality of service at an ever lower cost. Says Simon Grinstead, 'When I say ever lower cost, that is the cost of the selected level of service we are delivering. We are not "stack 'em high and sell 'em cheap". This is a different level of service, a different strategy. Our prices are under pressure more and more as the integrated flexible workforce concept takes root in the form of contracts, outsourcing, on-site management of the workforce etc. We are placing higher volumes of people, and with higher volumes of people customers want to see price discounts. It is a fact of life that we have to live with a lower price.'

In the 1980s, Alfred Marks was reactive. It used to wait for people to come to its door, or wait for orders to come over the telephone, or visit the customers for orders. According to Simon Grinstead, it never spoke to the customers about addressing their productivity, quality and customer service, the way they worked with their people, how they organized themselves, or how they could benefit from working with a company such as Alfred Marks. 'Today, there is a whole new source of revenue in terms of our managing the recruitment budgets of our clients, which they always used to manage themselves, of outsourcing some of the personnel function, taking care of routine matters, everything from payrolling through to assessing people, interviewing, and removing arduous tasks from our clients in order for them to concentrate on their core business.'

How does Alfred Marks manage to sell the new concept of total

15

people management for clients, when its image is of a company providing temporary secretaries? Simon Grinstead explains: 'In the UK we have encompassed a group-wide strategy, led by Adia as holding company, wherein we keep what we call our bread-and-butter business going while we make the change. Alfred Marks is our bread-and-butter business. When people think about secretaries, secretarial related and office support sector related work, they think Alfred Marks. We want to play to our strengths. We have used the concept of specialist brands operating under the Adia name to provide our new, broader range of services, which includes outplacement and career transition management. It is a specialized division that focuses on not only selling but delivering partnership-based services, such as on-site services, outsource services, a computer specialist business, an accountancy specialist business, financial staff and other specialist businesses in the financial services, industrial and technical sectors. Our clients have told us that is what they want and we have organized ourselves accordingly.'

The Adia International Group has a great advantage in that it owns the second largest outplacement business in the world and the second largest accountancy specialist business in the USA. It is able, therefore, to draw on a worldwide expertise on all fronts, including technological applications to the industry, which many of its competitors lack. 'From that perspective we are able to differentiate ourselves and show we have moved from the eighties into the nineties as a modern and forward-looking company – a company which delivers solutions to a customer, even over-delivers. Our task is to take care of problems which historically the client was burdened with. That is our mission.'

To introduce these new services, Alfred Marks persuaded long-standing clients to agree to pilot something with it on a small basis, so they could see how it would work, get a feel for it, and progress from there. To Simon Grinstead it is actually breaking the mould of the traditional way of working with the workforce and coming up with that solution. 'Effectively , we set up an on-site office. We also have the branch network in the surrounding towns, and our strength is the ability to recruit people, to test and select them, exclusively for the client. Take for example, a food manufacturer. Using assessment techniques which are applicable to the work that needs to be done within the factory, we manage the staff who work in three eight-hour shifts a day, twenty-four hours a day, seven days a week. If we don't supply the people, the factory comes to a standstill. This is what we do now – total people presentation and management, to take the pressure off the client's managers so they can focus on their core competences, which is the production management and financial management of the food business.'

Into the early 1990s the recruitment industry was not interested in investing in technology to any great extent. Today, successful companies are spending anything from 2 to 5 per cent of sales on technology, because increasingly that is how they can differentiate themselves and gain cost advantages. What Alfred Marks used to spend money on was high street property. Says Simon Grinstead, 'People in our industry cannot afford to be on the high street any more because of the cost of premises. IT allows you to provide more and more remote recruitment services, to think more of hub-and-spoke kind of networks. The hub would be in a much cheaper office location with more space and a lot more administrative services. At the end of the spokes would be recruitment centres which could be anything from a kiosk in a shopping centre, through to mobile booths set in the suburbs where people live, where electronic application services would allow someone to sign up, or view the jobs that are available.'

The fourth strategy template is distribution. Says Simon Grinstead, 'Off high street, with much lower property costs, we have more money to spend on marketing, which means we can have a more targeted recruitment campaign to find the people in an area that clients need. My view towards 2000 is that we are finding new ways of delivering our service at an ever lower cost. The highest cost in our business after people is property. We must arrange our network to be ready for the next recession, hence our ideas such as hub–and–spoke, remote recruitment techniques using technological applications. Everything to provide a customer with much richer information about the candidates in a much shorter time.'

For a customer calling Alfred Marks with an immediate vacancy to fill, it used to take from two to three weeks to organize a set of interviews. Today Adia Alfred Marks intends to deliver that one hour later. 'We are even looking at three-dimensional presentation, a virtual reality system, where a client can see how the applicants present themselves. They see the applicant answering the ten most-asked questions in an interview, making the elimination process much faster. We can take a quantum leap via technology to improve the time and richness of information. That is going to become the entry ticket into the future, a prerequisite just to compete in the industry.'

In Simon Grinstead's industry, it is people that count from A to Z. 'It is that ability to work with people, to lead and motivate people, that counts. It is not an industry like investment banking in the late eighties, where the average age was twenty-seven, and anybody who moved up into the second half of their thirties was out of it. Our industry can still appeal to anybody who understands that it is a people-centred business and works on that basis.'

The recruitment industry has been as tough as any other in terms of reorganizing and changing the way it proceeds. It is far more customer driven. 'The organizational structure, the way people were organized in offices, which was the interface, the cutting edge of working with our clients, has moved to a team-based approach. Many clients used to say it was a greed-driven industry, it was very individualistic. People were driven by commission. Today, it is more a team of people working in an office who need to deliver customer service, and if somebody is out of the office it is not good enough any more to say to a client, "Sorry, we don't know anything about you, this person will have to call you when they come back." Everybody has to be focused and work around the client. That is a notable change.'

Today, Alfred Marks organizes itself according to three different categories of customers. 'The first one is the customer who uses us on a traditional contingency basis,' says Simon Grinstead. 'That would be an *ad hoc* user. They would use us for probably up to twelve weeks in a year for holiday relief and absences through sickness, etc. They would be the smaller customer. Then, there are those customers who would use us on a fifty-two weeks a year basis. They would use us continuously, but they would still be doing so on a contingency basis. They would be a medium-sized company. The third category would be the large user, who also uses us fifty-two weeks a year, but they are spending a large amount of money, sufficient to warrant having account management concepts and building in quality programmes to make sure our company matches their company's quality programmes. Theirs is a more planned and strategic use of flexible labour.'

Simon Grinstead believes the medium-sized companies, and the larger ones, could outsource many of their personnel functions, starting from the recruitment end, where they use agencies because they are not sure what to do internally, maybe due to the status of the job or the technicalities in a job specification. 'Towards 2000 I see a new step coming in between the way the clients address their recruitment needs and our industry. That step is a virtual organization structure. Step 1 is, if you have a vacancy you look internally first, to see if you have someone you could use to fill that role. Step 2 is that you then call one of the recruitment services. Now many people still see the recruitment industry as a multiple shopping industry, that is, if they give the business to only one agency they are not sure that the agency could actually source the right person, so they give it to three, four or even five agencies. It means that agencies are in competition, often on price, or it is first come, first served, whoever can get there quicker. That leads to all sorts of tricky salesmanship situations. In the new step, which fits between 1 and 2, I see the client going to their virtual organization, the people in that area who have maybe worked for them before, who already understand their business, who have already gone through their training courses, who could be considered associates of their company and who may be available. If you build up a model like this over several years, you will have a much larger organization to draw on, not only in your local area, but also regionally and nationally. You can then configure a team of people according to the needs of the company as you go forward, you can contract and expand, according to the needs of the business.'

Simon Grinstead is suggesting into the millennium such people could be contracted to a company and not be on a permanent payroll. 'The key point is that the organization has created a memory of people and built up a database of human resources that fit with their organization. They can draw on that resource as a second step before they approach their traditional agencies. I see our company being able to manage that virtual organization for them. To provide them with that corporate memory that can lead to their being far more efficient in the way they deal with their manpower and human resource issues. The type of customer we see must embrace these changes and move away from traditional management.'

This concept is as applicable to the larger company as to a small or medium-sized business, if not more so. 'In many cases,' says Simon Grinstead, 'there is the argument of scale, that small can be beautiful. Small is beautiful, even within large corporations, where there are specialist departments, and business units that have specialist recruitment needs. Often people find it difficult to source technicians or a particular person with the expertise they require. Building up this memory bank over years helps solve that problem as it originates, helps to configure new teams in new areas. However, with larger companies working in partnership with a company such as ours, which embraces the whole employment services life cycle – from when somebody enters his career through to when they are placed – the concept of on-site human resource services is just growing like wildfire, particularly in the United States.'

Adia's own turnover in the US rose by 2,400 per cent between 1991 and 1994. The total service concept is on a rising curve, and clients love it for it is really producing what they want.

'Take, for instance, a client company with 2,000 employees on one site. The new concept is to have a career centre which is managed by an independent company who can deal with people on an independent basis, and which is therefore non-threatening. We would put together a group in this career centre who would specialize in outplacement for people whose roles in the client company are being changed and who are no longer specifically needed right then and there. We would be a job centre which helps these people find jobs, an assessment centre which helps people entering or leaving the company, and provide induction and other forms of training which might be applicable to the client company. Everything happens in the career centre which is managed by us, the experts, and is a symbiotic relationship, because the client company provides our employment services with a well-trained, good stock of people, who we can then place out to other customers. It makes good sense for us, because our recruitment costs are lowered, and we have a ready source of people. It also makes good sense to our other clients who will benefit from these well-qualified people. It is an advantageous situation for everyone, and the service is delivered at far lower cost because it is on-site. From our perspective, it means we can put our money into the added value end and make investments to keep moving ahead of the game. Those are the exciting ways in which we can work with our large customers, particularly towards the millennium.'

Within its own industry Adia UK's internal recruitment policies have gone through a revolution. It is raising the concept of the employment services industry providing expert-led, tailored consultancy. 'We used to recruit people internally to deliver our service, who came from a generalist background. Today, we are employing people with personnel management experience, people with qualifications, who are working with both us and the customers, reviewing the customers' human resource base, assessing their manpower plan, and from that expert-led approach, coming up with solutions. This is becoming more and more a prerequisite of the more sophisticated buyer of employment services and the smaller companies who do not have the human resource expertise can benefit as well. This certainly is the trend. In ten years' time this industry will require a minimum entry level in order to provide the consultancy necessary and to be expert-led, because otherwise the industry will not be able to address the customers' productivity. That is the whole key – to address their bottom line through better human resource management.'

Adia UK is building sector specialisms which will give it deeper insights into why some companies are more successful than others. 'That is why today our sales and account managers are trained in total quality management, business process re-engineering, and a very high level of financial analysis, in order for them to look at a company's organization structure and say, "Hey, we know that if you do it like this, you will gain higher productivity levels." They understand the customer's business and how the services could be delivered. One of the advantages of consultants is they have a breadth of knowledge in the industry and know who the winners are and how they do it. They work in many different companies, often in the same industry. Our industry will have the same attributes in the future, specializing in human resources.'

The whole drive towards professionalism is one which Grinstead's industry is embracing. 'Our federation, the Federation of Recruitment and Employment Services [FRES], has really geared up over the past five years. FRES is the legitimate voice of the recruitment industry, playing a vital role in guiding, advising and monitoring us – increasingly important now that the government licensing of agencies has been scrapped. With this de-licensing, the industry is open to self-regulation, and members of the industry that sign up with FRES agree to a code of conduct and standards of service. We are driving for ever higher professionalism.

'It is not just the relationship-driven aspects that count, it is also the skills we provide to our customers, through to very high standards of health and safety. We certainly are health and safety consultants. If we are sending people to work on an industrial site, whether as contractors or temps, we have to be sure they will be safe in all respects. We give them information and training. Before we are prepared to work with clients, we check they have the same attitude to health and safety. We drive for health and safety throughout the organization. The Adia Group throughout the world follows the same policy. We are moving into countries in the Far East, Southeast Asia etc., where the health and safety records are often not as good as in the UK, and our companies are driving for change in health and safety provisions. It is almost an international mission of ours into the millennium, to bring corporate responsibility in the health and safety area to a higher level than it has been before.

Simon Grinstead believes the management of change has been made much easier because the industry went through turbulent trouble in the recession. 'It has helped tremendously to focus on change and on listening to clients' needs. In the eighties the industry did not really listen to the clients, it worked in the way that it had always done, and because the marketplace was so buoyant one did not need to listen. We have all listened far more, and it is becoming more and more appreciated. For the future, the challenge is to keep the momentum of that change going. It will take a lot of leadership. Whereas in recessionary times, people got together to decide which way to proceed because they were under threat, now it will require much stronger leadership – sometimes authoritarian, sometimes visionary leaders, who are going to go forth.'

Simon Grinstead feels that both styles of leadership are useful. 'You do get different styles of management which are more appropriate to different cycles in the market. It might mean that the manager has to realize where his strengths and weaknesses lie. Nowadays, leaders need to be more chameleon-like and take on different management styles according to circumstances. More and more we are working in a team, and on a project basis, which has delivered a higher level of productivity in many areas. Being the catalyst, the consultant, the coach, is an important part of managing today.

'What I would like to see by the year 2005, is that our industry is professional and equivalent to the best of the auditing and consulting world – where it can be seen with that level of respect, because it provides an added value service. That is my dream. Not to be seen as just another high-street shop, as it was in the eighties. We are in the middle of that transition now, and to get us to that point is going to take the strong-headed leadership of people who will force through the changes. Our industry has still more "pain" to go through before we get the gain!'

The year 1992 was the worst year for this industry in living memory. About 30 per cent of Alfred Marks's competitors went under, mostly the smaller ones. But then Simon Grinstead saw signs of better things ahead. 'I had a lot of faith that things were going to come right. In the years since 1992 we, as an organization, have doubled our income and increased our return on sales quite dramatically. There are still gloom and doom merchants who say we have to prepare for the next recession, but I actually believe that as a whole we are moving into a golden period of a much longer sustained business growth cycle, what Sir Michael Angus of Whitbread in your book refers to as an industrial renaissance. I believe our industry, in particular, is moving into a golden period as well, when our services will be used, accepted and integrated with our customers to a much greater extent. That belief has led me to lay out a strategy for our company which takes us into the next millennium.'

Market research has shown that many people on the opposite side of the fence from the client companies have had disappointing experiences at the hands of the recruitment industry when registering as job candidates. Simon Grinstead is aware of this and is striving towards 2000 to ensure that Adia delivers a much better service experience to candidates. 'We take the view that there are three parties who should be made to feel they are our valued customers – our candidates, our clients and our own staff. It is a great source of pride to me that our Alfred Marks brand has the highest name-awareness in the recruitment industry amongst both employers and applicants. I intend to do everything in my power to maintain that position as the number one, and to be at the absolute forefront of the industry.'

A millennium wish? The reason Simon Grinstead is passionate about his industry is that he sees, in the longer run, that he can play a far greater role in helping young people integrate into careers. 'It is terribly important if you look at key problems today. Some people would cite as key problems a lack of direction during their younger days. I would like to think our industry could play a greater role in helping the transition and integration of the younger people into careers and society. It is vital to set up links with the educational services to advise them on what employers want from new school leavers or college leavers.

'I also think the role of women is vital and we should be addressing as a social issue the integration of women into fulfilment and satisfaction through a career, especially the mother who wishes to return to work.'

Simon Grinstead also feels we must be concerned about those people at the more mature end of the spectrum. 'I believe people want to contribute more, yet society is cutting them off earlier and earlier today. Our industry can play a role in helping those more mature people to find satisfaction through work, jobs and careers. That is the intellectual attraction to our industry. We may not think about it like that yet, but more and more, to be successful, we must provide a service not only for clients who buy our services, but for the people who come to us for help, for our applicants, our temps, and candidates. Formerly, when they registered with us, we used to say "Don't contact us, we'll contact you." Often we didn't even write back to them. That is starting to change. They are our clients too, and we must give customer satisfaction to them. The emphasis has to be shared between both the buying client and the people we place in work. If I have helped at all, I hope I have helped to focus attention in that direction.'

For those members of society whose careers are poorly integrated, Simon Grinstead believes Alfred Marks can help make their entry into work smoother in the future, which means more people can gain satisfaction through careers. 'My life has been enriched and nourished by my career, and I have gained a tremendous amount of satisfaction out of it. For people who don't have those opportunities, for whatever reason, our company can play a social role as well. That could be to the benefit of all, a win–win for everyone!'

ASDA GROUP PLC

Turnover (1994–1995)	£5,285.3 million
Operating Profit	£251.1 million
Profit before tax	£257.2 million
Total fixed assets	£2,020.1 million
(inc. investments and share ownership plan)	
Employees	65,000

Leading UK superstore retailer, serving over 5 million customers each week, with sales performance from existing stores, outstripping the industry since 1992.

Archie J Norman – Chief Executive

Appointed as Chief Executive in November 1991.

Other appointments:
  Non-Executive Director of Railtrack plc.
  Former Director of British Rail.
  Former Finance Director of Kingfisher plc.
  Member of the DTI Deregulation Taskforce and Anglo–German Deregulation Taskforce.

ASDA Stores Ltd

Operates 203 stores in the UK, with 6 further stores under construction and due to open during 1995, two of which will replace existing stores.

ASDA was founded in 1965 and pioneered the development of superstores in the UK. Initial success came through providing deeply discounted prices on branded goods through large, single-level superstores with adjacent, free, surface-level parking.

Following a financial crisis in 1991, the business returned to its value-for-money heritage under a new management team led by Archie Norman.

ASDA Group PLC
Archie Norman, Chief Executive

When Archie Norman arrived at ASDA, it had been through six months with little or no leadership, was running out of cash, had been under-performing in the industry for five years, had nearly 2,000 people in headquarters, 65,000 in the country, owned a number of other failing businesses, and was generally regarded to be a shipwreck. In fact it was sinking fast – a sad state of affairs for an organization that pioneered the move to edge-of-town, one-stop family shopping with trouble-free parking and large superstores offering a wide range of customer services from in-store restaurants to cash-point machines.

In that grave situation Archie Norman had no option but to be tough. 'You have to do what is required. It is much easier to be tough in a situation where the ship is sinking, because you know if you are not ruthless in solving the problems you won't be a business for much longer. When I arrived, in my first half hour I said to all the management together: "Look, no change is not an option." I said we had to be lower cost and better value, we had to be radical in what we did, that there would be changes in management but there was room on board for anybody who could pull on an oar. As you cannot recruit people anyway in that situation, it is best to motivate the ones you've got. You do rely on them, depend on them.'

ASDA re-established a direction, embarked on a programme of corporate renewal and changed large parts of the organization. It has obviously reduced its costs. It has stripped down and sold off or closed all the other businesses, except for its property developing arm. It has repaid its debt, in the space of three years. Last year ASDA reinforced its survival and sailed into a sound future with a 35 per cent jump to £246 million in underlying pre-tax profits, declaring it

27

had overtaken Safeway to become the UK's third largest supermarket chain. Archie Norman has announced a programme to the millennium which will see ASDA aggressively attacking fresh food and non-food areas, plus an undertaking to make ASDA's George range of clothing into the UK's second largest mass-marketed clothes brand.

ASDA was formed by a group of northern dairy farmers some three decades ago, and by chance developed the first native food superstore in Britain. By 1984 it was operating some sixty stores very successfully and moving south. By 1987 the business had a billion pounds in cash and was still expanding, had twenty-one years unbroken growth in earnings per share of profit, and very strong earnings generation.

By 1991 it was a billion pounds in debt and profits were in decline. The core business had diversified unsuccessfully into a number of different businesses, losing sight of its role in the marketplace. ASDA had moved from adolescence towards senility as an organization in a very short period of time, adding enormous overheads and delusions of corporate grandeur with layers of management without ever really delivering the quality. By mid-1991 this had developed into not just an organizational crisis but a cash crisis. Archie Norman's predecessors, the chief executive and chairman, both departed after the shareholders complained. The new non-executive chairman, Patrick Gillam from BP, came in just in time to find the business running on to the rocks of receivership. In consequence, ASDA announced in September 1991 an emergency rights issue to raise £350m, and in order to support the rights issue they needed, amongst everything else, a new chief executive. Archie Norman agreed to join the company from Kingfisher, charged with turning ASDA into what chairman Patrick Gillam said must be 'a leaner, more responsive business, well-equipped to exploit the challenging market conditions' of the nineties.

All corporate failure of that magnitude stems from organization weakness and most organizational weakness stems from lack of leadership, or misguided leadership. ASDA was no exception. Says Archie Norman, 'The organization was not able to perform because it had lost sight of its customers, the northern heritage, the value for money which is what ASDA stands for. There were too many layers of management – one had the feeling decisions cascaded down their own drainpipes.' ASDA was building bigger and bigger and more heavily designed stores to try and compete with Sainsbury's and Tesco – endeavouring to compete on designs and expenditure and not competing by retailing. In Archie Norman's book the results were very poor, the underlying results were becoming disastrous, and the accounting was aggressive because every year ASDA was under pressure to make more money. In order to revive and recover the profit that had failed to arise, the margins were put up every year, a malignancy in retailing resulting in worse value for money, and fewer customers.

'Our strategy now is to reduce our margins,' says Archie Norman. 'As more and more food capacity is being established in a stagnant market, where there is no real demand for the increased output, it is inevitable that margins will become depressed. There's no point in sitting around saying, we hope the margins will grow, because they won't. Our overall policy is to reduce the margin, because we believe by doing that first, we will be ahead of the market. On balance, reducing the margin offers better value because we're passing the value on to the customers. Our policy is to provide better value so that we have more customers, to increase the sales and reduce the cost ratios. That's intrinsic to our way of competing.' It obviously makes sense – ASDA has recruited more than a million extra customers in the last couple of years to take their total over five million.

ASDA's philosophy has been that success depends on growing sales in the stores it already has. 'It is no achievement to spend money on new stores,' says Archie Norman, 'anybody can do that, if they have the money. The achievement is to grow the business you have. On average, British superstore retailing has not been successful for three years, despite the fact we've got some magnificent companies. That's because the whole industry has been very slow to wake up to the change in what is happening. The industry in general is still caught in the 1980s syndrome of growing the margin, spending more and more money every year on new stores, building things that cannot really be afforded, the superstore palaces we see. That is not our philosophy. Our philosophy is to grow the business we have.'

Its real measure for success is if it can make a store that has been trading for a while, trade even better and attract more customers. Archie Norman wants existing stores to 'punch their weight'. These are on average 60 per cent bigger than Tesco's and Sainsbury's and should, as such, enjoy advantages in non-food areas – entertainment, clothing and gardening. Its competitors are squeezed to fit these ranges into their floor space.

With its stronger balance sheet, ASDA is interested in replacing some of the failed superstores it had, and in finding opportunities to build new ones on a cost effective basis. It certainly can afford it, 'But we are parsimonious with our money,' reminds Archie Norman, 'it is part of our attitude. Where there is a good opportunity we will take it, but our traditional roots are in the North, the North Midlands, Lancashire, Yorkshire, the North-east, and Scotland – where we're largest.'

He is not a trendy manager. This business paid a high price for the loss of customer focus, and it is not a mistake that will recur under his management. 'Our philosophy is to create a company which is value for money, which is action oriented and very high on communications. With good communication you create a stronger awareness, better motivation and, ultimately, better customer service. We believe all good communication happens verbally. Basically, 90 per cent of real communication is word of mouth, and all the newsletters, posters and manuals add up to a row of beans compared to what the first line manager says. That is why it is important for us to have what is fashionably called a flatter structure. Reduce the number of layers you get between me and the check-out operator, because each layer is another diffusion of communication.'

Archie Norman also expects people to work across the business. 'We like to employ business people, not functional specialists. In retailing you want to have a totally integrated approach to management. And one way of doing that is to have fewer layers, because with fewer layers you tend to get less functional specialists. For instance, we have four executive directors and a management board of thirteen. We expect most management board members to have two or three different portfolios they are working on. At the moment I have about twenty direct reports. Obviously the whole business reports to me or the chief executive, but I also act as marketing director and HR director. Someone else looks after building construction, renewal, design, our Dales business, and retail operations. That is the way we like to work. In the stores, we want to have a team of people who are close to their colleagues and are good at communicating. We don't want to have a hierarchy.'

Getting rid of layers and hierarchy, is all part of the attempt to get ASDA people involved and motivated about what they do. The ASDA philosophy is that all staff must want to work hard and feel good about ASDA. This attitude will reflect on customer service. 'It is very important every member of the firm feels they are involved in what they are doing,' says Archie Norman, 'and you cannot have that if you have those stultifying layers of hierarchy. Retail businesses are often a bit military. They have to be to some extent because they are very fast moving but you don't need to be hierarchical in order to be action-oriented and decision-oriented. You can be involving. That's our belief.' As such, ASDA removes not just hierarchy, but also symbols of hierarchy. Visit head office in Leeds and you will see it is genuinely open plan. Too often in 'open' organizations you find the junior staff have open plan but the élite sit in offices. Not at ASDA! Everyone is equal. The directors wear clothes from the George range on Fridays, don't have any dedicated car parking, and try to avoid status-oriented titles. Archie Norman believes titles should say what people do, not what they are or what their rank is.

Of the top 200 people now in the organization about 30 per cent were with the company prior to the 1991 overhaul, including one member of the group board, and three out of thirteen on the management board. It is important to avoid 'new and old' syndrome when discussing ASDA. As Archie Norman explains, 'One of the features about ASDA is that we have people who are very dedicated to it. They have been very loyal to the business, are totally committed, and we depend on them a great deal for the way forward. We had to make a lot of changes, obviously, but we are through that with a great team now.' He also has some powerful non-executive directors which is important to him in the sense that he is at ASDA because the shareholders and non-executives hired him. 'The shareholders suffered the previous experience, loss of money and destruction of wealth. They were prepared to see the earlier management go and someone like me come, and I came here to do a job for them. Obviously, the shareholders are the ultimate stake holder, because whilst there are other people who have an interest in the business and care about it a lot, I do think that given the history of this company, it is very important to put in place some reassurance and protection for people who saw a lot of their money disappear down the plughole. It's right, therefore, we should have some strong non-executives, to avoid a recurrence of the previous situation.'

In Archie Norman's experience, very few boards really work. 'Lots of them work formally, but very few of them actually contribute value to the business. One reason is that most boards consist of a litany of a company's history – someone who has been around for years and retired, the semi-retired chairman, somebody who was involved in financing the company, somebody whose company was bought – such a gathering is not formed to be a working boardroom. They reflect what has already happened, and various vested interests, so when it comes to board meetings they don't actually *work*.'

What ASDA has been able to do is recruit a complete new team of non-executives and by doing so has been able to create a team which is right for the company, who are able to contribute to it, and who, when they meet together, work well together. 'I think the executive directors generally look forward to board days!' says Archie Norman. 'We are given the chance to talk about things we are doing, about the problems, and the non-executives have the chance to say, "Well from my experience this, that and the other," or "You know, I've got an idea you might like to think about." That has worked well.'

Many organizations in this book have formed ways of keeping in touch with their customers and ASDA is no different. Fundamentally, 'listening groups', 'customer clinics', 'focus groups' and market research of any kind are secondary to the way people actually behave. Most importantly, ASDA has managers who are constantly in the stores, and visible. They talk to customers, talk about their products, see how the store layout works. They understand the business and they are close to it. As Archie Norman puts it, 'The management and the traders here are close to the people who are close to the business. I can never be as close to my customers as the store manager is, he is there every day. We employ 65,000 people and the vast majority of them work in the stores with the customers. What's more, our focus in life is on ordinary working people and their families who demand value, and the people who work for us are just like their customers. There is a perfect fit.

He explains that ASDA's market base focus is on the type of individuals who work with ASDA, working people and their families. 'Our people are inevitably fairly budget-constrained, because the supermarket industry does not pay enormous amounts of money. A lot of them are women who are the second bread-earner in the family, so by definition they work to supplement the family income. The point I'm making is that if you are close to them, then you are close to your customers. If you give your staff involvement and avenues to contribute to the running of the business, you will know what is going on with the customers. Everything we do organizationally is part of the jigsaw, and a jigsaw with one piece missing isn't acceptable. So it is very important to us to be a *listening* organization, not just because it is the top management priority to keep in touch with customers, but also because, unless you give your people involvement, appreciation and recognition, they won't be motivated to achieve what we want them to achieve. Unmotivated, they will not feel good about the company and they will not deliver a proper customer service, essential towards 2000.'

The 'ASDA way of working' (AWW) is the definition of how it wants people (the internal customer) to behave towards each other. It is ASDA culture, with staff known as 'colleagues'. 'AWW is really about how we want management and colleagues to interact with each other,' says Archie Norman. 'It is about our style of leadership. My object here is to have discipline and motivation simultaneously. That is why we need to have a management style which is visible, leadership orientated, capable of decision-making and exacting in standards, yet, at the same time, is involving, listening, respectful of people and rewarding in the way we work.'

The attitudes within ASDA used to be very formal, authoritarian, heavy, hierarchical and deadly dull. All the managers sat in offices and the staff, which they were then called, did all the work. Admits Archie Norman, 'There was a very strong fear culture – basically, if you did not perform, you were out; a mistake, you were out. That was the way it worked. Lots of retail businesses run very successfully like that and especially the ones with good systems, good tradition, who know exactly what they want to achieve. I recognize there are different role models, but for us we do not have particularly good systems, and we try a rather more decentralized business anyway, so it is much more important to create a management like this which is involving and motivating.'

One of the things Archie Norman believes very strongly is that all successful customer service emanates from a desire to sell, and this will only ever be delivered if you work first on improvement in attitudes and morale. 'It is not something you can ever train in. We do relatively little direct training on customer service. I don't really believe in it. We strongly believe all our colleagues benefit from knowing more about their business and contributing to sales.' He is right to assert this. Selling is the most measurable, instantly rewarding and challenging activity in retailing. 'Selling is a universal responsibility,' he says. 'Everybody here is expected to be part of the sales effort. It doesn't matter where you work in the business. Knowing what the sales are, contributing to the sales, is vital. I expect everybody in the organization to be briefed on Monday on the previous week's sales, on this week's sales, because that's the way we ensure all our colleagues are in the picture and involved in what we are doing.'

At ASDA there are six core values, written down everywhere. Archie Norman states them:

- Selling is a universal responsibility.
- Colleagues are our staff and staff are our colleagues. In other words, everybody is part of the same organization and there is no distinction. They are all equal. Everybody is equally valued.
- What we sell will be better value because we are totally committed to value, that is part of the ethic.
- Through selling we will deliver legendary (for want of a better word) customer service because customer service in our business emanates from the desire to sell.

    In a business like ours, selling is tangible. You can relate it to sending people away happy with what they have spent, see the figures. That is really easy to relate to. Whereas ephemeral ideas, like better-served customers, are more difficult to relate to, more difficult to measure. With us you can measure service.
- We hate waste of any kind, because waste is such a big cost in our business. If you deliver better value then you have to lower cost. Therefore, waste is a corrupting influence on the business, it corrupts attitude. However small it is, you must have an attitude which supports the delivery of value.
- Everyone's responsibility is to improve the business. In other words, what we say to people is your role is not just to be finance director or personnel manager. Your role is to improve the business and take on an ownership attitude.

There exists a humility within ASDA – which is a rare commodity in management. Archie Norman recognizes that he is not going to ingrain these six core values into the lives of 65,000 people. Two-thirds of ASDA people are part-time, 75 per cent are women and many of them bring up families. So ASDA realizes it is probably somewhere around 135th on their list of priorities in life. In other words, it is not that ASDA is not important to all its staff, but one has got to recognize that the family, schools, the husband or wife, the pub, television, and so on, are very much more important. 'So while I think it is very important to recognize that we are not trying to dominate their lives, my objective is,' says Archie Norman, 'to try to relate in simple ways. If we try to be too sophisticated, we'll never achieve it. I would just like ASDA to be number 35, not 135, and what you want people to think is that ASDA is a great place to work. To get people to think, "I enjoy coming to work. I get paid a very fair wage. If I make a contribution it is really recognized. I like my boss. He always takes the trouble to say hello, and looks after me if there is a problem."'

Archie Norman is always out and about, enjoying talking to the customers. 'The good thing about ASDA is it's doing something worthwhile. Colleagues are able to say, "It is helping people I know, customers I recognize, who get their food and clothing at better value." That is where we want to get to.'

How do ASDA do that? 'We start off by recruiting people interested in serving customers in the first place. Lots of people in the great British public are not interested in doing what we want them to do. That is no criticism of them. They may be great bricklayers or chemical engineers, but they are not going to be great check-out operators. Great check-out operators are people who like hard work, are dextrous, enjoy people and that buzz of being in the stores. Finding those people is very important. That is of the essence. Secondly, when they arrive they have to be well treated in basic ways. It is important the facilities are good, are kept clean, that there is somewhere they can have a decent cup of coffee and a break, and they have a decent uniform to wear. Uniforms are a very difficult issue.'

The next thing for Archie Norman is the buzz around the place. 'We want friendly colleagues, motivated to sell. We want everybody to know what is happening in the stores, how the selling is going, how they are performing in relation to the selling, and we measure everything we can and feed it back. We're very high on measuring results and information. Finally, we do make a real point of trying to measure motivation attitudes all the time.'

To achieve this, every store in the company gets a roving We're Listening Survey. It has around forty multiple choice questions on people's attitudes to management, to the business, their pay, how they enjoy working, and the opportunities. Every survey result is fed back explicitly to all the colleagues in the store. If they get a bad result, it is vital it is fed back in order that problems can be discussed and resolved. The survey is anonymous, going out to all employees, and ASDA expect at least 70 per cent return. 'If we don't get 70 per cent,' says Archie Norman, 'we are not doing the job. It is the manager's role to make sure we have a high return. Most colleagues see it as being important, whilst some are a bit suspicious. You know: "Where is this going to go? How do I know it is anonymous?" Inevitably, some people think it will not make a difference anyway. If you look at the results, however, at the comments that are written, a lot of people regard it as a great opportunity to say what they think. We find the results generally encouraging. The morale in the company is high and that's where it shows.'

Archie Norman is adamant that the one thing that is more important than ASDA customers is its 'colleagues'. 'That is at the heart of it. We believe if you work all the time on colleague motivation, communication and attitudes, then you will deliver a good customer service. Whereas if you work on customer service as an end point in itself, which is the mistake most people fall into, then it will not happen in our business. The other thing we believe is that there is a lot of customer service that is easy to do, but only if you want to add cost. There have been competitors who have advertised on national television that they will pack your bags for you at check-out, or reduce the queues for you. We can do that too. If you want, we'll pack your bags for you, carry them to the car and even drive you home. It's just going to cost more money, so you're going to pay more for your shopping!'

Can ASDA pack my bags for me and carry them to my car at a lower cost than their competitors? 'I honestly have to tell you, no!' admits Archie Norman. 'It's going to cost about the same.' So, if all supermarkets can do it, that's not competing. Competing is doing something the others can't do. What can ASDA do that the others cannot? 'Well obviously we strive to execute everything better, but also we can do it with a different personality. When we get people to express their personality, and the ASDA personality, in the store, then we have something which will be different. Remember, the reason people come shopping with us is for the product, the prices, value, the range, and maybe because we are the only store locally, but if they have a choice, then the unique ASDA service is one of the things which may persuade them.'

ASDA try to express that personality at the point of sale in the store, in the way they do displays, the way the people on the deli counter, for example, or check-out operators interact, what they wear on their badges, on their nameplates. They try to get the whole spirit of the enterprise throughout, and in the ASDA stores I have visited, this is working, and is consistent. ASDA used to be grey, disciplined and uniform. Archie Norman insists, 'We need to be disciplined, but good customer service requires character and initiative. We encourage colleagues to express themselves through our stores and have *fun* doing so. I do expect them to look professional, but above and beyond that, we are very tolerant of the issues and events people want to take on board locally. We encourage it through our store managers.'

The ASDA ambience and atmosphere at head office to my mind was one of action and a strong belief that every single one of the 65,000 employees could actually influence the ASDA way of working. At a desk opposite Archie Norman, for instance, I met two ladies whose job was to manage the company's suggestion scheme. Close to the ASDA boardroom, this team sifted the innovations and ideas emanating from the employees. What better example of involvement and business improvement can one have than the knowledge that an ASDA pizza team trainer, check-out operator or produce assistant has an idea listened to and acted upon, less than a dozen footsteps from the chief executive himself? ASDA operates in a market which, in a sense, is one commodity. In other words, it is all very 'samey', and therefore little differences become big differences. Archie Norman says, 'I think that what one really wants is to create a company where, in our sort of business, there is widespread motivation to find improvement, a thousand small improvements. One of the difficulties with this innovation language is that it conjures up images of massive technological change, or breakthroughs of one kind or another. Our real success in the late nineties depends on doing a thousand little things better.' That does not depend on Archie Norman. He knows it depends on 65,000 ASDA people coming out with a thousand little things and constantly edging forward. Of course, product innovation is vital to them. But they are not going to change 20,000 lines whenever necessary very quickly. 'What we can do,' he says, 'is to have every trader, every buyer, every marketing person looking for little ways of improving items – the can of baked beans, the yoghurt, the labelling, the packaging, the product, coming in with new suggestions, new thoughts, things that are quite easy to put through individually. That adds up to a total difference and that is innovation in our business.' His commitment to that is epitomized by those two ladies opposite his head office desk.

ASDA's own label lines jumped from 2,500 lines in 1987 to 8,000 in 1993, with many more constantly coming on stream. They have taken a lot out, too. ASDA used to be all branded up till 1985, but launched a big drive into ASDA brand and unlabelled product from 1987 onwards. Unfortunately, it was something of a cavalry charge, with a great deal of poor product and packaging. The difficulty with own-label is that if customers experience one disappointing own-label product that will put them off the whole lot. Therefore, quality is of the essence. Under the new management ASDA has taken every single ASDA brand product and put it through its quality control, a customer panel. Quite a few of them failed. In fact, ASDA brand penetration declined initially for two years. It is only in the last year that the brand has been growing again because the company is now redeveloping, repackaging, and improving the product. Archie Norman says, 'We set up last year a new division here, just to concentrate on product development. We have hired a chef, which I think is very important. This is a food company and people have to understand what good food is. All our buyers should understand a bit about cooking. What makes up good food, how you taste and eat it. How you distinguish between taste, texture, appearance. We are what we eat. In our case, we are what we sell.'

ASDA people are encouraged to 'eat their own cooking'. 'If your people don't shop in your own stores, then you have a problem,' says Archie Norman, 'a real problem of lack of pride. If our people are proud of what we are doing here, they will shop in our stores. One of the things we did, which is not unique to us, was introduce a discount card – all colleagues get a card, whereby they get ten per cent off their shopping at ASDA. That's a tremendous deal. It's worth three or four hundred pounds a year to most households. It is very important to me that our people shop here. If our people aren't shopping with us, then we had better go out and shoot ourselves!'

Regulation is a big issue for ASDA. 'There is probably a less business-friendly attitude in government than there was. In too many ministries civil servants are still knee-jerk regulators, looking for opportunities to regulate rather than opportunities to free up and motivate. We have a very substantial increase in bureaucratic regulation coming from Brussels which has added to the cost of running a business like ours in Britain, and added most to the cost of many small businesses. It looks likely, for the next five years if we are not very careful, that we will see another substantial increase in regulation which will slow the pace of change. The character of European legislation, especially, is death by a thousand cuts. Many small areas, individual pieces of regulation, food labelling for instance, add to the total bureaucracy.

'Employment is a very big problem: a lot of the European companies still work with employment concepts from the sixties or seventies. In other words, the basic attitude is that there is a clear polarity of interests between management and trade unionist employees. Employment regulation is framed around protection and rights, instead of around motivation and enterprise. Britain must come away from an awful lot of that. Adopting somebody else's legislative structure which is a little of what the Social Chapter is obviously about, is very dangerous. We can live with anything, but it is a step backwards.'

Another concern is executive pay and the issues that led to the 1995 Greenbury Inquiry. 'A very unfortunate development. That gets down to self-interest, and at the end of the day, nobody works here purely for the money. But I think this whole thing over boardroom pay is denigrating of management. Whilst there is no doubt that a lot of British management have brought it on themselves, especially in the public utilities, where there has been a help-yourself mentality, it is a very unfortunate development, because the press can then portray management and business bosses as being greedy, self-interested and unprofessional. The country's success may not depend on shop-keeping, but it does depend on having people going into professional management. I think one of the things we achieved in the eighties was to generate a new attitude towards business and management which was more enticing and motivating for bright young people. The danger is, all that could be lost.'

What gives Archie Norman the greatest joy is last week's sales figures. If last week was a good week, then he is happy. That is the way ASDA works. 'We are driven by the progress and achievement: whether we had more customers last week, and on our measures, such as if colleagues are more motivated, whether we're delivering better service, whether our prices are lower. Those are the things that really matter to us. Those are the things that really matter to us.

Those are the things that we worry about all the time. Very specifically, every Monday, I have twenty people in the boardroom and we trawl through the sales by line, by store, the complaints we've had, the results we have had.'

He is critical on customer complaints. 'The most important thing is for a complainant to go to the store. If you get the store handling things well, then you have satisfied customers. Once a complainant writes to me, you have already failed, because the reality, with the best will in the world, is that it is going to take a few days for me to reply. And it is putting customers to a lot of trouble. The best complaint handling happens there and then on the shop floor. If it is our mistake, then one of our people must say, "I'm very sorry, can we get you a new product, can we replace it, or can we give you some vouchers or your money back?" That way a complaint never becomes a big complaint. All our products have our address on, and we have a money-back guarantee. Everyone knows where to write, and we have a customer helpline, but if people write to me, they're going to get bad service. However well I try and do it, I am not here full-time answering letters. It takes time — a four-day delay is bad service, isn't it? But it's fantastic for a managing director to achieve that. Go next door, you'll see we have a performance board and we have all the turnaround times for complaints on it. Once a complaint gets to that level, you've already lost, unfortunately. You are in recovery mode. Recovery mode is me writing an apologetic letter, trying to put things right. By that stage you're trying to climb back, and of course you can climb back well or badly. But it's better to get it right in the first instance!'

ASDA's objective towards the millennium is to be Britain's best-value fresh food retailer, and to really extend its points of difference. To Norman, these are, 'a wider range, larger stores, more "theatre", better clothing, better quality fresh food, more in-store preparation and finishing of fresh food; a sense of excitement in the personality, and service delivered through happy people; and a business which is more decentralized in its way of working so each store is run more as a collection of small businesses than as an operational unit with a place where you open the doors at the beginning of the day and shut them at the end of the day.'

He does not believe, as a general rule, that joint ventures such as ASDA has with the George Davies partnership (the George range of clothes) is necessarily the way forward. What is important, 'is to work very closely with our suppliers. It is our objective to be the most important customer to as many of our suppliers as we can. If we can do that we will get them to focus their development work and align their supply chain, their production methods, to our needs. But that result is best achieved, in my experience, by working closely with people, generating business together, not by inventing complicated joint venture arrangements. We are great believers in outsourcing. We do not do anything we are unhappy to do ourselves here. We much prefer to depend on people who are more expert in doing things than we are. Success in doing that into 2000 does depend on having suppliers who are very much geared to our attitudes, our culture and what we want to achieve.'

How would he summarize his millennial wish for ASDA? 'We would want to be an employer of first choice. We would want to be Britain's best-value, best quality fresh-food superstore, and we would want to be somewhere that, as a place to shop, is recognized above all as different, with a different personality and different service.'

To this end ASDA is relentlessly pursuing policies designed to return it to its traditional customer base – ordinary working people and their families who demand 'value'. It is certainly creating the foundation of a selling and service organization that is so good that customers will find it worth driving past its rival to reach it. Five million customers – and growing – will agree. Competitors – watch out!

BMP DDB NEEDHAM WORLDWIDE LTD

UK	Billings (1994)	£290 million
	Employees	330
Worldwide	Billings (1994)	$6,722 million
	Employees	6,329

BMP DDB Needham is the UK's fifth largest advertising agency, offering effective, creative advertising solutions to commercial problems. It is the London office of the DDB Needham Worldwide network, which has 183 offices in 75 countries.

James Best – Chairman
Joined BMP as a trainee planner in 1975 and appointed to the Board in 1980 as a Planning Director. After BMP's flotation, he was appointed to the Board of BMP plc in 1987 as Corporate Development Director, building up the BMP Group of companies. He rejoined the agency as Chairman on its merger with DDB Needham in 1989 and was appointed to the Board of DDB Needham Worldwide in 1991.

The Agency
BMP was founded in 1968 and has won more creative awards for television advertising at home (BCTAA) and abroad (the Cannes Advertising Festival) and for effective advertising (the Institute of Practitioners in Advertising Effectiveness Awards) than any other agency.

BMP DDB Needham
James Best, Chairman

Near the top of the business league table of advertising agencies is BMP DDB Needham. It is a healthy business, growing throughout the recession, with clients ranging from Sony to Walkers Crisps, Barclaycard to Volkswagen, Schweppes to British Gas. A remarkable variety of products, services and companies make up its list of winning advertising campaigns that work in their marketplace and delight the clients. Today, few agencies can claim to have netted so many awards for their work.

To quote *Campaign* magazine, 'BMP DDB is the source of consistently excellent creative and strategic advertising solutions that – crucially – appear to work hard for their paymasters' money.' I have selected BMP DDB for this book because it has achieved consistent excellence, a tall order in recession. It is the agency that established John Smith's Bitter as a national brand, and created campaigns ranging from NDC's dancing milk bottles to Rowan Atkinson's bungling secret agent, Latham, for Barclaycard. The commercials are beautifully produced and can be funny or sad, high-brow or oblique.

Three people founded the agency in 1968 – Boase, Massimi and Pollitt (BMP) - and they pioneered account planning, placing the consumer at the centre of decision making about advertising: 'We are not just talking *at* people, we need to *listen* to the consumers.' Planners analyse research, conduct group discussions, and are charged with bringing the consumer's point of view to all the advertising processes within the agency – strategic, creative, evaluative and so on. This was the first ad agency to employ this way of working.

According to chairman James Best, 'We ourselves grew, prospered, went public, bought other companies, played at being Saatchis without perhaps having their entrepreneurial exuberance. In 1989 we became part of a big American outfit called Omnicom, and merged with the UK office of their network, DDB Needham. So we became this awkward mouthful of initials BMP DDB Needham!'

The agency's name is known, its creative work is admired and, most importantly, its campaigns are effective. Its ads make people behave or see things in a slightly different way. This focus on effectiveness means BMP DDB has got to understand the consumer, and put resource behind that understanding. Frankly, this is not done in a lot of agencies.

The advertising industry famously suffered in the recession. The 1980s had been ludicrously good to it but that lead to bad habits, and luxuries unnecessary to the business and not justifiable to clients. When recession came there was a lot of room for cutting fat and improved working but BMP DDB went forward. According to James Best, 'We benefited because we were able, throughout the recession, to wave the banner of work that works, work that makes money for clients and we suffered less than some. It was a cruel time for advertising agencies and the industry reduced from 15,000 to about 11,000 people. We had to focus on what we were best at and what was most important to us and to our clients, and that did involve reducing the total head count by some 10 per cent; but we kept on growing.'

For the agency, establishing a client relationship means exploring and understanding the client's business and product, and turning this understanding into a relevant way to crack the client's problem. The client is involved as much as they can or want to be. Around half a dozen disciplines from within the agency are involved on each piece of client business, working *with* the client through every stage of the process. Advertising requires the creative process to be disciplined – a process in which 90 per cent is perspiration and 10 per cent inspiration, but none the less the inspiration and intuition are vital and the type of people who are able to produce new ways of looking at things are not on the whole nine-to-five suit and tie folk.

James Best believes that traditionally in Britain, there have been agencies which have fallen each side of a divide: 'There have been those which have been clearly commercially switched on but whose work you might not admire. And then there are those whose ads make you think, "Wow, look at that!" Then you think, "What was that all about? Is that ad really shifting product or people's perceptions of the product?" The discipline BMP DDB always tries to put on the creative process is, we hope, one that is totally understandable to creative people. The account planning function means that our creatives know exactly to whom each ad should be talking, the way to approach these people so that they respond. By using this thinking to lead to a good, creative solution, we are able to discipline the creative process, without giving in to arbitrary demands, "I want it done this way," or "The client says it has to be done like that." If creative people are answering a question and they are able to provide the solution, then their work will see the light of day. It will have a good chance of being put to clients and consumers, and then, perhaps, into the big wide world!'

Creative people aren't totally weird! There are creative people in every business and it is not something peculiar to one department of an advertising agency. When James Best talks of creative people, he does not mean solely those people in the agency who write the ads. 'We also need creative thinking from our planners at the strategic end, so that when they look at a client's commercial or communication problem, they can find a solution to it which will be expressible by the creative department.'

What is often frustrating to clients and business managers in advertising is that solutions may take a while to arrive at. It is a messy process. As James Best says, 'So often you have to go back to the drawing board – even though you think you've gone quite a long way down the path. It turns out you haven't got quite the correct creative brief and the work you have will not make a piece of communication. You then have to re-think what you can say, narrow it down perhaps, be realistic about how much you can expect to communicate to people in one 30-second TV commercial or one page of the newspaper.' The difficulty of bringing together the commercial pressures, and what has to be a creative solution, can be fraught. Plans can slip behind time and over budget, and the agency has to be able to legislate for that. Sometimes someone has to say, 'No, it's got to be redone, rescheduled, repriced,' otherwise the solution will not be right.

The financial clock starts ticking once the ad has been approved by the client. Although the production cost in making a TV or press ad can be high – film crews or photographers have to be commissioned, actors and actresses paid, locations found and assessed, even the film used must be accounted for – by far the greatest cost is the media spend – buying airtime or print space. As we move to the millennium

James Best sees the bulk of the cost to clients, the media spend, increasing. 'Production costs are very seldom more than 10 per cent of the media cost. It's buying the audience that's getting more expensive. Not many years ago there was just ITV and a number of newspapers and magazines. Now there has been enormous growth of commercial radio and of new TV channels, particularly satellite and cable. The whole media scene has broadened out. There are more ways of reaching particular audiences than ever before. Conversely, there are fewer easy blockbuster ways to reach everybody – and these few ways will cost more and more as time goes on.'

In the old days, one spot in a big movie on ITV would reach a vast proportion of the population, but that is no longer the case. According to James Best, 'As cable becomes more and more accessible to more households, and other satellite channels come on, gradually the audience fragments. To some advertisers it is very helpful because they can target different audiences more effectively than ever before – perhaps young people through particular music or sports programmes. To other advertisers who have been used to getting a big audience, it can be more difficult because they have now to buy in a more complex marketplace, and pay more because of that. This process will intensify.'

Over the years, BMP DDB's media department has grown, and is now a substantial media business. Says James Best: 'It pulls in a lot of money from clients who may not use the agency on a full service basis. These clients come to BMP DDB purely for our media buying and thinking, the wit and muscle that we've got in the media marketplace to negotiate the best rate. The media department is now the largest in the agency, winning non-creative clients' independent media business, thus ensuring that our media offering is as good as, indeed better than, anybody else's in the country. This protects our existing clients because they know they're with the best. And it gives us the opportunity to develop a bigger business into the future.'

The agency's prime purpose is to give their existing clients the very best service by having a top quality media business, and to build their own total business by attracting that independent media income through total media solutions. Explains James Best, 'For a major client, such as the Boots Group, with a key image in lifestyle retailing and stores such as Boots the Chemist, Halfords and FADS in every high street, we handle all of their media planning and buying centrally here. The idea is that we can give each store brand individual attention, in terms of the audience to target and the right way to reach that audience, but also, by co-ordinating the expenditure of the group under one umbrella, we can ensure the very best deals in the marketplace are available to each of those individual businesses. When there are local needs, there are local solutions. Every store opening has its own programme tailored to what is appropriate to that locality: the media available, the audience and population – demographics. We have specialists in regional media, radio, cinema and now, increasingly, in the media which doesn't exist yet - interactive media – an area where we see growth into the twenty-first century.'

Interactive media will mean that any person sitting at home will have the ability to use their television as a two-way communication tool – to look for products on it and buy direct – rather than just receiving pictures and messages. Just imagine you are thinking about a holiday. Instead of going to a travel agent and getting a lot of brochures you could look at different travel company offerings on your TV at home then, having selected which details you want, have them put straight down the line for you to view and ultimately book your holiday via the TV screen.

The idea of interactivity is not just programme selection, it is getting back what we, the customer, want: asking questions of the advertiser, and having the ability to get individualized answers. It is an area which James Best thinks is destined to grow: 'How big it will grow, nobody knows. We have been involved very heavily in one of the early trials in Cambridge, where there is a limited number of households which are cabled both ways. They have the ability to try new services, maybe home banking, which would enable them to do their banking through their television screen. Maybe interactive media will work for insurance, giving quotes and calculating insurance needs; maybe it will look at different models of cars and allow someone to take a video test drive of the car before making a decision to see one in reality and talk to a real person about it. Already we have car manufacturers looking forward to marketing their cars without a sales force and without a chain of retail agents. All sorts of things might develop.'

James Best is enthusiastic about this media vehicle for the future. 'There are ways in which interactive media could become a very useful commercial tool for a host of enquiries. Maybe an individual has something as personal and problematic as an illness or disease; they could access detailed information and ask questions of the TV screen and gain valuable personal information to either reassure themselves or set them on a trail of further enquiry.'

The agency has a team concentrating purely on interactive opportunities, getting their clients interested and providing the resources for them to experiment through an initial trial to learn if it can work for them. As James Best says, 'There are always new media opportunities coming along. Interactive selling opportunities are happening because the technology is beginning to make it possible.'

The use of 'personalities' can be important in a campaign. In the early 1980s, Barclaycard had had Alan Whicker as their spokesman in its successful, long-running TV campaign, giving the brand a certain cachet, an internationalism. When BMP DDB took over the account in the 1990s they enlisted the help of another personality, Rowan Atkinson, who created a whole new character and used it, through his constant interplay with his assistant Bough, to convey a new way of looking at Barclaycard's uses and its extra services whilst still developing the humorous and international context. It has been an enormously successful campaign.

This use of humour is a trend towards the millennium. James Best says, 'The reality is that consumers aren't usually as involved, interested and as serious-minded about the product as the manufacturer. We have to convince out client that humour can play an enormous role in gaining people's empathy, getting people on the seller's side, as it were, making people listen and winning them over. It is the reason that the best teachers often use parables, stories and anecdotes to get a point across. If you can involve people, get them to enjoy you and what you are doing, you are saying something about yourselves. You are likeable people if you are doing that. And, of course, different audiences, such as the late teens and twenties, expect advertising to entertain, stimulate and offer a good laugh.'

Competition in the advertising business is fierce and growing more so. A lot of BMP DDB's work is repeat business but every year it has to win new clients. Every year, for a good reason or not, the agency will part company with some clients and others perhaps will spend less money. BMP DDB has to constantly replenish the well, prove itself in the marketplace and win business. This is, however, always a relatively modest proportion of the whole operation – it is more like eighty/twenty in favour of existing clients. The agency believes relationships should be long-term. As James Best says, 'We aim to get under the skin of a client's business. If we are closely involved with the client we are more likely to do a good job; if we do a good job we are more likely to retain the business year in year out. We have had some of our clients for twenty-five years.'

To sustain such excellence the agency must attract good staff. Recruitment and retention of key compatible people is therefore essential towards the millennium but, as James Best points out, 'There has to be a corporate culture which is bigger than any individual, because individuals will come and go. Those agencies which are founded on the merits and talents of an individual will rise and fall with that individual. If you have something which is bigger than that, then it has to be a culture which can infect lots of people. That doesn't mean everyone has to sing the company's song, because these are all highly intelligent and individual people, but they must be aware there are certain ways of doing things at this agency.'

According to James Best, building that corporate culture has become very broad-based. 'Understanding the right way to do things is important. "The way we do things round here", is a phrase that is often used, a concept that is shared and becomes part of the language. The people we hire from outside - because, of course, people change, people move on, people move in – almost universally seem to be struck by the way we do things here, but find nothing is written down terribly clearly anywhere, although occasionally we make an effort to do so. The culture is not proselytized succinctly in management speeches, but it permeates the way people talk, act and work together. It is very open: there is hierarchy, but it is pretty transparent and informal. If you look at the evidence you'll see we can't get away with short cuts or ego trips because our conscience is our concern for the consumer, which keeps us on the straight and narrow.'

Going into the mid-nineties there have been a number of changes in how advertising agencies operate their business. Some have been positive, and some not. James Best explains, 'One significant change in the agency business is that people have realized that "being creative" is not just a department, it is a whole way of collective operating. Moving to the year 2000, I think more client companies also believe marketing is not just a department. In fact, the principles of marketing are fundamental to their business, particularly as markets mature and there is less new territory conquest, less organic growth through population, and more emphasis on serving your customer, communicating with your consumer, developing the answer to real needs. Marketing is absolutely, intrinsically part of all management thinking and decisions. In that respect, we are on the whole the servants of marketing.'

An unmistakable change has been the increasing globalization of BMP DDB's client list. Maybe five years ago, 15 per cent of its business was international, now it is around 40 per cent. In 1994, it was fortunate to win the Sony account across Europe. This was the first time that Sony put all of its advertising eggs in the one basket, seeking a co-ordinated and coherent European presentation of its products and of itself. BMP DDB is based in London, but has required its planners to conduct their research and qualitative interviewing in other countries, not just in the UK, building strategies which are valid *across* frontiers. This has required new thinking, and is a strong trend towards Year 2000.

James Best believes he must attract the right people to serve this globalization. 'Every year since 1971, we have hired graduate trainees – I was one, as were several of my senior colleagues. In selecting them, the essential qualities of an enquiring mind, energy, an interest in people, the sort of values that we look for, will not have changed because of internationalization. Increasingly, people coming into the industry are interested in working elsewhere in the world. Or at least they will always say they are, then it will turn out they really only want to work in New York, Hong Kong or Sydney! In fact, when you suggest to them that they go to Caracas or Seoul it may not be quite the posting they expected! Languages now matter more. Although we are lucky enough to have English as the business language of the world, it is none the less much more comfortable for clients and our colleagues around the world to speak in their own tongue. To organize things at a distance, we must also have people who are extremely good delegators. These are to some extent different skills from those we have needed before, so we have to have a good catholic mix of talents to cover all the things we need to do into 2000.'

As BMP DDB goes into the process of planning and developing a campaign, it puts in place appropriate measurement tools, to see whether the ads are having the result it hoped to achieve: selling more products; not letting the competition take existing customers away; changing attitudes and perceptions. As James Best says, 'In each case you've got to determine just what the advertising can be expected to contribute. You must be as specific as possible and quantify it as best you can. Then, put in the right measuring checks to see whether you are doing what you set out to achieve. To some extent we are paid – by a few but an increasing proportion of clients – in part according to whether we hit those performance targets. It is a small element of our remuneration, but it is growing and we're very aware of a trend for the millennium of performance related pay [PRP].'

James Best believes you can only go so far with PRP in his business, not least because there are so many factors involved that often make it impossible to tease out the contribution the advertising made: 'It can't be more than a relatively modest proportion of remuneration. You can't wait for three years until the campaign has had its effectiveness measured in order to be paid. But as a way of incentivising an agency and as a way perhaps of ensuring they are focused on the end result for the client, it is a growing trend.'

The regulatory regime for advertising in the UK is regarded by James Best as 'a pretty sensible one'. Advertising is self-regulatory to a large degree, but is subject to any Trading Standards legislation. 'You must be honest. It's really the TV companies, aided and abetted by the advertising agencies, that ensure whatever goes on screen, on posters, or in the press, is acceptable and appropriate. On the whole, the media and advertising need good policing in order that the irresponsible lunatic fringe doesn't do daft things and give everybody a bad name.' He fears the bugbear is 'Brussels' which tends to require everybody to live up to or down to the tightest and strictest regulation. For example: 'Because alcohol advertising is not allowed on TV in France, there is the danger that we will no longer be able to advertise alcohol on TV anywhere. That concerns people. On the whole, however, Brussels is not the restrictive villain that people fear, and there are certainly parts of the Commission which are in favour of deregulation rather than one more regulation. However, we must ensure that silly rules and regulations are not landed on us by surprise.'

He thinks that it is important that regulation is seen by the public to exist. 'It is vital that people believe advertising to be properly supervised, so they believe what they are told in advertisements, and they know those ads are not made in such a way as to upset or anger people for the wrong reasons, particularly if there are animals or children involved. It's important that we are seen to keep our house in order and be properly and appropriately managed. The popularity of advertising in this country is greater than almost any other country in the world, so we must regulate ourselves properly.'

He believes that the UK has very high standards, particularly in broadcast television programming and production. This he feels allows advertising to be intelligent, provocative, amusing and entertaining. 'In fact advertising has to live up to the programme standards, and people expect this when they have you come into their living room without being asked! We've been fortunate, having high standards around us in the UK to live up to. Obviously, one of the sad things about the future, with the increase in TV programmes potentially leading to a lot more junk TV, is that you're going to get more junk advertising, because viewers lose their level of discrimination and expectation. Look at America and Italy. I don't know if we can stop this happening. It's a relatively free economy and liberal democracy that we work and live within, so what works will win. If junk television works and makes a lot of money for people, if those junk newspapers and magazines sell a lot of copies and make a lot of money, then they'll be allowed to exist and the advertising that goes with them will follow.'

What of BMP DDB's future? James Best insists that advertising and 'our part in it', will develop considerably in the run up to the millennium. 'It will be recognizable, but it will not be the same. We will have developed new strings to our bow. I suspect that some things we now do may be hived off and turned into businesses in their own right. I'm sure we will be doing things that we currently haven't the foggiest idea about, that will become part of this industry, such as the interactive media, media based on new technology, new ways of talking to people or helping our clients talk to people and market products and services – all that will grow and change. I want our firm to continue to be regarded as the best advertising agency in the UK, particularly by people who know anything about advertising agencies. We are the advertising man's advertising agency, and that matters a lot because reputation is as great an asset as anything else we have. Reputation is founded on people and the culture as well as the product, and if we can sustain that reputation then we sustain a great business.'

He also feels that BMP DDB may well find it is necessary to have several smaller business units rather than making their one central office bigger and bigger. 'Size is nice, but flexibility and the ability to answer client needs in different areas is more important. Technology gives us the ability to co-ordinate such business units much better than before, for example, through IT networks.'

For agencies, James Best feels the greatest focus for long-term growth is the Far East. The DDB Network, to which BMP DDB belongs, now has four offices in China and is devoting a lot of network time and money to their support. India, Indonesia, Taiwan, and some of the other younger economies are also showing growth. In those areas there is a need to grow more professional, to provide higher quality of service. Latin America is the second most important growth area where DDB is establishing a properly connected coherent network.

As far as Eastern Europe and Russia are concerned, James Best feels they cannot be looked at as one block, or one market. DDB has been in Budapest for a long time, which has a well-developed marketplace, as well as in Prague, working in a country of great technical and commercial sophistication. As he says, 'As you go farther east, the legacy of state socialism is increasingly hard to cope with, and certainly Russia is a difficult place to build a business. One day it will happen. We have representation there – but it will take time, and for many companies looking to expand their markets it may not be a big priority.'

He believes there are other areas of development in the media apart from TV and the press, such as in the field of sponsorship, sport and music, delivering commercial messages to consumers in non-traditional ways. 'We have a joint venture with a music management company where their artists, if they are interested, can perhaps work in part with our clients, represent those clients, be sponsored by and build a promotional programme around a concert tour backed by a client. We can buy the media for those artists, and bring everything together into a useful commercial enterprise. Another example is a joint venture on TV, a programme can be sponsored by an advertiser, and then the project can be developed as a major business activity in its own right, appropriate to the client and interesting to the consumer, the viewer. They are adding value to the core business by helping clients to communicate through major advertising media and move our business forward by so doing.'

Towards 2000, James Best suggests agencies must help change views in the global marketplace. A product's country of origin confers a certain status and image. Sometimes this is an asset, at other times it is not. There is a clearly identifiable British character, concocted from Merchant Ivory films, our literature and our colonial past, which, while not necessarily squaring with how the British actually see themselves, is still how they project themselves abroad. National heritage is often an intrinsic part of a brand's make-up and, well-handled, can help steal an edge on the competition. America is the world of the rugged loners who wear jeans and smoke Marlboro. Coca-Cola, for example, appropriated this broad outdoor canvas and extended it into the invigorating world of youth, optimism and fun, giving us the all-American uniform, cigarette and soft drink. American values sell these global brands and they, in their turn, sell America and shape our perceptions of that country. James Best states, 'There is increasing cultural dialogue between countries and exposure to each other's foods, customs, styles and values. Instead of viewing this globalization as shrinking the pool of advertising imagery by removing differences, we see this new level of identifiable national characteristics as an opportunity to re-examine the old, primitive national stereotypes and discover new sources of imagery.'

BMP DDB researched all these issues and discovered that Britain is perceived as decidedly strange: 'The island which lives its own life'; 'Ugly people with bad taste'; 'Narrow, constrained, dull, conventional, stuffy yet picturesque.' The British are seen as contrary, always doing the opposite to everyone else, refusing to fit in. Sports are viewed as symptomatic of this – croquet, cricket, darts, are uniquely British. On the positive side, much of the pomp and ceremony that surrounds great institutions such as the Royal Family, Parliament, the old universities and Law Courts, are unique. Most countries have time-honoured rituals, but England has the edge here, famed for its ability to preserve tradition and keep history alive.

Such characteristics can help steal an edge on competition by some industries' ability to capitalize on them. Explains James Best, 'If you are selling shortbread, classic clothes, or country house holidays, that's the England you very much want people to respond to, because your products are fully dependent on that heritage. Whereas if you're selling computers or fly-by-wire systems, aeroplanes etc., you would rather those characteristics were a well-guarded secret and that other aspects of the British spirit and UK abilities were to the fore. If "Made in Britain" is to be used on products and to mean anything, you've got to be cognisant of what that meaning is, and try to ensure it is reflecting reality not just an historical myth. There is an aspect of Englishness that people have ignored because they are too busy creating either some Sherlock Holmes ethos or country cottage rose pot pourris. To succeed in the millennium we can and must do more to present UK individualism, creativity and inventiveness, through our high technology, design, music, and the like.'

If you talk to the CBI or DTI they will say, 'Hang on a bit, half the investment in Europe from other parts of the world is in the UK, and our exports are doing well.' James Best responds, 'Great, terrific. Thank God for that! Those people are working very hard to continue the trend, which is excellent. But it doesn't stop there being a brake on our exports, or on our ability to make things and feel good about making them. That brake is created by an aura of olde worldeiness and heritage holidays. In the same way, Japan's products have led people's perspectives of Japan, so it may be seen as a cold and soulless place where people are automatons, work-obsessed, and uniform. Much of that perception is entirely wrong but that is what has happened to our image of Japan, as being not very attractive at the moment. That thinking spills over into what we might accept or want to buy from Japan. America manufactures images rather than products and has an enormous image range, from the Wild West to the streets, from the Southern Gentlemen to Marlboro' man. These images are rich and internationally understood. There are a lot of different themes to play on, a much richer heritage to use. Those images exist in the minds of British consumers, and are ripe for exploitation by advertising.'

Even given all this globalization and brave new world, BMP DDB is a service business, and as such knows it must respond and react to the needs of its clients. As James Best admits, 'It is very important we do not just sit back and wait for them to tell us what to do. Sitting back and waiting for somebody else is probably seen as a more comfortable way to serve. But, as a business, BMP DDB cannot pretend that it can rush off and create a new world; if it's not relevant to our client's existing, everyday needs then we're going to fall flat on our face in terms of forward movement. We must restore the balance between the conservative, traditional, refined image of Britain and the opposite end of the scale – the image of being creative, inventive and original.'

And he concludes, 'If the parent brand "Ad UK" is to be kept strong, healthy and relevant so it can provide unique umbrella support to a broader range of brands and product categories, it is critical that Britain plays to its new-found strengths which are rooted in the reality of the country today. Planning for change must be to serve our customers today and move their minds for tomorrow. That is the business we are in towards the year 2000 and beyond.'

BUSINESS IN THE COMMUNITY

Turnover (1994)	£4.86 million	
Operating surplus	£101,852	
Total fixed assets	£147,125	} Pre-merger figures
Employees:		
Full time	108	
Part time	5	
Secondees	40	

Leading UK charity in the field of corporate community involvement. Its president is HRH the Prince of Wales and its chairman is the Lord Sheppard of Didgemere.

Julia Cleverdon – Chief Executive

Julia Cleverdon joined BITC in 1988, having previously been Director of the Industrial Society's Education and Inner City Division. Under her leadership the Industrial Society became the leading provider of management training for educational and voluntary organizations.

She has also served as Chairman of the National Curriculum Council's Economic Awareness Committee and as Foundation Governor of Camden School for Girls (London). She is a Board Director of Trident, the Employers' Forum for Disability, and of the Princes' Trust Volunteers.

Major Campaigns

BITC has launched major campaigns on education, economic regeneration, employee involvement, the environment and women and ethnic minorities in employment. Its 'Seeing is Believing' programme, introducing senior business leaders to successful community projects, was instigated by HRH the Prince of Wales.

Business In The Community
Julia Cleverdon,
Chief Executive

Towards the millennium many organizations highlighted in this book insist they will have an increasing corporate responsibility to society and will be more committed to helping the communities in which they operate. Many of the chief executives endorse the need to raise the quality and extent of business involvement in the community and to make it a part of successful business practice. What happens to society matters to business, and for this reason I have chosen to highlight the work of Business In The Community [BITC] a not-for-profit organization at the leading edge of corporate community involvement (CCI) towards 2000.

BITC was founded in the wake of the Toxteth riots in the early eighties by a group of business people (founder members included Pilkington's and M&S) who believed business should be more involved in the communities from which they drew their profits, future prosperity and customers. They were much influenced by the American experience, where corporate organizations see CCI as an element of good business practice – with no welfare state, there is a great tradition of volunteerism in America. They brought that idea to Britain and said, 'Come on, we ought to try to engage business in the community.' Since 1982 the movement has grown, and BITC now has about 450 member companies, nearly all blue chip, many out of the top 200 FTSE companies. BITC mainly targets large corporates, on the basis that their influence has a domino effect, not only on all their suppliers and the small businesses around them but also on their customers.

Julia Cleverdon is BITC's dynamic chief executive. 'We encourage our member companies to work in partnership with each other, with local and central government, and particularly with the com-

59

munity and the voluntary sector, so that they target their efforts to address real community and social needs. Our role is sometimes to advise, make suggestions and help to bring on these partnerships. When a new company becomes a member of BITC and says, "We know little about CCI, what shall we do?" we help them to build the partnerships on the ground, to write the policies; we provide advice on good practice. There's a big task for BITC in encouraging our membership to do it well. If they're going to be involved in the community there must be benefit for the community as well as benefit for business.'

Readers will note in the Marks and Spencer chapter how its boardroom is involved in BITC and 'Seeing is Believing' [SiB]. Explains Julia, 'BITC runs SiB for senior level managers in companies. Each year we take some 200 top business leaders into the community to see for themselves what is going on, what the issues and the problems are, and what they as individuals and companies think they could do to help. HRH The Prince of Wales is the President of BITC and invites individuals to come on the visits and to report back to him on what they've seen and what they are going to do. The first thing we would do if a UK company was not in membership would be to target its most senior person with an invitation to join the SiB programme.

'We would benchmark where that company was in the community against similar companies, both in the UK and internationally. Before we went anywhere near them we would have much evidence about what they were already doing, what their management issues and challenges were, the ways in which they, for instance, were using their advertising to send messages to customers about community activities. We would research what they were doing with their own staff – where they were on employee involvement in the community, what support they gave, let's say, as governors of schools, what they were doing about using the community involvement as a tool to grow young managers and young people. Were they, for example, running, as M&S do, 100-hour development assignments for 150 managers a year, attached to a community organization, with a clearly defined project to carry out and with real learning objectives?'

Community involvement is firmly about business, not charity. 'With any organization, BITC will review the business arguments for getting involved in the community. In the early days of the CCI movement the idea was to get involved because it was a good thing to do. It was altruistic, it was right, common sense. All those things are true, but increasingly as we move to the millennium, it's about the business case for a company, what are the business arguments for doing this? If you look at our two equal opportunities programmes – Opportunity 2000, which gets companies to set goals and targets as to where they will be on the employment of women by the year 2000, and our new campaign about race – they say that it is in the business interest of companies to do better on their promotion and retention of female and ethnic minority talents.'

If you segment the companies into 'will and skill' you get a strategic view of what BITC is doing. 'There are some companies who I will call novices, who are low skill in the whole area. They have little experience or knowledge about CCI. Then there are the companies who are very high skill and very high will. These are the sophisticates who win everything. They are the ones who can give you the best examples of quality, of really making an impact. They are the ones who, when running conferences on measuring the management development benefits of getting employees into the community, will have actually *done* the measurement.

'Then there's a large number of companies who have high will, but not very high skill. These are the committeds. We have to try and use the sophisticates to build up the committeds, and the committeds to build up the novices. Our strategic objective is to keep up with the sophisticates at the leading edge and to understand what they are doing, to get the novices to do better, to do it in a more skilled way, and to keep wanting to do it, that is, to continue to see the business benefit of it.'

In the old days CCI was very top down. It was the chairman's wife, the chairman's charitable committee, or the sub-committee of the board, who drove it on. Now the whole issue is about delegation to strategic business units. Whether it's called social responsibility, employee involvement, a new way of motivating people or making them feel part of their local working community, it means that the whole organization has to be engaged in the community, as part of the community.

'Towards 2000, the aim,' says Julia, 'is to send the message down through the organization, so that you actually affect the local community in Gloucester, Liverpool or wherever. GKN, for instance, is saying, "Right, we have a commitment to all of this; we believe this is good for business and good for the community; we are a socially responsible company; we want to encourage people who work with us to believe in us but also to care about the things we care about. We will therefore care about the things *they* care about – we will care about schools, and will care about their difficulties in their particular area. We will try and make it easier for our strategic business units to get involved in the community." Our task at BITC is to help companies at regional and local level find the networks and opportunities to engage in the community.'

BITC has committed itself to strategic objectives towards the millennium. One is to measure improving quality and the impact of what companies do in the community. Says Julia, 'There isn't enough evidence at the moment about the quality of what companies do. It is quite easy to say, "Let's throw some more money at it, get some more people to go and do something about it," – to concentrate on quantity and not to measure the quality. One of our major concerns is to measure the quality, the impact and sustainability of private sector investment into the community. Part of this involves the political climate in which companies are working. As we go through into the latter end of the nineties, the possibility is that there will be a major political change, influencing the way in which government treats private sector investment in the community, how it encourages it and recognizes it is important.'

Another objective is to increase the number of key companies who are engaged in corporate community involvement and thus encourage a domino effect. For instance, the focus for BITC at the moment is the communications companies. Says Julia, 'Granada came on a "Seeing is Believing" programme three or four years ago. Their executive said, "I don't want *Seeing is Believing*, I want *Seeing is Doing*. How do we use the camera's eye to move this on?" As a result we supported Granada in running a highly innovative and very brave piece of work. We found five other companies in the north-west, Manweb, British Aerospace, Greenhalls, Norweb and British Nuclear Fuels, and we ran a "Community Challenge" for them. We found five of the toughest housing estates in the north-west and got each company to give us five middle managers for five hours a week of company time and, we hoped, five hours a week of their own time. We put them into company teams, each team working with the community on one of the housing estates, in order to achieve the dream of the people there to make life better into the future. All of them came back and said what is needed is a provision for young people; there is nothing for them to do in this area.

'So, all the teams set out to raise the cash and make things happen, to provide a community centre for young people in the centre of the Warrington housing estate or wherever. They had nine months. Because Granada used the power of the camera to broadcast a regular update every week about how the challenges were going, the whole of the north-west got tremendously excited and enthusiastic about how we were doing on the Blakon estate in Chester, how we were progressing on the Warrington estate, what was happening with the BNFL work in Wedlock, and so on. It made excellent television!'

An evaluation done by Manchester University reviewed the management development benefits of the scheme for the companies and what was achieved for those communities. It's most heartening reading. 'Staggering stuff,' says Julia. 'About £7.5 million worth of effort has been put into those five estates and some of the results are tremendous.'

BITC targets companies who have the power to influence others to get involved. BITC works on the five 'P's – profits, people, products, premises and power – as the ways in which companies can make a difference. They could help by putting some of their *profits* into the community. Many companies are now part of the Per Cent Club which means they give half a per cent of pre-tax profits into the community as a commitment.

According to Julia, 'Probably the biggest growth will be in the *people* skills put into the community, using community involvement as a developmental tool, supporting things that employees are already doing. Four out of ten of all blue chip employees are already involved in the community. If companies do what NatWest do – run a recognition scheme for community action by their staff – we can raise this number to probably six or seven out of ten, because you give permission, you encourage, you make it clear you want people to be involved in the community. I think people growth will be enormous.

'Then there's the *product*. In America they run a vast operation called "Gifts in Kind America", where things that companies throw away go to the community. There's a scheme running in Britain with the food industry, who have been extremely quick in picking this up, called Provision, where they have food which is not past its sell-by date but is wrong on the packaging or whatever. Through Provision that food goes to the homeless hostels or the Salvation Army, instead of the land fill site. It's good for business, and it's good for the community too. Those product initiatives are growing towards 2000.'

Julia gives an example: 'Gestetner run a scheme whereby they've said to all companies, "If you have laser printers and you want to upgrade, give us your old printer; whether it's a Gestetner printer or another, it doesn't matter. You give us that printer, we'll take the indemnity off you, we'll mend it, recycle it and put it into a school. We'll do that because it's good for business and good for the community." If they get 4 per cent of the companies who are giving them printers to buy a laser printer from Gestetner, it's really worth their while.

'With the *premises* – companies can put their surplus premises to use to help the community. BITC was able to persuade Ladbrokes hotels, to let us have a 40,000 sq ft building they had in Liverpool. It has now been turned into a hostel for thirty-four homeless young people who have just come off the Liverpool care registers. They have given us the building for ten years and they have used their muscle to get other people to help us fit it out. A marvellous new provision for unemployed, homeless young people in the Scotland Road.'

Power is the last 'P'. That is about the power which companies often don't realize they have to make a difference in the community. Explains Julia, 'I was with Andrew Cameron who runs the *Daily Express* on a visit to see John Bird who runs the homelessness magazine, the *Big Issue*. John was saying, "We can't get the newsprint to print the mag, they're charging us an absolute mint for it." To which Cameron replied, "For heaven's sake, one thing I could do for you is ring up every week and ask how much newsprint you need and we'll add it on to the end of our order. You'll have to pay something for it, but you'll pay a damned sight less, because it's on our power rather than on yours."'

Increasing the number of key companies and being a broker between business and the voluntary sector are key objectives for BITC, plus trying to change business behaviour by running a certain number of selective campaigns, particularly in the social responsibility area. 'There are campaigns on the environment, on education, on equal opportunities, including race and women, on employees in the community – what companies are doing to get their employees into the community – and on economic development, particularly at local level. What are the things that companies can do to recruit from the unemployed, or to back the community entrepreneurs who make a difference in inner cities? All various ways in which companies can move on these crucial campaigns.'

The whole of BITC is business driven. Julia is very clear that, into the millennium, although its key customer is the community, its constituency is business. 'BITC has a structure of boards, with people from the business world, government and the voluntary sector, but the actual leadership teams, as they are called, are driven by business. I have chief execs or managing directors or top flight people sitting on those leadership teams. If you take education, that's chaired by Mike Heron, chairman of the Post Office, ex-Unilever. It has the top people from Toyota, M&S, Whitbread and many others, all wrapped round the education issue. Tony Cleaver, ex-IBM, chairs the environment work. Employees in the Community is chaired by IBM and is about to be chaired by GrandMet, and you find Sandy Leitch of Allied Dunbar, David Rocks of W H Smith, David Barnes of Zeneca, on those teams. It's driven by the business world and by individual leaders in the business world who drive it through on a two-year focus.'

Another BITC strategy concerns developing as a centre of expertise on corporate and social responsibility. Explains Julia, 'There's a lot of work going on in companies which has always been known as corporate community involvement – what companies do in the community. Of course, a lot of what they do has to be driven from their own social responsibility and ethics, and their own belief in where they're going, what they want to do and how they want to behave. Over the next few years we think the social responsibility side will gain prominence. Companies will be saying, "We're doing this in our business because it makes good business sense, it is right and sensible for us to be a socially responsible company. We should be recruiting from ethnic minority areas, targeting customer support in particular parts of the country, doing different things which are much more about social responsibility than just what a company does in the community."'

Companies have long-term business interest in social cohesion in Britain. It is not in their interest to have pockets of prosperity in a sea of deprivation into 2000. Says Julia, 'Not only does it mean the costs for business are stupendous, but you are doing business in a society where there are no-go areas and, for example, you're paying out benefits to 68 per cent of people on one housing estate who are unemployed, unemployable and are effectively now an under class which you cannot touch.'

From my experience, a change in attitude is going on at the moment in Britain, in thinking about the responsibilities of companies to the stakeholder, not seeing this as a narrow world that only shareholders care about. Julia agrees: 'Companies are now, and will increasingly be, in a world where a wider group of stakeholders can have an effect on their profitability and their licence to operate, whether that be Greenpeace or Shell, or in a global way. We see global corporate community involvement strategies. There was a rather good line the other day about "companies, who are concerned to be seen, need to be seen to be concerned." That is a change, you know, they're not doing this hidden away behind the corner now.'

Julia has noted companies' business plans are more likely to have a social responsibility string to them towards 2000. 'The more sophisticated companies are clear that how their customers and employees see them can be affected by the way in which they do their community work. There's not enough research yet to show how customers view this although there does seem to be some evidence indicating customers will change their purchasing allegiance on the basis of what they perceive a company is doing in the community. That does have an impact. For example, Tesco's "Computers in Schools" has been an outstanding success at the tills – they certainly wouldn't be running it for the fourth year if it wasn't. You shop at Tesco's, get £25 vouchers which you give to a local school and the school claims a computer as part of the deal.'

On the other hand, customers are darkly suspicious about companies doing things in the community when they can't understand why they're doing them. Julia agrees. 'If Company A sets out and says, "We're very keen on Guide Dogs for the Blind, we're going to do a lot about that, and we want to tell you customers about Guide Dogs for the Blind," customers think, "What have Guide Dogs got to do with A?" If the company happens to be making spectacles, or it happens to be called Optrex Eyes, fine, we see the connection, but if not, we don't understand it and we're rather suspicious.' When, however, W H Smith said, 'We're really keen on getting books into schools, on encouraging volunteer readers, getting more parents to read with their children in inner cities,' the customers said, 'Got it. You want people to buy books because you're in the business of selling books.

Fine. I understand that, and I endorse it.'

Texaco's a very interesting example, too, with its 'Children Should be Seen and Not Hurt' campaign. That was a brilliant piece of advertising. It was in their garages, service stations and all over the place. Big advertising was spent on it and it had a profound effect. There's real evidence that as a result Texaco gets much higher recognition as a caring company.

Julia says, 'Texaco is also a leading example of another BITC strategy – corporate community involvement – and did some very clever and ingenious work in the East End. It adopted an organization called Community Links, which is one of the outstanding operations down in Canary Wharf. They worked in partnership with a community entrepreneur and Tate & Lyle. Canning Town Hall was bought for a pound from the local authority, who didn't have a clue what to do with this great building with pigeons flying about inside it. As a result of the support of Texaco and Tate & Lyle it was transformed, and it's now the most marvellous centre for volunteering, for community use, for kids at risk, for everything you could possibly find. That was a very clever piece of work by Texaco.'

The quality part of BITC's strategy is getting this activity to bring benefit to the community and not to be seen as a get-rich-quick tactic and a rip-off by capitalists. That means companies and BITC need to be very careful about too much gung-ho over how marvellous the private sector is. 'Companies are only one of a range of partners working with the community. They need to work very clearly in partnership with local authorities, community organizations, voluntary groups, the community itself. There can be no suggestion of "We're telling you what to do," or "We're the cavalry coming over the hill."'

The member companies have a vast array of different views as to what BITC ought to do. Some see it as a guiding hand, others as the recipient of their experience which it can pass on to others. Says Julia, 'Some see us as enthusiast; creative swiper; hooverer of thoughts and different things to do – others as a lobbyist, an advocate, a partnership builder. Some of the most sophisticated companies say, "You don't need to worry about persuading us to do the stuff, we now wish you to get on and persuade others, so the whole road is not taken up by us."'

BITC works very closely with the Prince's Trust. The Prince of Wales was concerned about the way in which the BITC internal organization was sending a message of potential confusion to the out-side marketplace. If you've heard of organizations called the Prince's Trust, the Prince's Youth Business Trust and the Prince's Trust Volunteers, it is not immediately obvious what the difference is between all of them, because surely all of them are concerned with inspiring young people to set up their own small business, to be a vol-unteer, to climb a mountain or whatever. Julia thinks his concern was whether 'we were doing everything we should to get a common, coherent and clear message out, not only to thousands of young people but also to many supporters and funders.

'As far as BITC is concerned, the Prince of Wales has been a very active president for the last ten years, and he will go on, we hope, for the rest of the nineties. His hope is that BITC will help to get busi-ness to make a real difference on the ground. He is absolutely driven by results. When you attempt to do the evaluation of what BITC achieves, his concern is always "where has the grass come off the mowing machine, where has something happened which may be innovative, which may be tough, which may be difficult, but which has made a difference to the lives of the inner cities", since that's what he's particularly concerned about. He has a tremendous memory for ideas and initiatives, so I don't get away with much as the chief exec-utive! He is continually saying, "What happened to that idea for regenerating mills in the north-east, where are we on that very inter-esting idea about running an investment fund for community entre-preneurs?" and so on. The Prince will be saying in the year 2000, how have we made a difference? Where's the evidence, where are the results? Where are forty examples over the last year or so of the things that companies have done as a result of their "Seeing is Believing" visits?'

Julia's biggest hassle is trying to keep at the leading edge of com-munity involvement: to keep the ideas, the creativity, the campaign-ing, the sparkle and the bite of it all, while also managing a recent massive merger with another voluntary organization in order to give BITC the strength on the regional ring that it needs for the millen-nium. 'I need that strength to be able to deliver to all those com-panies out there who keep saying, "Yes, it's all absolutely fine, Julia, but what do we do in Lincolnshire?"'

Everybody's mergers are tough, but voluntary organization mergers are particularly so, because you're dealing with people who care deeply about their particular thing. Says Julia, 'I think the voluntary sector will do more merging. I'm sure that will happen, in the same way business is streamlining and trying to decide what its core business is. There will be more strategic alliances even if there aren't more mergers. For the voluntary sector, life is dependent partly on government handouts, donations and fund raising. Many organizations now increasingly believe that business is somehow going to back them, while businesses are increasingly saying, well, we might back you, but how do we differentiate you from the others? That causes a pressure for the voluntary sector to explain what it does and why it's unique.'

BITC is concerned to support the social and economic regeneration of the communities by raising the quality and extent of business involvement. For Julia, a millennium wish would be that whatever government is in power at that time, it should recognize the contribution business can bring to the community fabric of society. 'Government should make it easier for companies to do that, not more difficult. Until recently great problems were caused by government either changing its mind or producing new initiatives all the time. Every time a minister got into a post, up came a new idea for something that businesses might do.

'So far the government has proved very impractical on trying to find incentives for business to do more in the community. In the States there are enormous tax breaks and very helpful financial incentives for both individuals and companies to get engaged. I would be very keen to see the government make it easier for everyone to do more, perhaps linking substantial economic regeneration to awards from the National Lottery.'

Julia is keen for BITC to raise the quality and extent of business involvement in the community and to make it a natural part of successful business practice. She is not a great believer that you get business to do things because other people do things. 'My real millennium wish would be that all the top 500 UK companies, which would include those with headquarters internationally, should see their role and responsibility and the benefit they could bring to both business and the community.'

DAVID LLOYD LEISURE PLC

The UK market leader in ownership and operation of tennis- and fitness-based leisure clubs, and one of the largest sport and leisure groups in Europe. Listed on the Stock Exchange since 1993, it currently has a market value of approximately £120 million.

David Lloyd – Chief Executive

For seventeen years David Lloyd was one of Britain's foremost professional tennis players on the international circuit. He played many times at Wimbledon and was doubles specialist in the British Davis Cup team, being ranked in the world's top 30. He worked as a coach in Canada and the Netherlands and was coach to the British Wightman Cup team for several years, also to the Israeli National Team. He retired from the circuit in 1981 and devoted himself to his new company.

In 1986, with Jim Slater, he set up the Slater Foundation, which trains young boys with the ultimate aim of producing a Wimbledon champion.

In 1995 he became Captain of the British Davis Cup team, in which position he has responsibility for team selection and training.

He was named Entrepreneur of the Year in 1994 PLC Awards – the City's Oscars – sponsored by Coopers & Lybrand.

The Company

Founded in 1980, the company built and ran the first commercially successful indoor tennis club in Britain. There are now 13 clubs, six of them in the Greater London area, the rest throughout England and Scotland. Further new clubs are planned throughout the country. The company also manages a tennis centre in Portugal and has an 18-hole golf course in Bristol.

All the clubs offer:

indoor and outdoor tennis courts, a gymnasium, an indoor swimming pool, a dance and aerobics exercise studio, bars, restaurants and corporate entertaining facilities and a creche.

and, according to local demand:

ten-pin bowling facilities, squash and badminton courts, an outdoor swimming pool, an indoor bowling green, an indoor running track and a Laser-Quest arena.

Except for ten-pin bowling in selected clubs, facilities are open only to members and their guests.

David Lloyd Leisure PLC
David Lloyd, Chief Executive

I wanted to include in this book an entrepreneur; I wanted to write about small business excellence; and about leisure and sport. To achieve those ambitions in the one individual is a bonus. That individual is tennis player David Lloyd.

When David Lloyd played the professional tennis circuit, he travelled to different places in the world where tennis clubs were lovely country clubs with family memberships. Britain had nothing similar. He decided, when he left the pro game, to start a chain of clubs similar to those in North America where he had worked. There, clubs were not just tennis clubs but part and parcel of people's lives. For David Lloyd they were the place to go, to meet people, the social scene, unlike the UK-type terrible club where people weren't allowed to mix, had no showers that worked and so on. The UK was living in the dark ages.

Returning to Britain, he discovered the right piece of land around London for a club to be built; it was at Heston, near London airport. He invested all his money earned from tennis, and tried to raise the rest of the money for the project. The cost was around £1.6m, a lot of money in 1981. It was difficult for him, because everyone he approached said, 'Well, show us the sort of club.' His reply was, 'There isn't one in Britain, and that is why I want to do it.'

Now, in the mid-nineties David Lloyd Leisure [DLL] has a turnover of £25m and there are tennis and fitness centres from Renfrew to Ringwood, Cardiff to Chigwell. Clubs are mushrooming across the UK, expanding at a rate of two or three each year – and the company is set for further expansion with the recommended Whitbread takeover. Advantage Lloyd! How did it start – and was it easy?

David Lloyd left school at fifteen, with only two O levels, but one was maths. 'I was always good at maths.' He did all the feasibility studies for his proposal himself. 'I was lucky. When working in Canada I ran a club, learning how the figures stacked up, how margins worked, and how many members you needed to balance the books. The only thing I needed investors to believe in was the fact that a club, totally different from any before, was going to attract 3,000 people. That was the difficulty. When you have the 3,000 people a club can make money, but people did not believe you could get 3,000 people. We did. It took off immediately – opened in 1982 and was sold out within a month.'

David had invested his money, bought plans, an office, paid an architect. He had no pieces of jigsaw in place in order to convince investors, therefore he made a model to support his idea. 'I must have seen a hundred people in six months. Most would have given up. People here are nervous about something new. It was a heartbreak job. I remember coming home, saying, "This is ridiculous, no one believes me, I can't get the money." I was playing Davis Cup and my name was still reasonably well known. I had an income coming in. A lot of sports people retire, wait a couple of years and then try to go back in. Well, people have forgotten you, and you've lost your credibility. Unless you put your own money in, you aren't going to get past the door. At the end of the day people invested because I put in every single penny I earned. I wasn't someone who said, "Here's my name and I want you to put up all the money." It was, "I'm putting it all in." I had many meetings where I just walked away and said, "What am I doing this for?" No one believed me, it was a terrible situation.

'The banks have always been negative. Because I couldn't show them anything similar in the UK we kept knocking on doors to no avail. Finally Barratts the builder became interested, but wanted 50 per cent. I didn't want to give away 50 per cent of the club but we were considering that deal when a chap phoned me out of the blue and said, "Look, I've got some money to invest. I love tennis." He invested some extra money, which encouraged another venture capitalist.' That enabled David to keep the same amount of money in the project and strike a deal enabling him to keep control of the company. 'It was vital the financial structure allowed me control because it is difficult to put all your own money into something and have no control over it. After a long struggle we had the finance ready to go.'

David Lloyd recalls how choice of location for their first club was vital. To this day his company puts considerable effort into identifying new sites with a view to maintaining the pace of opening new clubs. 'I learned well from the short association with Barratts, about location, location, location. That is something we based our whole concept on. It doesn't matter how good you are or how well you manage, if it is in the wrong place it is not going to make money. Take all the retail, sports, leisure businesses, the night clubs, where location is number one: simply if it isn't in the right place, it's not going to work. At that stage, in 1982, with the M25 starting and the M4 the busiest road in Britain, we needed some twelve acres of land without paying a fortune for it. Around the major roads of London, that is a difficult mix to achieve. Location was the key: Heston was the right place, and in our talks with Hounslow Council we found them willing to rent land rather than require me to purchase it. With planning consent it took off better than anyone imagined.'

After opening the first successful centre, David found another site. 'We brought in a partner who put all the money in with a management contract. This was a mistake. As soon as it was running, the guy who had invested made my life impossible. Every time I journeyed between clubs, the rules changed in the one I had just left. I said, enough is enough, my name is on there. We got out. With hindsight, it would have been better to borrow the money for the second development because my concept worked. I made a commercial decision that it was wrong to risk the club that was going so well to support 100 per cent finance on the new one. I was being too cautious.'

DLL gradually expanded to the thirteen clubs it has today but David Lloyd still feels they are worried in the City about leisure's reputation of people coming in, changing course, spending lots of money and diversifying. 'What the City must understand is that *all* my money is in the business. I've taken none out, not sold a share, only bought shares. Every decision I value enormously, and I value the pound in my company more than anyone else. I teach all my staff to say, "Look, that's your pound, would you spend it? If that's your name over the door would you allow it to be dirty?" That is the concept throughout the company, and we will not do stupid things, I hope. We have built up slowly, and I think the City now realize we are not going to be one of those fly-by-night companies. We are here to stay!'

DLL has a reputation for being well run. Yes, business is a risk, any new centre is a risk, with £6m development costs. How does David know any new centre is going to work? 'I study the area, do all my homework, the demographics, I build it correctly.' In order to turn a possible site into a definite project his key requirements are price, suitable location, stringent demographic criteria and agreement with the local council on planning permission. Somewhere along the line, you might pick a bad site that doesn't work. That can happen. It did at Beckenham, which became an abortive project, courtesy of failed Department of the Environment planning permission.

'I am very disappointed at what has happened in government. Take the planning side. Sport is difficult to get going in this country unless certain types of land can be used for it. We are light years behind in facilities. Not just tennis. Speak with Seb Coe on athletic grounds. We are living in the dark ages, miles behind. The only way we can build is by acquiring a big area that can be used for nothing else but sport. But we are treated as a planning issue, the same as a supermarket. Well, I cannot pay £1m an acre, it will not stack up. I have constant battles with the government and the minister, because planning authorities are giving approval and then the government are calling it in and saying no. Sadly, the government are ignoring local views.'

David says, 'It's important that the government should give better help. To own your own business you've got VAT returns, lots of things where you have to hire professionals. Accountants and solicitors charge a fortune, and at the end of the day you are paying so many fees you don't make the thing stack up. There must be ways of making small businesses easier to run. Government should look at lowering VAT thresholds. People starting up should have a clear run rather than have to fill in a thousand forms.'

He has strong views on legislation. 'Some of the rules and regulations coming through to us leisure operators are staggering. At the end of the day, you won't be able to run your business. People in government don't know what happens in the field. I train my staff, all my managers have to know how to serve a pint, they have to know how the plumbing works, because if you're not in the field, you can't make a judgement. You have no clue. A lot of people say, "We do this and we do that", but they're not down on the floor. They don't know what happens. Every single council in the land has a different interpretation of safety and fire regulations. I go from Heston to Finchley, and the rules and regulations on what I have to do only two miles away are different. You sometimes don't know until you open a new club! The guy says, "No, you're not opening because your glass is the wrong type." The legislation is amazing. It's going to swamp everybody – no one will be able to function.'

On Europe, David thinks trade agreements are productive but doesn't believe one currency is going to work. 'We are so different from the French and Germans, I am not sure how we are going to combine. Look at history. It will not work the way it's been outlined. We need a trade agreement, that's about it, then work that way. To have one currency? I just can't contemplate how Germany can have the same as Portugal, they are chalk and cheese. Trade agreements, yes, but cultures do not change.'

For the future, tennis is still at DLL's helm but it's important for the company to be able to do other things. 'We believe the way forward for us into 2000 is to carry on the tennis units, with the health and fitness, and gradually try one or two other things like golf and bowls. Introduce them slowly, and if they work we can do more. We will not do more golf until we know the one we own in Bristol works. We are young enough to do a little bit here and there until we find out what works.'

Today DLL are capitalized at £154.5m, with some 1,000 staff. From when it started fifteen years ago, it has grown rapidly. With his recent takeover he is winning aces. That would benefit all his staff. 'I am proud of the fact we have a share option scheme, all the way down to the people serving behind the bar. I don't think any company does that. Our bonus scheme and our share options are not linked to the staffing salary, I don't think that is the right way.'

He believes people should be incentivized, but does not agree with across the board percentage increases: 'If you give someone 10 per cent of £20,000 he's getting so much more than the person on 10 per cent of £10,000. That might not be the right reward. We don't do it that way. We reward absolutely on what we believe that person has deserved that year, not linked to salary.'

Each club is run autonomously with the manager doing his own budgets, deciding whether pay should go up, within certain parameters. 'We always raise by the amount of inflation. Then we say to the manager, right, you have done very well this year, a lot of you deserve a share of the rewards, so here is £20,000, you give it out to your staff, how you like, your choice. That's how we do it.'

David believes the shareholders should have the right to have some say on executive pay. 'They are the people you are working for at the end of the day. I have three very strong non-executive directors, and, quite rightly so, there is no way they will allow pay rises for myself or anyone else that are not linked to what we do in the company. I am very "pro" non-exec directors. People view me as DLL, and believe I make all the decisions. It's absolutely the opposite, I see my non-execs every week. They have a lot to give. Somebody's got to make a decision, but you've got to listen. The three non-execs we brought on at the time of the float have been a tremendous help. They have different backgrounds. We have Peter Goldstein, who started Superdrug, then sold out, he is probably one of the wealthiest men in Britain, but has come from a barrow boy to a multi-millionaire. Knows the cash business, knows all the things that are necessary to know from that side. We have John Rogers, who has been on many boards and knows a lot about the City. And John Hunter who was a main board director and the chairman of Smith, Kline and Beechams from a products side. So he's got a marketing background. On any pay rises, or whatever, they decide. If someone does something really special, and is very important to the company, it has to be rewarded. I don't believe in ladders. That is why we are successful. That is why people are coming to work for us. A guy can come in and work for me tomorrow as the front of desk reception manager, and in six months can be the manager. There are no ladders. You have to have certain attributes, but you mustn't say, "Well, you start there, and by the time you're 99 you can still be there." I think it would be a very bad incentive, and we won't have any of that.'

To make a club run, you need to know the people, because there are completely different cultures in each club. A club is successful because the manager is king and knows his unit.

To work in a leisure club you have to love, live, eat and drink that club. It is a tough job, seven days a week. Outside London staff seem to do this, are much more loyal and love the work. Open a club in London and there is probably 80-90 per cent turnover of staff in the first year. Says David, 'That's what you get in London, because they don't like work, they don't want to work hard, and they have somewhere else to go. A lot of companies, Whitbread for example, bring staff down from the North, because they work better. There's no question about it, they do. That is something we're looking at into the future. We are only as good as our staff – that is the key to it all.'

DLL are always planning two years forward. David's time is spent mostly on location. 'I would say 80 per cent of my time is spent driving around looking at sites, talking to councils. I now have seven architects working for me full time, because we have so many building projects on the go. Last year I would have paid nearly £1m in fees to architectural firms, so I said, what am I doing that for? Now, they are all in-house and they will be working full out to get our next five projects – Edinburgh, Manchester, Leeds, Sidcup and Newcastle – under way and built.'

For the future, David believes there is a golden triangle between Cheltenham and Gloucester. 'We know that. We have probably got two years of what we would call Triple A sites such as Cardiff, then you have to look at the Brightons, Gloucesters, Nottinghams and Leicesters. At the moment you can go to many major cities in Britain and there isn't a David Lloyd Centre. Leeds and Manchester have nothing, it's mind-blowing when you think about it.'

Let me turn now to sport and its future in the UK towards 2000. 'It's getting better but from a parent's background, and those running the sport, many think sport is not a job. Parents won't let their children go into it, associations are still amateur. The amount of money raised, spent and earned in sport, if you add it up, is gi-normous. Look at these racing drivers – it's mega money. Agassi's on $24m for three years, just to use Nike clothing. It's unbelievable how much money is spent.

'The more money comes in, the more you get agents, drugs, and a feeling we must win at all costs. To get more people in Britain back to my sport, tennis, it's very important for everybody to realize that it is a business, with big money out there. The club I learnt at is lovely, but the showers don't work and there's nowhere to go afterwards. They have playing-in tests and you have to wear white all the time. We are dreaming, you know. If we want people to play the game, we've got to make it easy, not difficult. Young kids aren't allowed to play at half the UK clubs. They say, "Oh you can't play on a Saturday or a Sunday if you are a junior." Well, when can they play? That can be changed overnight. You have to encourage people to play the game. My brother lives in the States and the facilities are just out of this world compared with here. When you speak to Coe and all these athletics guys, they will say exactly the same thing. Golf is the only sport that is getting better here, because we have some winners to follow.'

In order to get us better in sport towards 2000, David believes the lottery might help people with funds, but there have to be tax breaks to encourage people to invest in sport. 'I'm not talking about bingo and bowling. I wouldn't dream of trying to get a grant for ten-pin bowling. But for some sport you need financial breaks, because it is very expensive. Take tennis. You can only get four people on a tennis course, and an indoor court costs £150,000, a lot of money for four people. With our weather, unless you have indoor facilities all over the country how are you going to play? Central government has to give breaks for the people who invest a lot of money. From a tennis point of view, schools have got to be encouraged. We are better at cricket, but at school I wasn't allowed to play tennis because I could get into the cricket team! This is fine, but I was the best in the country at tennis, yet I had to play cricket, because the school was cricket, cricket, cricket. Some girls' schools are good, but at boy's schools tennis was way back – no deal on that.'

When David talks to councils, he explains that he allows memberships where local people come in for a day without becoming a full member, as long as they behave. 'We do that. It's important, getting children off the streets. I worked in Israel as their national coach for a bit. They started their first national tennis centre in Tel Aviv out of donations from people all round the world. Their concept was to allow any child to come in; they were given a racquet, free; they were helped, tested and played. One guy goes round the world raising money to build more tennis centres, and they have, I think, twelve, all free, any kid can attend. And you know, they have higher ranking tennis players in Israel, with about a million people, than we do in Britain with nearly sixty million. If you go to areas like Tel Aviv and speak to the mayor, the crime rate, the kids kicking up things, has changed because they actually go down to the tennis centre and get on. It's a big scheme. There are a lot of things we can do in that way to get kids off the streets. We are getting better but we're light years behind.'

David is sad about our poor showing in tennis. 'I get really cross. Again, it's a matter of admitting mistakes. If the LTA had said, "Yeah, we're not in great shape, but look what we're going to do," they would have a lot more credibility than saying, "Oh we're actually doing quite well." You don't have to be a brain surgeon to know we're doing very badly, because you just look at where we are in world rankings. At last the LTA have accepted the fact they need to go forward. That is why I was appointed Davis Cup Captain – which was a shock obviously because of the things I've said! Now they are starting to look at changing: to become a professional body in a professional way, rather than all amateurs. The beauty about the game in this country is we do have a very wealthy LTA, because of Wimbledon, which raises millions of pounds, so we're getting the structure and the funds in place. Those two together with a bit of luck, three or four years down the line, might start to produce a few players, and then the base will get bigger and we might gain some winners.'

Towards the millennium, David's aim, obviously, as Davis Cup captain is to start to win a few matches. 'Winning is a drug, losing is a drug, and we have been losing for so long, everybody expects us to lose. It's a terrible thing to think you're a loser. You've got to really believe in what you do. If you don't, you're never going to win, and that is important.'

Are sports champions born? 'To a degree, but if you look at someone like Chrissie Evert, who I know very well [brother John was married to the Wimbledon Ladies' champion] you can learn from these people. The most important thing to be a success in sport, or in business, is dedication of the mind, a selfish, completely blinkered vision of what you want and nothing will get in the way of that. Training 100 per cent to succeed. Chrissie used to play for hours and hours hitting the forehand. She didn't have the racquet talent of a lot of people, but she had the talent of being able to say, "Right, that's what I want and that's what I'm going to get." Nothing got in the way. That is very important. When I'm looking at young players to make it, I'm looking at the mental side rather than the racquet talent.'

David goes on, 'I am worried about tennis from a spectator point of view, apart from Agassi. All they do now is serve the ball, hit it at a million miles an hour, it is not a rally. I want to see some action, some fun, see some balls coming back over the net. The game's gone too quick.'

Towards the millennium David Lloyd is trying to base his centres more round families. 'Look again at Whitbread, in this book. Its pubs are becoming family pubs, and I agree, that is the way to go. I think it important that a concept is built round family life in Britain. I want more people in this country to come to a club, and not pay a fortune for it, to join in something that is social as well as sport. It's a way of life, and it's important to get that across. On our golf courses we're encouraging ladies, not discouraging them. We want ladies to come. We have a crèche in the golf club. America has country clubs where everybody mixes. You don't have all-male preserves as in Scotland. Half the clubs in Scotland, ladies aren't even allowed to change in the clubhouse. That's scandalous. What sort of country are we living in here!?'

All his clubs have predominantly ABs memberships, which is the nature of tennis and gym, but David wants that to change. 'What we did at our centre in Glasgow, was build it big enough to lower the price. We have a lot of ABs but we also have many Cs. It really is a friendly club and they all mix together. That is why it works, there are no social barriers. I haven't said, "Right, here's a £2,000 membership club." If I set membership at that price I'm going to get one class of person, and that is not what I want. I want the mix of people that makes it happy. That is what makes our clubs work successfully.'

He recognizes there are other clubs who don't want families. 'That will happen and they will carry on like that. But that is not my concept, not something we endorse. All the managers do a club showround and tell customers, "Look, if you don't like kids, don't come on Saturday and Sunday, because it's all kids." We are into kid's gyms, kid's play areas, we have nursery schools in all the clubs. Big business and good service. Kids are part and parcel of our business towards 2000.'

David Lloyd thinks he can take his concept and expertise to other parts of the world. 'I don't see our future only in the UK, absolutely not. We believe we're very good at managing and I don't think it needs to be just tennis. We've managed to convince the City that we're good operators. People look at the returns. We get a margin of 32–33 per cent which is double that achieved by many others. Competitors or would-be imitators will look at us, no question about that, but we have two things going for us. We have a brand name which stands us in great stead, and our motto is Marks and Spencer's: five-star quality for three-star price. This is important, and to give the same quality every day, which is something we haven't achieved yet, but are trying to do.'

DLL are growing at double digit figures by using all areas on their sites. They are very similar to a supermarket. 'They are clever,' says David. 'They move their sales and product line around. If something doesn't sell, they change it. They all do it, and watch carefully what the other guy does. Suddenly everybody comes down in price, which is great, it's competition. We do the same. If we have an area that is not making money, we will change it into something that will prosper, and we'll give members something extra. That's the move to the millennium. It is not just making money, you have to give the service as well, otherwise the memberships will not come.'

Where DLL has fallen down is the customer service bit. 'We have been complacent because we are the only market player out there. Our facilities are second to none, and we can't be beaten on price, but in the past we have not concentrated on giving the service the facilities demanded. We have now invested a lot of money in setting up a training department. When growing, that is probably something business companies don't spend on because they are looking at a short-term gain and it is one area you think, "Pshew, what money is that going to earn me?" So you shut it off. That is wrong; yet we did, there's no question we did. If we were not the only player in town that could have caused us enormous problems. I hope we caught it in time, and now we are investing in our people. We are making sure they are trained, rewarded and go forward as part of a very success-ful company.'

A millennium wish? 'I would wish we could win the Davis Cup and have a Wimbledon champion, because that is my life! I am a ten-nis player, and if that happened, the business spin-off would be enor-mous. I would love it to happen. It would change the whole concept of tennis. You would have sports shops making money again, tennis clubs playing everywhere. You would have every kid wanting to be a champion. The game would just blossom. We could take our cen-tres to anywhere in Britain and know they are going to work!'

As an individual, David feels he has something to prove. He thinks people felt the first club was luck and the second one was more luck. The City, however, has realized DLL is a good company. It has done what it said it was going to do when it was floated. It has done more. 'We had to decide which way to go forward. One or two clubs a year or a dramatic explosion. We decided the way forward, since we liked the product, was growing big quicker rather than as a trickle. It was a major decision and everybody was 100 per cent for it, that is why we floated.'

David enjoys going into the City because he has a good story to tell. They like the product and are beginning to understand it. Leisure has a bad image, and he tells analysts DLL is 'clean' leisure because DLL is more than that. 'We are ready-made sport rather than leisure. I've got great respect for those leaders in leisure with very well-run companies. They are more for the passing trade. We are about membership. There is a difference. I'm not saying they're better, or we are, but a lot of good leisure companies have been blackened by bad leisure companies, and it is an image that we have to change.'

DLL wants to be one of the most respected leisure companies in Britain. In five years time David will be disappointed if he hasn't got fifty centres, with masses of smaller satellite facilities tacked on. He has a lot of ambition and a recommended £201m take-over by Whitbread as this book went to press should see DLL achieve that goal.

Personally David would like to be remembered for what he's done for British tennis. He would like to think he's done his bit. 'It's a game I love, and I've got to put that above everything else. I don't think any single person or any association should be bigger than the game. They have to put the game first.'

For DLL, he is happy knowing that lots of Americans come to the clubs, saying they are the best-run they've ever been to. 'That gives us a lot of pleasure, because America's the best in sport. Ultimately, our asset is our people. We haven't ever ignored them in making them part of the company. We haven't always helped them enough in training, but they are the business. Without them we have nothing.'

I doubt if we'll have a Wimbledon champion by the year 2000, but many more kids – and their parents – will be happily playing tennis if David Lloyd has his way – and he'll be a millionaire.

Footnote
While this book was in preparation Whitbread was in the process of making an offer for David Lloyd Leisure. The offer became unconditional and DLL is now part of the Whitbread Group of Companies.

EMAP

Turnover (1994–1995)	£547.1 million
Advertising	£251.8 million
Circulation	£227.9 million
Exhibitions	£35.7 million
Newspaper printing	£11.0 million
Other	£20.7 million
Operating profit	£67.6 million
Staff at 1 April 1995	6,934

Publishes consumer magazines, provides business information, publishes and prints newspapers and operates radio stations, with 70% of its business in the UK, 26% in France, 3% in Germany and 1% elsewhere.

Robin Miller – Group Chief Executive

Robin Miller joined EMAP in 1965 as a reporter on *Motor Cycle News*. He was appointed General Manager of the Magazine Division in 1974 and joined the board in 1976. He was appointed Group Chief Executive in 1985.

Business is in the following divisions:

Consumer magazines: 56% of group turnover

Titles include *Elle, Q, More!, New Woman, Just Seventeen, Match Weekly, Here's Health, Angling Times, Smash Hits, The Garden, Practical Photography, Motor Cycle News, Looks, Sky, Slimming* and many, many more. French titles include *Télé Poche*, with a circulation of over 1 million.

Business communications: 22% of group turnover
This includes business magazines and other business and specialist information services, including exhibitions.

Newspapers & printing: 18% of group turnover
Local weekly and daily papers.

Radio: 4% of group turnover
Local stations in London, Liverpool, Manchester, Preston, Leeds, Cardiff, Newcastle, Sheffield, Hull and Teeside.

EMAP
Robin Miller, Chief Executive

A hundred years ago East Midland Allied Press began life as a local newspaper company, its founder being a local MP. He decided he wanted to buy one or two local papers to support his cause, and formed the Winfrey family-owned company. When parts of the stock were sold off in the market in 1947 it became a publicly quoted company. Now it has moved on from being a family-owned, although Richard Winfrey is still a non-executive director, and today it is a full-blown PLC.

EMAP got into magazines in 1953 by accident. It had some spare capacity on the presses and someone came up with the idea of publishing a fishing magazine as a tabloid newspaper. The bulk of its business has today grown into consumer magazines – some ninety in the UK; business magazines, which it started effectively fifteen years ago with the acquisition of a title called *Which Computer?*; and exhibitions, born at the same time. EMAP is now the biggest exhibition organizer in the UK. It still has local newspapers – in 1995 it celebrated the 300th anniversary of the *Stamford Mercury*, which is pretty remarkable, as it is the oldest newspaper in the UK to have been continuously published since its first issue.

Recently EMAP has expanded into radio in the UK, and also into Europe with consumer and business magazines. Those parts of the business now outstrip its local newspaper activities and it is a broadly based media company, although it has no national newspapers and no television.

Robin Miller, the chief executive, explores the transformation of the business publishing side. 'We ran the business publishing and exhibitions sides separately, until we came to the conclusion that what we were really trying to do was serve the market by whatever means it wished to make contact with its customers. We are really acting as a conduit between seller and buyer. What we aim to do is serve our clients in whichever way they want, and by whichever form of media they wish, whether it be on-the-page advertising through a magazine, organizing a conference, holding an exhibition, doing an awards night, by newsletters, directories, or whatever.'

A good example of their approach and appeal is in the motoring market, where they have a magazine called *Fleet News*. 'The fleet market represents over 50 per cent of the sales of cars in the UK – it is a huge market. Half the cars you see running around the roads are company cars; this is unique in the world, though it is now starting to happen in Europe, which is why we have a magazine in Germany and organize a fleet show over there. In the UK fleet market we have a weekly magazine and a monthly; we have a fleet show; a fleet awards night; fleet conferences; price guides called *CAP* (Car Auction Prices) – they're the Bible of the new and second-hand car market.'

Advertising is cyclical: it depends on the state of the economy. In 1990, when the economy fell down, business advertising went off the edge of a cliff. It is now recovering slowly. What EMAP wants to do is get more balanced revenue streams and not rely almost wholly on advertising revenue, which was up to 90 per cent, at one particular point, on their journals. As Robin Miller explains, 'We want to reduce our reliance on advertising by upping the value of the editorial information we provide, and persuading people to pay for that. People are prepared to pay for high-value or topical information. They are much less prepared to pay for editorial that simply fills the gaps between the ads. We are trying to improve the value of the information we provide. Our acquisition of *CAP*, for example, is a good illustration of that, because people who are selling second-hand cars need up-to-date car prices in order to keep abreast of what the market is doing and what they can charge.'

UK job advertising has been growing about 40 per cent year on year. That is greatly influenced by the recovery, or the return to normality more like it, which EMAP has been experiencing. It is slightly unusual this time: in many ways job advertising has in fact led the recovery. 'It is curious why this has happened,' says Robin Miller. 'I think it is partly because there is a definite sea-change in the structure of employment in this country. People no longer see themselves being employed for life. There are many more short-term contracts.

Employers see people coming in and out; it is much more flexible. There is much more part-time working. There are many more women employed.' Also, according to Miller, 'This recovery has to a large extent been export led. Many could not quite understand that, because we have never seen it before. Previous recoveries have mostly been consumer led. Many of the jobs now advertised are being provided by small to medium sized businesses selling their goods abroad.'

The fact is, advertising is an excellent barometer of the state of the economy. Much of the growth in EMAP's consumer magazine advertising revenue has been due to many of the big brands coming back in and trying to re-establish themselves. Explains Robin Miller, 'In the recession, both here and abroad, brand advertising, if not dropped, slowed down a lot. Many of the big companies went into short-term promotions, below-the-line advertising, as opposed to long-term brand advertising, above-the-line. There was a huge switch, particularly in the States. What we are now seeing is the building up of long-term brand values again. That is coming through in some of the advertising seen in our magazines and newspapers.'

Looking at the way forward to the year 2000, Robin Miller has already mentioned a change in employment in society. 'Whether we like it or not (it depends on your view of life), I think employment is going to become much more flexible, much more short-term. If you've put a lot of money into the training of an individual, that is going to be shared by maybe even your competitors. Good people are going to become ever more valuable. That does pose some long-term social problems, because that might imply there is going to be a greater divide between the skilled and the unskilled.'

On the business publication side, EMAP has restructured the business to suit the market, as opposed to the particular structure of the company. Says Robin Miller, 'Too many companies – and we are not free of this – structure themselves to suit themselves. That is the way it has been, that is the way it suits the particular management team etc. Every company does it, we do. But we feel there is such a need to serve the market, we just had to restructure. That was a pretty painful process because it meant merging one business with another. It meant some important people became redundant.'

In some cases EMAP makes the mergers and theming physical. Where it has computer exhibitions they will be in the same building as the computer magazines. Despite all the wonders of E-mail and

IT, for Robin Miller nothing beats being geographically close. 'That is a definite aid to communication. Nothing beats meeting people, being on the same floor. Being on a different floor can cause problems, being in a different building causes greater problems, however much you use the telephone, video conferencing, E-mail, and all that. There is a very definite interaction when people can pop next door and discuss it, talk about it, or bump into each other. We try, wherever possible, to put people in close proximity, if not in each other's pocket.'

The other big change which, plainly, print media businesses are contemplating, is the exchange of electronic information. It undoubtedly has greatest application towards 2000 in business communication, where you have detailed or topical information, pricing and so on. Robin Miller says, 'In our own modest way, and fairly cautiously, we are pushing through with that. For example, we have a magazine called *Local Government Chronicle* which is a weekly, but we also offer a daily, something called *LGC Net*, which chief executives of all local authorities can have on their desks, either through their PC or on a separate screen. They tap into it and get updated information on a daily or hourly basis. So we're supplementing our weekly, using our team of journalists to provide daily bulletins electronically. That is one little instance. Again, having bought BRAD, we are doing an electronic version so rate changes can be pushed through electronically to the market user. This is happening within our business communications division, and some of it will start happening elsewhere in EMAP.'

Basically EMAP wants to serve its customers every which way they want. It wants to serve them whether they want advertising on a page, sponsored sections, exhibitions, conferences or whatever. Says Robin Miller, 'We want to be able to deliver that information by whatever means – electronically, by paper, pigeon post if that is what they want. Let us have that facility to give them. I do believe the death of the printed word is much exaggerated, but plainly, by Internet or other mechanisms, people are going to be more geared to getting information through their PC as the years go by. The younger the individual the more likely she is to use her PC to receive information. Into 2001 that will become increasingly important. In ten years' time I see us being an information provider in the way we are now, but the way we deliver that information will have evolved, and much more of it will be delivered electronically – some still by

CD ROM, but that's likely to be superseded by more sophisticated on-line mechanisms . . . call it real time or whatever. The information delivery methods are going to change, and we have just got to be up with those.

'There is a different relationship between the consumer and his hobby magazine, and the businessman and his desire for quick and accurate information. In consumer publishing, there is a certain chemistry, a magic between the magazine and the individual. It's a personal thing, almost a badge. When girls get *Just 17* they take it to their bedrooms and read it. It is a private thing, they read it on their own, it is a very close relationship they have. When my mother gets *Yours* for the over sixty-fives, it is a friend dropping in, a personal communication, she loves that, and lots of its stories apply to her.'

The consumer magazine business is undergoing tremendous change in its distribution mechanisms, as there are now many more outlets. All the major supermarkets are selling magazines, like Superdrug, Woolworths and Asda. There are now almost 50,000 outlets, compared to around 35,000 five years ago. Says Robin Miller, 'The whole business of distribution, of getting magazines to the right place and displayed in the right way, is becoming a big issue now. But while distribution outlets are growing over the years, the market has become increasingly segmented. We started out with *Angling Times*, one magazine to cover the whole fishing activity. Now we have eight fishing magazines. There are another twenty on the news-stands, dealing with specialized fishing interests.' People who are interested in fishing on Grafham Reservoir don't automatically want to read about fishing on the Tweed in Scotland or the Wye in the Royal Forest of Dean or *vice versa*. And, of course advertisers want to get at the particular, as opposed to the general. 'That is why specialist magazines are very cost effective,' says Robin Miller. 'Advertising page rates are relatively high because the response is high. There is little wastage. Either way, the industry has become more and more segmented, and we have led the way in that. It will continue to get more so into the millennium, and there will be more magazines dealing with bits of markets.'

The magazine industry last year, saw some 600 new magazines being launched. 'I am not quite sure what the record of failure is, but it is obviously fairly high,' says Robin Miller. 'Lots of people are launching, very often one man bands, so only a small proportion of those are coming from the major publishers. New product development is fantastically important, in my view, for any business, certainly for publishing. It is a real ideas business. People love it. I guess it is like someone's new baby, it is the ultimate in creativity. Seeing your idea emerge and be there, on the news-stand. It is fantastic. We do it because it makes people feel good and is a great motivator internally; it gives EMAP a progressive image outside and attracts good people; and because when you get it right, you actually make pretty good money out of it.'

Launching new publications is high risk, because the probability of failure is high, but the rewards are worth it if EMAP gets it right. Acquisitions are a lower risk because you're buying a known quantity, but you are paying quite a high price for it. It is a balance, and EMAP has to do both. 'Many of our best magazines are launches which we started from scratch, whether it be *Garden News* and *Angling Times*, going back many, many years, or whether it be *Q*, *Mojo*, *Empire*, *Maxpower*, *Your Cat*, *It's Bliss*, or whatever. We have had failures. We had a very high profile failure called *Car Week* which cost many millions of pounds. We got it badly wrong. We had to get out. As a guy who rides a motorbike every now and again there's an old motorcycle racing analogy which says, "If you don't fall off every now and again, you aren't trying hard enough." Our track record is very, very good, but occasionally anyone will come a cropper. We got on again. We've launched *It's Bliss*, which is doing pretty well, and we will be launching many other magazines as well over the next few years.'

Product innovation is vital to the growth of EMAP towards 2000. Growing the company just by acquisitions would mean the return on capital was quite slow because acquisitions are expensive. In Robin Miller's view you have to get the mix right. 'When you can get successful launches, your return on capital employed is very high. You need that. Sometimes you have to buy to get yourself into a market – but then do a launch or relaunch off that. We got into the motoring market by buying *Car Magazine* from Murdoch, which was a well-established magazine, and it brought us a fund of expertise and a presence in that market, off which we can now launch new products.'

He gives two more reasons for product innovation: 'First, it is important for the culture of the company to have people who are able to see their ideas come to fruition. You have to be an ideas-driven company, and the ultimate idea is a launch. Of course, in every newspaper, every magazine you produce, every issue, you are going to want some new ideas, but the ultimate idea is a new product. Second, externally it is important to be seen as an innovative company because you then attract the best people. Our people, especially those in marketing and journalists, enjoy the idea of inventing new things. They like knowing that their ideas might just work one day. Having that culture is terrifically important and will ever be thus.'

Most journalists are highly disciplined people. They have to get a paper out every day, and they know the press has got to run dead on a particular time. Miller thankfully agrees. 'It is a *very* disciplined business. People make a mistake when they think journalists, as creative people, are sitting simply waiting for inspiration. Plainly there's a lot of that going on, but the discipline is vital. I suppose being a "hack" by trade, I don't have a particular problem dealing with people who are creative. In fact, it's bloody marvellous that people keep throwing ideas at you. It is great. The most important thing you must do as you get older – not necessarily wiser – is to receive ideas openly, with enthusiasm. Some you know will never work. Sometimes they do work, and the fact that it did not work last time should not prevent you trying again. That is why it is important to keep our whole business decentralized, to have young or young at heart people running the companies, people with very open minds, who will be receptive to anything which an 21-year-old, straight out of college, throws at them, and not turn it down.'

To my mind, the strength of EMAP's young companies is they often have no fear. They will have a go at anything. The most important thing about launches is to get the mix right, with a bunch of people who are committed, enthusiastic and without fear, and a bunch of slightly more sceptical people, who just knock an edge or two off it, and say, 'Well OK, but what about this, or what about that?' Robin agrees. 'I think with that picture you can get something which is likely to succeed. But it is really important to keep that balance just right; sometimes we don't do it, but 51 per cent of the time we probably do.'

Just like pressure in society to conform, there is a great pressure in business to get bigger at the centre, and that has to be resisted, at all costs. Robin Miller insists the HQ has to be kept to a minimum, and you have to push out responsibility as much as you possibly can to the people who are closest to the market. EMAP in total has about

6,000 people, of whom about thirty are in its head office. Ten years from now, he states, there may be more people, but certainly no more in head office. 'Our objective is a flatter organization for the millennium. The line people are going to make the decisions. That means, of course, those men and women are going to have to be bloody good, because you are going to have to give them responsibility, and they are going to fail every now and again just like I have. But as long as they don't fail too often, you have to keep letting them have a go at it. *I* cannot decide whether a launch into the heavy metal market is going to work or not, but the people in those marketing and editorial offices, alongside a bit of experience from the guys heading that particular company, will get as near right as dammit, and they should be allowed to get on with it. Only the big decisions will come to our main board.'

To the future. Although EMAP has dabbled in radio for many years – as local newspaper people they were allowed to share some local radio stations and did so – it did not seriously get involved until about four or five years ago. It is a new area for the company. Robin Miller says, 'It is part of the media business, it is effectively packaging a product, through programming, selling advertising on the back of that, and delivering an audience. Rather like the circulation of magazines, the relationship of a radio station to its audience is very important. We are relatively familiar with the fundamentals of the business, although the techniques are different. Plainly, radio has been a Cinderella business, which hasn't gone anywhere for many years. Not any more. Now it is going somewhere, because it's being managed better, the shackles are off, it has a lighter regulatory touch, and it is proving to be an effective medium; it works for people.'

It is not unlike consumer magazines. The markets are being segmented. Look at the London market, there are radio stations dealing with all taste buds, whether it be Jazz FM or Kiss 100 FM. Radio is a legitimate and exciting area for EMAP. 'There are going to be more stations, there are going to be more frequencies available, and there is the possibility of building a much bigger business than we currently have.'

What about EMAP and Europe? 'I see EMAP growing and developing globally. However, on the basis that you can only do so many things at once, we initially established ourselves in France around five years ago in joint ventures. We learnt enough about it to take a larger plunge. We want to build up our market share in France. We are the third biggest publisher now, with some 11 per cent of the market, and we want to do more. We are in Germany with some business titles, and we can do more. There are many structural changes going on in businesses there. Germany has been a very protected and private society; now, fifty years on from the war, many of the families and dynasties are changing and it is becoming much more open.'

Robin Miller would love to see, let's say, a launch of *Just 17* in Russia. And why not? 'There are millions of teenage girls who are thinking of sex and worrying about spots and all those sorts of things, and they want to read magazines like *Just 17* which are all about that. There are big markets out there, and that is where we would like to be towards 2000. We just have to get the timing right. We could be there by the millennium. By then I think we will be in a number of places, certainly in the Far East and almost certainly in the States. We will be much more global by the year 2000.'

He doesn't bother about politics very much. He only bothers about what governments either allow or prevent you from doing, and there is little doubt it is slightly frustrating. 'Looking at a regulated environment like television and radio, if we had to suffer that same regulation in consumer magazines, we would be nowhere by now. And yet, here we are, in an unregulated market, and the consumer has fantastic choice. Look at the number of consumer magazines there are on the news-stands. What remarkable choice the consumer has in a self-regulated industry, no interference by government. The market prevails, marvellous! I realize the airwaves are a slightly rarer commodity. However, governments, in my view, use these matters as an excuse for exercising a bit of control which they would love to have had on the print media if they had thought of it early enough. In terms of politics, I want as little state control, state interference, state support, state whatever, as possible, and freedom for individuals and markets to prosper. The more we have of that, the better.

'In some ways, France is like England twenty years ago, but things there are having to change. The world around them is changing. Things have to be freed up, through mobility of labour and so on. The UK is now an extremely healthy place, and when history is written, Margaret Thatcher will be seen to have done a tremendous job before she passed her sell-by date. If people could only remember how difficult it was to operate businesses – I do because I'm old enough – fifteen or twenty years ago, in the media, newspapers, magazines, in printing and in many another business. Well, how lucky we are now, and how lucky everybody is! I think the world has to go that way, and things will loosen up in these other European countries, and people will drop some of their more fanciful ideas.'

For Robin Miller trade unions exist and that's fine. He's relaxed about that. 'People are perfectly free to join and be members should they wish to do so. The fact is we negotiate locally with our people in every area now, and that is the right way to do it. No longer do we have people trotting down to the NGA at Bedford, or NUJ head-quarters, and all that kind of stuff. I went through that when we had a 23-week journalistic strike at Kettering in 1976. It doesn't do any-body any good. We negotiate locally or individually; most of our negotiations are on an individual basis with individual people.'

In 1997, if we have a Tony Blair government, does he see the trade unions regaining the powers they historically had? 'I think that is water under the bridge. Tony Blair is a social democrat, and I think he is doing all the right things. There are a number of backwoods-men who would like to return to the status quo, who are in sheep's clothing right now, until they get elected, and they will emerge at that time. Blair, and the people around him, seem to be pretty clear in what they want to do, and I hope they are strong enough to be allowed to do it, should they get to that point.'

A man of conviction, Miller is uncertain about being remembered at all for his thirty years at EMAP, because somebody else will come along and say 'Who the hell was that guy beforehand?' 'It's an irrel-evance. What my partner, David Arculus, and I did at EMAP will be judged by the magazines, the newspapers and the exhibitions that we got off the ground; the titles we did, and those still successful, prod-ucts like *Smash Hits* which is still going great guns after fifteen years, *Angling Times* after forty. We launch titles to be here a long time, for a sustained future. It's a constant process of tweaking the title as it changes with society and fashion. Obviously *Angling Times* today is not the *Angling Times* it was forty years ago. Always there's that con-stant living with the future. They're not here today, gone tomorrow things.'

For Robin Miller and EMAP it is just good to see those great titles still there and know they have played a little part in them. 'That is the feeling all our people get, Lynda, when they see the results of their work every day, week, month or year, in a product, whether it is a magazine, a newspaper or an exhibition. It is a living thing, it is dynamic. It changes every time it comes out, it is different. The people all make a little contribution to it, and they can see their work in front of them. It plops on to their desk, every week, every month. It's wonderful, wonderful!'

The vision of EMAP into the next century is that it will be a completely international company, doing what it is doing, delivering some of the entertainment and information in different ways, but also in many of the same. It might be delivering some spin-offs of its consumer magazines in terms of television channels. Or it might have a specialist car channel, or a *Golf World* channel, based on its magazines, where people who are prepared to pay can watch their favourite sport as well as read about it. As Robin Miller says, 'Advertisers will be happy because we will be delivering to that audience clearly, using cable or satellite. Much of our business information will be going by electronic means. We cannot even contemplate what technology will be in ten years' time, because what there is now will be completely obsolete. We will be international, we will be publishing magazines, we will be staging exhibitions all over the world.'

Miller doesn't think EMAP has any major headaches. 'What we try to do is produce even more ideas, and produce even more good people. At the end of the day, it is all about the companies who employ the best people, and treat them in the best way. These are the companies who will win. It has ever been thus and it will continue to be thus until I'm too old to worry about it, like forever.'

Corporate excellence and the social problems of a divide between the haves and the have-nots is a major issue as far as Robin Miller is concerned, and one which all nations and governments have to investigate. 'What has made companies good, what does make companies good, and what will continue to do so into the millennium, is not technology in itself, it is how it is used. I do not believe in computer intelligence – if you put rubbish in, you get rubbish out. The companies which employ the best people, which motivate them best and organize them best, will win. If we are going to win in the year 2005, we must have the best people, who are most enthusiastic, most dedicated and with the best ideas. And the best recommendation is their saying to their friends, come and work in EMAP, it is a great place to be. That is my aim.'

Robin Miller rarely looks back. 'What has happened has happened,' he says, 'and it's there and it's fine, but the only important thing is the next step. What happened yesterday or five minutes ago is irrelevant. We can learn from it, but we cannot change it. There is no point agonizing over what has gone wrong or right, except to do a bit of analysis and say, let us do it slightly differently next time. That is all. I rarely look back and I don't see much point in putting epitaphs on headstones, it is all bunk. I don't give tuppence for what has happened, quite frankly. Because when you're dead, you're dead, and the only point for doing things is when people are alive. It's looking forward that's important, not back.'

FILOFAX GROUP PLC

Turnover (1994–1995)	£31.2 million
Operating profit	£5.0 million
Profit before tax	£4.9 million
Employees	221

A group of consumer supply businesses offering specialized products under strong brand names in over forty countries worldwide.

Robin Field – Chief Executive

Robin Field started his business career working for Jardine Matheson & Co in Hong Kong and Taiwan. After obtaining his MBA he joined LEK/Strategy Ventures as a strategy consultant and did extensive work for Esselte Group.

After acting as a consultant to Filofax Group he was appointed their Chief Executive in 1990.

The Company

The origins of the Filofax go back to World War I, when Colonel Disney, an Englishman working in the USA, came across an American organizing system of technical leaves for engineers and scientists. This was taken up by a London company, Norman & Hill Ltd, who registered the name 'Filofax' in 1921. Despite proving its worth in the London 'blitz' of 1940, when it was instrumental in reconstructing Norman & Hill's business when their premises were destroyed, it did not attract much attention until the 1980s.

Since then it has set up or acquired subsidiaries in the USA, France, Sweden, Germany and Denmark, and has bought out some of its competitors, continuing their products as separate brands aimed at different markets. It has also diversified into complementary businesses able to benefit from its distribution network.

Its business currently unites nine brands:

Filofax	The world's best recognized name in personal organizers
Lefax	Stylish organizers for those seeking differentiation
Systemplan	Time management organizers with a business orientation
Microfile	Mid-priced organizers
Stylofax	Lower priced organizers for mass market channels
Mercato	Diaries and calendars
Drakes	Carbonless message pads, self-adhesive pads, telephone accessories
Yard-O-Led	Hand-made gold and sterling silver writing instruments
Ling	Greetings cards, gift wrap and accessories

Filofax Group PLC
Robin Field, Chief Executive

For half a century, Filofax was a tiny operation, with mail order sales mainly to British clergy and army officers. By 1981, with sales of less than £100,000 per year, it could not survive. One of its customers, David Collischon, who had a small mail order business himself serving the home office market, bought it for £11,000. One of his stories is of arriving for the first time as owner and meeting the old gentleman who was running the company, who said, 'Oh, Mr Collischon, we have one of those funny orders today. Someone has ordered a hundred pieces. Of course, we couldn't possibly supply that many, so I have put it in the bin as I always do.' He got it out of the bin and supplied the order.

To some extent when David Collischon started in 1981, there was a pent-up demand for what is now the world's best recognized name in personal organizers and his acquisition was fortunate in that it coincided with a few fashion leaders discovering the brand. Whether that was something that would have happened anyway, or whether it was something that happened because David was more adept at supplying what demand there was, we shall never know. At that time, one or two retailers noticed the Filofax range, put it in their shop windows, and sold some. Thus commenced the second phase of the company's fortunes, when it moved from having been exclusively a mail order supplier, to becoming the supplier of a fashionable accessory to up-market stores.

The product was spotted by journalists and copious complimentary copy was written about it. More and more retailers became interested, and wider retail distribution was established between 1981 and 1985. Chief executive, Robin Field, has an explanation for the increase in popularity.

'Prices had been kept down as much as possible since 1921, only being pushed up very gradually by increases in costs. David took the view, particularly in the inflationary environment of the early eighties, that he would put prices up much faster than costs. That had a very interesting effect. The product suddenly became very, very expensive – people were expecting to pay £60, £80 and more for a Filofax. This in itself generated interest and was something journalists noticed. There arose the phenomenon of paying not £4 for a pocket diary, but £60 or £80 for something to organize your life. Therefore, just in the same way as advice is supposed to be worth what you pay for it, it became peculiarly valuable!'

Sales in 1981 were around £100,000 per annum, sales in 1987 were about £12 million. During this second phase, says Robin Field, 'although everything went very well, and obviously through this price-led sales growth the company became very profitable, there were two worrying aspects: the amount of interest in Filofax had spawned a lot of competition and, as a result of constant price increases, the company itself had lost track of what its growth was doing in unit terms.'

Because sales were doubling every year in value terms, the company rather assumed the business itself was growing and doubling every year. 'Of course it wasn't,' says Robin Field. 'The prices were very nearly doubling every year, but the volume was remaining almost static. That was very dangerous. First, it meant the enormous amount of interest that had been spawned in the phenomenon of a ring-binder organizer, was being fuelled more by imitations, copies, and competitors' products than it was by the Filofax itself. Second, it meant the company had its own internal structure completely out of order, in that it assumed it was a much bigger company than it really was. This assumption had Filofax believing it needed many more staff and that it could afford to make many more inserts to go in the Filofax, with a much wider variety – golf and bridge score cards, wind-surfing records, bird watcher's check lists and the like – which were all duly published and put into stock.'

Externally, competition was growing fast and taking a large share of the market. Internally, costs were escalating, and in particular, stock-keeping costs were racing out of control. The years 1987 to 1990 were a period of worsening crisis, when these problems started to come home to roost. David Collischon tried to sell the company between 1989 and 1990. No one would buy it. He tried to borrow some more money from his bankers to go on operating the company, but by May 1990 he had a £2 million overdraft and the bankers said: 'No more.' When Robin Field first came to meet David at this time Filofax was on the brink of receivership.

As Robin Field explains, 'David came along to our consultancy company and said, "Is it sensible to try to operate Filofax? Is there any value there, or should I close it down?" We looked at the company for a three-week period in the spring of 1990, and made three discoveries, all of which were quite surprising to the company itself.'

First, the company had lost massive market share – Filofax had never really appreciated it had competitors. They discovered that competitor products were on the whole very much more user-friendly, having features superior to Filofax in many cases, and were at vastly cheaper retail prices. Second, Filofax's costs were very much greater than its competitors' costs – as much as 70 per cent higher; and third, the product line was much too wide. There was a huge proliferation of different papers, inserts and wallets in exotic skins, many of them with low turnover rates. This imposed not just high stockholding costs, but a heavy administrative burden on the company in keeping track of these products – publishing more papers, keeping them current, and the like, while not actually providing the simple basics that the customer wanted.

'These were some alarming pieces of data,' says Robin Field, 'but there were two quite cheerful pieces of news as well. First, the Filofax brand was still very widely recognized and wanted. People would go into stores and ask for "a Filofax". Shopkeepers acknowledged they could sell more product bearing the Filofax brand name, provided prices were competitive. Second, Filofax was not tied to any single source of supply or any single factory and did not have factories of its own. It could buy the cheapest product anywhere in the world, whereas its principal UK competitor had its own factory and its own UK employees and therefore had a cost floor beneath which it could not go.'

On the basis of that review the advice to David Collischon and the Filofax board was that the company should be saved, and it was worth someone injecting cash to do it. A consortium of investors was found in the summer of 1990 and a £2 million rights issue was put into the company on the basis that David Collischon would retire from an executive role and the man who had been running the UK subsidiary would step up and run the entire company. That did not work and it transpired that the consultants, who had intended to do just a short study, give their recommendations and walk away, found that the new management was constantly returning for further advice on a day-to-day basis. Robin Field became increasingly involved with giving this advice, until eventually he said, 'Look, this is enough. If you want me to run the company I will, but I'm not going to continue to do it through other chaps.' In October 1990 he took over as chief executive.

Filofax made a lot of changes. The total number of employees of the group went from over 250 down to seventy: 'It was not difficult to achieve,' Robin says, 'because an awful lot of people who went were very highly paid "management staff". It was not as if we had a factory with people doing what they perceived to be a useful job, coming in and working hard. We had rafts of so-called managers doing nothing. It was obvious what we had to do. We also had to reduce the cost of product dramatically and get a new source of supply to do that. We had to narrow the product line and cut out the "ostrich and alligator" type organizers being held in stock. We had to reduce the amount of handling the company itself was involved in and contract out the warehousing. All those things were very obvious, broad brush things. There was nothing complex in any of them. Getting them done, once we had decided to do them, was not terribly difficult.'

The most difficult thing, according to Robin Field, was introducing a new, cheaper product. 'Retailers who have already bought from a company cannot be told "Dear Mr Retailer, we sold that to you yesterday at a price of £30 and you retailed it for £60. We're now going to reduce the retail price of the thing to £30 and you're going to make no margin at all." A new product has to be introduced. We also needed to find new sources to produce more product which we did very fast, so fast that over 80 per cent of the binders sold in 1991 were new models which had been introduced since October 1990.'

Up to that stage, Filofax product manufacture was 100 per cent UK based. Today, the majority of the product is being manufactured in the USA, Italy and the Far East. Filofax has a diversity of global manufacturing points, not just because of raw material or production costs, but simply because it sells in forty countries round the world with only a minority of the sales in Britain, so it would be entirely unbalanced to have all its supply in the UK where there is less than a third of its turnover.

The entire turn-round strategy was based on quantitative analysis. What Robin Field did was simply to look at numbers, in terms of the market share, cost position and growth of product probability. He says, 'Taking the staff through the trauma without losing confidence in themselves in a period that saw our business drop so dramatically, keeping a team together at the time, called for human skills – but the blueprint was very much analytically driven.'

Looking ahead to the millennium for Filofax, he suggests there are two elements of growth: 'One is organic – the ring binder organizer business is still growing very nicely worldwide. The growth is in double figures in any country you care to look at. Then you can add to this the acquisitive growth of other products which share a common channel of distribution.' Filofax has already made two highly successful UK acquisitions in the last couple of years and is actively looking for more, while keeping a firm hand on what it already has. Indeed, strong organic growth and successful acquisitions have contributed to sales in mainland Europe alone increasing by nearly 60 per cent in the last year. Drakes, the commercial stationers, was acquired at the end of 1993 with all the advantages of shared customer relationship: 'In Drakes' particular business it's got a market share of over 90 per cent in the UK. That market share and brand support from its customers is always going to be of value and the channels of distribution are surprisingly similar. Over 50 per cent of Drakes' customers by sales value were already Filofax customers. So there is considerable commonality and savings potential in distribution channels.'

Greeting cards have been of interest to Filofax for a long time. They are a vast market and the acquisition of Ling contributed sales of £5 million and operational profits of £800,000 to Filofax's last financial year sales of £31.2 million. With a market share of less than 1 per cent the potential for share gain is considerable. With Ling, there is brand defensibility which made it interesting to Filofax. It was also an appropriate size: 'We wanted to keep the company separate. Anything much larger would have been betting the entire company without having personally been exposed to the greeting card market. It was a nice first toe into that water.'

According to Robin Field, 'In the UK I believe the little unit comprising the Filofax business, the Yard-O-Led pens and the Drakes business forms, which now has a turnover of about £10 million, is about as large as I want a single unit to be. Everyone can know everyone else and work very closely in an informal manner. In that whole unit we have about forty people office-based and another fifteen on the road. That's a nice, clear unit size where people can know each other and feel a sense of camaraderie. Much larger than that, it becomes rather more difficult to manage.'

Apart from size, another consideration is: how much of an infrastructure does any particular product need? Robin Field explains, 'If you take the Drakes or the Organizer business, there is very little individual product design and development that needs to happen in a specialist way and which cannot be married into what happens in any case with the Filofax product. In greeting cards, on the other hand, design is absolutely crucial, and the integrity and individuality of particular design in a company like Ling is all the value there is in its product. So if you were to try to bolt that on to something else you would risk killing the golden goose in no uncertain terms. In that business the integrity of the design is so very important.'

Robin Field's operation has a flat management structure, with no separate or central group head office. He says, 'What we have fundamentally, is a unit of perhaps fifty-five people in the UK serving the base Filofax product and the two other small subsidiaries. Within that are the small number of people – a total of perhaps five, myself included – who manage the group overall, and also manage the ownership of the Ling business, the American, French, German, Swedish and Danish subsidiaries, and our operation in Hong Kong. I, in particular, and my colleague Richard Eteson, who is responsible for group sales and marketing across the world, and indeed our finance director Chris Brace, keep very close to the detail of the individual products, the customers, and the individual brand policy of the organizers.' Having said that, empowerment is very much their philosophy. From 1990 to 1993 all the Filofax business was run directly in a hands-on way by Robin Field and Richard Eteson. Every instruction, every decision, everything was done by them directly, but now Robin Field is delighted that the last eighteen months have seen a real change. 'We have been able to develop line managers who run the Filofax business and the other Organizer brands on a day-to-day basis, with absolutely no interference at all. I guess it has happened simply because we have withdrawn. Given that we've got seven other subsidiaries to run round the world, we are not here most of the time. I hope we've given people encouragement to come up. We've created a vacuum into which people have grown, very successfully. Now the truth of the matter is, I could certainly go away for a year, and my two colleagues for at least three months, without the smallest hiccup in our base business.'

To achieve this empowerment Filofax gives much attention to staff training. It has, for example, one person in the US and one in London, both attending business schools part time for MBAs at company expense. 'We've devoted a lot of time to training and fundamentally, I think, we have developed Filofax by giving good people opportunity. MBA programmes are great fun. When someone has an ambition to do anything that might be related to their work and help them in their job – whether it's learning a language, or doing an MBA programme or some specific vocational training in credit control or customer service – the important part is to encourage and help them to do what they want to do. This approach has a good effect on morale and adds to your opportunity to recruit good people. I would be very sceptical of saying that because someone has gone on an MBA programme, they will be a better manager for it, but the fact that they wanted to do it in the first place, they made the commitment to take the time and effort to do it, that is valuable.'

Since 1990, in every country in which it operates, Filofax has had a *salaried* sales force and it has made a big difference. Robin Field says why. 'Our concept is to sell not a single product but a system. There's no point going into a store and seeing just a Filofax binder for sale. You need to see that there is a range of inserts that you can put into that binder, to justify buying it in the first place. The point of buying a ring-binder Organizer is that you see the whole system. This comes about through one of our staff going in there wanting to ensure each of those pockets with inserts in them is properly filled with the right produce. The salesman may make no sale whatsoever – but he has brought the stock up, he's seen that it is nicely displayed. He has serviced that retailer's requirement rather than making a hard sale. A commission salesman would never do that. Similarly, there is nothing more frustrating for a customer than going in to buy a card if the pockets are empty, or there are duplicates, or there aren't the appropriate cards for the season. We should help the retailer stock what is going to sell best for him in his store. Companies who try to sell cards with commission salesmen simply cannot do that.'

Despite the emphasis on empowerment, he advises that it is important to stay close to the business. 'One of the mistakes people certainly make in little businesses is trying to run them as if they were ICI. They like time off playing golf, rather than being very close to their business, answering the telephone for themselves, getting involved with the staff. My other advice is in precisely the opposite direction! The thing only grows when you are willing to delegate, when you are willing to encourage the staff beneath you. On the whole, to date, we have got the balance right, but it's difficult and I'm sure both sides are absolutely essential.'

Filofax serves forty countries round the world, but the area in which it sees most opportunity for growth that it can manage, understand and get its hands around, is continental Europe. 'We have a thriving business in the USA,' admits Robin Field, 'but I wouldn't say I was as confident about making an acquisition or doing business there as I am on the continent. Similarly, we have a healthy business in the Far East and Japan, but I wouldn't like to have to face the challenge of managing a subsidiary in Japan.' Whilst the Japanese retail scene remains depressed, Filofax's success in the rest of the Pacific rim suggests it should improve its performance towards 2000 even without any general recovery in consumer demand. From 1996, Filofax, for the first time, will be selling in both South Africa and Argentina. 'They are two countries that don't know about us yet, and there are plenty more to come,' says Robin Field, no doubt considering the Indian sub-continent with its increasingly affluent English-speaking middle class, and all of mainland China, offering significant long-term potential into the millennium.

Returning to Europe, interestingly, Robin Field does not believe a single Euro currency would help him: 'I don't have any difficulty at all in earning Deutschmarks and changing them into pounds or, indeed, where necessary earning pounds and changing them into Deutschmarks.' He also believes strongly that the one thing that Europe was meant to do was remove the trade barriers between countries within the Union. 'Even today, there are still considerable trade barriers. Every single silver writing instrument we sell to the French, already hallmarked by the Assay Office in Birmingham, has to be hallmarked separately in France or they will not accept it. That sort of nonsensical barrier to trade within the EU does bother and irritate me.'

On the whole, Robin Field believes governments prevent business and get in the way. 'The less interference we have, the better. There is no conceivable way I believe governments can help small businesses, because governments are far too remote to understand the issues and inevitably, by their very nature, they are inefficient. They can't spend money appropriately. All governments, everywhere, have always wasted more money than they have spent efficiently. I would have a horror of the government trying to assist me.'

He also thinks competition is becoming more and more difficult and that is the real challenge into the millennium. 'People are going to be offered more choice and superior products all the time. We spend a lot of time and money on developing new products. Ling cards may look very traditional and classic but in fact more than half those cards every year are new. Similarly, within the Filofax business, last year over 80 per cent of our binders were ones we hadn't had the year before. Constantly we're bringing out new products. It will accelerate, it's bound to accelerate, it has to.'

Filofax's organic growth over the last few years has been somewhere in excess of 20 per cent and the company is regaining market share. In the UK, sales of binders continually exceed those of refills, demonstrating that there is a healthy amount of renewal, and that the UK market is far from saturated. In the greetings card field consumption is growing, particularly in Germany and France, and this is a market Filofax will be focusing on towards 2000. There are changes going on in outlets too. Multiple grocers in the UK have grown rapidly, although their share of the card market is, as yet, low. At the same time, specialist card shops have sprouted.

Robin Field is convinced Filofax's greatest asset is the distribution network and not the brand. The company take over its own distribution wherever this is economically viable. 'I think the distribution network, actually getting in to something like 10,000 retailers in forty countries, is more valuable than any one of the brands – probably more important than all the brands put together. Everything we do should be devoted to looking after the retailer, and improving our services to him. In many ways the whole sales thing for us is a complete misnomer. What we're doing is all about service and not about sales.'

To a large extent all the company's products, whether they be Filofax organizers or Ling cards, are bought not sold. After all, when you go into a card shop you look, you choose, you buy. As Robin Field says, 'It's not because someone in any way, either through advertising or otherwise, is pushing that particular product down your throat. It is being made available to you and you are buying it, no one is "selling" it to you. That is also true of Filofax products. Filofax doesn't do any advertising at all above the line. We invest money in stores so that they have decent store fixtures, ensuring the products are displayed properly in a way that is attractive to the consumer, but nothing could be more different from selling. Our product is not like soap powder where you are actually making a hard sell, and investing a huge amount of money in advertising to try and persuade the customer to buy.'

By the year 2001, Robin Field obviously hopes his business will have expanded and will be flourishing. However, his final millennial advice is that life should not be only business-related: 'I don't denigrate the importance of business, but running Filofax is not to me the most important thing in my life. I'm just as concerned about my family, my daughter getting through her Common Entrance, as I am about running Filofax.' And that is how it should be.

FIRST DIRECT

The first organization in the UK to provide full person-to-person banking and financial services over the telephone, 24 hours a day, 365 days a year, including current accounts, credit cards, savings and investments, loans, mortgages, share dealing, travel services and insurance. It has approximately 2,300 employees across two sites in Leeds.

Kevin Newman – Chief Executive

Still in his thirties, Kevin is one of the youngest chief executives in the UK banking community. He has held the position since 1991.

He joined First Direct as Operations Director in January 1989, having previously worked for Woolworths PLC and Mars Group Services.

The Company

First Direct was launched on 1 October 1989 and has never closed. As at August 1995 it had been open continuously for 50,000 hours. During that time a typical high street bank branch would have been open for less than 15,000 hours.

First Direct currently has approximately 500,000 customers, with 10,000 new customers joining each month. Almost a third of all new customers come through personal recommendation.

First Direct is an independent and autonomous division of the Midland Bank Group, itself part of HSBC Holdings PLC, one of the world's largest banking organizations.

Following substantial investment by HSBC and the Midland, First Direct became a profitable business in 1994. Profitability is set to increase significantly over the next five years.

First Direct
Kevin Newman, Chief
Executive

At midnight on Sunday, 1 October 1989, First Direct, the UK's first 24-hour direct telephone bank, was launched. Today, First Direct is acknowledged as the market leader in the UK for direct banking and financial services. It provides a full range of financial services by telephone, 24 hours a day, 365 days a year, ranging through cheque accounts, VISA credit cards, savings, mortgages, loans, share dealing, travel services and investments. Customers can call one of First Direct's banking representatives at any time of the day or night to conduct an extensive set of financial transactions, from a simple balance update to setting up a mortgage or giving instructions for share dealing.

First Direct is an independent and autonomous division of Midland Bank. Today it has over 500,000 customers and continues rapid growth with an average of 10,000 new customers joining every month. 35 per cent of customer acquisition is by word of mouth and over 75 per cent of customers come from Midland's competitors. Customers are broadly 'up-scale' in profile terms, with approximately 80 per cent in the ABCI socio-economic groupings, while over two-thirds are between the ages of twenty-five and forty-four.

First Direct was the brainchild of radical thinking by Midland. Midland wanted to grow its market share among upscale customers, something it was unable to do by acquisition and which was extremely difficult to do by organic growth. The banking industry has been over-supplied; profits have been hard to achieve, cost cutting has been an essential feature across all banks as they increasingly found themselves competing with the lower cost base of the building societies. Customers, particularly the more up-scale younger innovators, have become more discerning – even hostile – demand-

111

ing far higher levels of customer service and a return to a more personal approach from their banks. Midland knew there was a growing number of customers with a deep-rooted frustration with the traditional banking system, and its own research revealed customers were progressively making less use of the branch network. It is well known that consumer demand for better service is higher amongst banks than any other retail sector and friendly and knowledgeable staff are considered most important, alongside convenient opening hours and quick and easy transactions.

The way forward for the Midland seemed to be some form of direct banking – dealing with customers over the telephone – but there was still a need to have human contact. Research by the Midland indicated three-quarters of those interested in a telephone banking service wanted a person on the other end of the line – not a computer. To provide customers with the kind of service Midland believed they were now demanding meant starting from scratch. None of the traditional banking models could be adapted.

So the seeds of change were sown for the unique proposition that could be offered as an alternative service to Midland customers and to the banking market as a whole, thereby generating incremental business for Midland.

Kevin Newman is the chief executive of First Direct and was part of the original Midland team which conducted the feasibility research for such a banking operation. He discusses its concept and banking into the millennium: 'Midland had once been the UK's biggest bank. Its personal customer market share was falling off, and the view was they had to maintain a minimum of 15 per cent of the market or else they would get into a vicious spiral – if you lose your volume of business, you have to start reducing infrastructure costs. The initial idea was to come up with a differentiated service. The problem with banks is that 80 per cent of people think all the banks are the same, whether you bank with Lloyds, Midland, Barclays or NatWest. The perception is also that the service is getting worse but, because it is the same, very few people – about 3 per cent a year – actually move their bank accounts. That perception just adds to the inertia. Consequently the banks did not address some of the fundamental issues they needed to, because they had a relatively captive market. The fact is you are more likely to change your partner than your bank account. It is in that context one needs to look at the industry. So we had to come up with a substantially differentiated proposition.'

That proposition has four elements to it. Explains Kevin Newman, 'It recognizes personal banking is pretty much a commodity activity. A bit like filling your car at the petrol station, it is something you have to do, but people would far rather use their time to do more interesting things. Therefore banking has to be quick; speed is a fairly important component. Second, it has to be convenient, and that means not only does it need to be accessible but the bank needs to revolve around the individual customer and not the other way round.' Convenience is fundamental.

'Banking also has to deliver value, which is not just price, although price is a component of it. It has to give good value because as consumers, we all want to receive more and pay less for it. Fourth, and probably above all those things, it has to deliver service, and we can categorize service into two components: a hygiene component, which is getting it right, and what one could call a motivational component, which is how we go about it.'

First Direct set out to deliver a service against those four criteria. Anything you can get from a high street bank you can get from First Direct, only it never closes. So the vision was set. First Direct was launched, with the huge advantage of having a blank sheet of paper, a greenfield site. It was able to define not only the computing and infrastructure which is important, but the culture; the ability to hire people with the right attitude, to build something from scratch. Says Kevin Newman, 'I think it is fair to say we were envisaged as a niche business, and the original business case did not envisage we would ever have more than about 300,000 customers, limited, for a very particular market, predominantly but not exclusively in the south-east. We have become far bigger, certainly in terms of volume, with around half a million customers now, and we anticipate still growing strongly towards 2000, bigger than anybody ever really envisaged.'

Kevin Newman says First Direct is able to offer pretty competitive rates on all its products because it has no branches. 'There are no bricks and mortar. There is just a factory, two buildings, one about the size of the Wembley football pitch. We can keep costs very low and pass the benefit on to customers.'

Broadly speaking, staff in First Direct fall into two categories. There are the experts, the operational specialists, computing people, banking specialists, marketing people and so on; some will have come from Midland, others from elsewhere. The bulk of the people recruited, however, the people you talk to when you ring, 98 per cent of them have never worked in a bank before. Says Kevin Newman, 'They come from all walks of life. You name a profession, I bet you we have somebody who used to do it. We are recruiting against a set of criteria of which attitudes are not the least. Fundamentally, we want people who can relate to customers, who can listen, which is a pretty underrated skill, who probably have a level of aptitude in terms of numeracy, and are reasonably articulate. We think we can, with the investment we have made in computers, teach people the banking side of the operation. What we cannot teach people is the set of values, in the same way that we cannot force the culture on people. You can only create a culture, create an environment, if you bring the right people in who would hopefully thrive with it. So we are very particular about who we employ. In addition, we give our people a lot of training.'

Essentially, into the millennium First Direct is providing a service which really typifies an adult to adult, one to one relationship. Newman explains, 'One of the traditional problems with the banks is people perceive them as big organizations, talking down to little customers. I think many people can feel quite intimidated by this. We don't want that at all, and nor do our customers. We want this to be, frankly, business orientated. I don't believe I can ask the people in our business to treat our customers as adults unless we treat our staff in an identical way. It is two sides of the same coin as far as I am concerned. Let me give an example. The approach we take to hours of work is to say, "Look, these are the hours we have available, and those vary depending on the time of day and day of the week. Everybody leads different lives, you are an individual, what hours suit you?" We have some staff who work Mondays and Tuesdays, Thursday evenings and Sundays; others will say, "No, I would just like to work Monday to Friday 9 to 5." Some say, "I'd like to work overnight." We don't pay any shift premium because we are providing hours they want, with a service to our customers 24 hours a day, seven days a week.'

It must be a hassle on personnel structures, with staff numbers of approximately 2,000. Kevin Newman agrees. 'It certainly has a major disadvantage in that if you are a team leader and you are managing about ten people, the chances of all ten coming in at the same time, and at the same time as you, are non-existent. If you are not there when one of your ten has a query then another team leader will sort out the problem. That has forced us to put even more emphasis on getting regular feedback because you don't have the inherent advantages of starting and stopping together. The business never stops. First Direct never closes. You cannot just say, "Right, after work today we will do X," because work just never finishes.

'It really comes down to an all-embracing culture. We passionately believe it is a team game and there is no status in our organization at all. There are no offices. Everybody is on a first-name basis, everybody eats in the same restaurant. Everybody is highly valued within the organization, and I think everybody *feels* highly valued. That is probably the key to it.'

If you meet any of First Direct's banking representatives or speak to them on the phone, they do say, 'Yes, I make a difference.' There is a tremendous amount of pride in the business. In fact Kevin Newman carries out surveys to check they are not getting too carried away! 'We have something like 96% of people convinced First Direct is going to be a world class business. I think how we treat people on an ongoing basis has a lot to do with the values and culture within the organization. The teams, the team leaders and the approach by management help to facilitate that, but it's really an individual thing that brings us there.'

Heading for the millennium and beyond with an organization unheard of six years ago has challenges. Newman insists leadership is a big part of it. 'It can only come from the top. It is not what you say, it is how you act. Frankly, the best word to describe it is *trust*. If I am saying, which I am, that everybody in our business is equal, we treat everybody as an adult, I have to live that agreement every minute of the day. It is like porcelain: if you break it, you cannot put it back together again.'

Newman thinks the constant challenge is changing the mind-set in some of the senior managers within banking: 'I'll give you a trivial illustration of it, but I think it is quite a good one. If you talk to some of the longer-term executives within a typical clearing house or large organization, you will hear them saying, "Oh well, we are doing this through the branch network, and we need to keep it simple 'so the kids can understand it'." Now, some of those kids are fifty-five years old! I have to say I find that hugely derogatory, and when I am in the presence of somebody saying that, I get quite upset, because they are not kids at all. They are part of the same team. My belief is that this mind-set will manifest itself in terms of body language or whatever else. So the person out in the branch will feel, "That's how I am treated, a bit like a kid." Some people will react against it and say, "If that's the way you're going to treat me, that's the way I'm going to act." Other people act in different ways. Either way, nobody is going to be particularly motivated by it. We try very hard to make sure, throughout our organization, that we always talk with respect to each other. Whether you are, frankly, the guy cleaning the toilets or whether you are the chief executive, you are all part of the same team. And we all have to live that, as I say, day in day out.'

Newman always talks about the individual. 'The individual is most important. We do have departments and we have teams, and there will be a structure. That said, however, we have tried very hard not to do too much because you will get (and it is an issue within our business, as it is in others) the departmentalization of the business. We work very hard on getting people to talk across our business. We see the role of managers as very much one of facilitating – rather than instructing and ordering or whatever else it is - and trying to get people to talk to one another. I am in my department, you are in your department, if I do it this way, I might be able to help you even if to do so is less convenient for me. That is our job. We as managers create the opportunity. To give a good example, we hold a number of what we call "theme" days. They are usually fun and often people dress up for them. The people on the ground decide the theme and the rest of the team dress or act in keeping with the theme for the day. We really encourage individuals to communicate right across our business. We have been able to achieve that with well over 2,000 people, but whether we can continue as we get to 3,4,5,6,7 or 8,000, I don't know. What I do know is, it is a damn sight easier doing it in just two physical buildings, in one physical city, than it is over 1,500–2,000 branches throughout the UK. We have that big advantage; and it is a lot easier for me. Day in day out, people see me wandering around, I sit down and talk to people. By comparison, Richard Orgill [Deputy CEO at the Midland Bank], even if he was Superman, cannot do that, because of the physical problem of getting round to so many branches. Archie Norman [of Asda, also in this book] places a great deal of emphasis in getting his management out to the stores; but Asda has got around 200 stores, which is more "do-able" than 1,500 branches. We will need to get the culture institutionalized in some way, so it is not down to an individual, it is delivered through how we go about doing things around here. That is something we are working on quite hard at the moment for future success.'

116

This is probably one of First Direct's big strategic advantages. Kevin Newman explains the service which First Direct is trying to provide for the potential customer. First Direct acts in many ways like a gateway. 'The gateway is principally a physical gateway, wherever you have a telephone you have access to your bank. That in itself is not sufficient. We also need to make banking with First Direct a really positive experience and to do this we have to provide the service in the way the customer wants us to provide it, and that may well be different for every single customer. We listen to customers and some customers will be sharp, precise and to the point: "This is what I want, I want it now and I really want to get off the phone as quickly as possible." These people can be described as "functionalists", and are basically inner driven. Other customers will be more uncertain, less sure of what they want, more hesitant with their enquiry, maybe saying: "Well, I am not too sure. I've got to go on holiday, I am not sure, should I take some foreign currency, should I use my Visa card?" They need a very different sort of service. We have to train people to listen to all types of calls and to mirror them. If we can do that, then that leaves the caller with a feeling of "autonomy", which is simply that the customer is in absolute control of their money and other finances, and that is what we are trying to provide.'

If First Direct is able to provide me with whatever I want, is it tailor-made? Answers Kevin Newman, 'I think you will find the level of service very high. If you talk to people in terms of what it gives them, people will take different things out of it. Some customers will say, "I like it because it is extremely efficient," or, "I like it because it is extremely personable." Some say, "I love it because I am treated with courtesy, more than from any other service I've received in the last twenty years." Others say, "It's a bit idiosyncratic, a little bit on the edge, sometimes." That is how we are tailoring it, providing this service which mirrors the individual customer's requirement.'

Into the twenty-first century, two areas should keep First Direct one jump ahead of potential competitors. One will be the good attitude of its staff. 'That will be a major issue,' says Kevin Newman. 'We had to have that at the outset. It is not just about the mechanics of the telephone. One of our competitors suddenly decided all its telephones were going to be answered in three rings. When we first started we were paranoid about how quickly we picked up the phone. We were convinced if we picked up the phone quickly it equalled good service; if we did not pick up the phone quickly it meant poor service. Some time further on now, we have recognized that argument is totally flawed. That is not the prime issue that customers are after. What they are after is, when we answer the phone they have a quality service. Here is an actual example. Before we went away on holiday in the USA, I wanted to check whether the place I was going to was on our ATM network so I could draw cash. The banking representative [front line staff] patently cannot do that. [They will be able to answer approximately 85 per cent of all requests or queries, while others will be transferred to a specialist in a particular area.] After she had arranged my currency the banking representative said, "I'll just put you through to our foreign currency department." It took twenty-five seconds and I was thinking, they are taking a bit of time here. But then the person came on, and the difference was that the person in foreign currency said, "Ah, Mr Newman, I understand you are trying to find out whether you can use ATMs in Vail and Denver, is that right? Where are you precisely staying?" How often in other organizations would the caller have to repeat the whole enquiry all over again every time they were transferred to another person within that organization? We try to make the handover seamless.'

The other area Kevin Newman feels he will build on and go forward with, will be intelligence. 'I hope we will get to know you as a customer and establish a relationship. Customers don't always deal with the same member of First Direct staff. The approach we will be taking, will be to ask customers to provide information to allow us to build up our intelligence. We will use computers in a fairly major way to do that. To give an example of something we currently do, the banking representative will log the conversation in the system, then the next time the customer calls in (but not always, because it is down to the bank representative's discretion), they may say, "Did you have a good holiday? Did you manage to use the ATM?" because we have used the computer record of the previous transaction. This is an example of the intelligent gathering of information; ultimately, it benefits both First Direct and our customers.'

First Direct will use the computer to do the brain bit, in terms of the memory, and people in terms of communication. 'That is what we believe, fundamentally, we are trying to do here,' says Kevin Newman, 'use people for what people are good at, which is talking.

We are sceptical about voice response, touch-tone or similar devices. We are saying, people do a very good job talking to other people. Where the computers are good is in storing away this information and then passing it to the individual when that is appropriate, in an intelligent manner that adds value.'

First Direct can get pro-active about that approach. Kevin Newman offers an example: 'We can approach the marketing of car insurance in two ways. The conventional route, and we are reasonably good at it, is to use our marketing database to identify the people most likely to have cars, and mail them about car insurance. Typically when they next call in, it comes up on the screen and the banking representative will say, "Did you get our mailing? Is there anything else I can tell you about it to give you more information?" That's smart but it's not particularly efficient, because car insurance is an annual purchase. With this approach we have no idea when people's insurance is due for renewal, so probably for eight out of ten customers it is ill-timed which increases the chance of it being viewed as junk mail. What we would rather do, is say to customers, "If you are interested, tell us when your car insurance is due for renewal. If you would like us to give you a quote three weeks beforehand, we will do that." If it beats their existing quote, they have saved some money and we have won some business. But there is no "hard selling" involved in that process at all. If our quote is not competitive, that is our problem. We need to discover a way of making it more competitive. In this case the customer gets a good benchmark in terms of the competitiveness of their existing quote. We think that equals extremely good service.'

First Direct's typical customer age range is 25–44, professional people, ABCI, more educated and earning higher salaries than the average. Kevin Newman says, 'They are busy, confident people, predominantly living in the south-east, or major conurbations. At the moment we have nearly 2 per cent of the UK current account market and probably, depending on how it is measured, about 4–5 per cent of our target market. By the year 2000 we believe we will have approximately 1 million customers, which in today's terms, means our current account market share could be approximately 4 per cent.'

To the credit of Midland, it has taken the decision right from day one, that it cannot create a brand new business, with a brand new culture from within the bank. Therefore First Direct is managed as an independent division. It has functional lines into the Midland, and works closely with them, but remaining autonomous.

Can First Direct be transported globally into the millennium? Says Kevin Newman, 'The HSBC Group, of which Midland is a major component, is one of the world's largest banking and financial services organizations. I think our style of telephone operation is applicable in a number of different countries; but I don't think you can take a proven formula and just transplant it round the world, because different centres have different cultures and problems. For instance, in Canada or Australia they are interested in Direct Banking: they have a geographical issue which is readily resolved by the telephone. In south-east Asia there will tend to be limits on opening branches, and obviously it is a way to the retail market without those outlets.

'Midland itself has already started offering telephone transactions – for instance ordering statements and obtaining balances of accounts, and this will become the norm inside the next four or five years. The big difference for First Direct is, we have gone to what we feel is the logical end of this development, "Why have a branch at all?" Technology will be arguably faster. Mondex, electronic money – is here now. We spent a lot of time trying to find why certain customers don't join First Direct and one of the reservations has been, "You can't get money over the telephone, can you?" Well, now you can!'

What will First Direct look like on its tenth anniversary in October 1999? 'We are going to have approximately 1 million customers,' says Kevin Newman, 'and be recognized as a world class business. We'll have a strong reputation in financial services and amongst the media. I would hope by 2000 to be recognized by many people in the UK as a top quality organization providing outstanding levels of service. There is an element of the brand that is going to be different from Midland Bank. Midland will be developing a position as a bank respected in the community. I don't think First Direct is like that.'

The fact is that First Direct already provides an outstanding level of service, well before the millennium. Could that harbour an arrogance and complacency, breeding service contempt? Kevin Newman responds, 'What will stop us becoming complacent is the strong sense of pride within the organization. We think we can do considerably better than we currently do. I believe by the year 2000 we will achieve that. I expect to be making a significant contribution to the

Midland in terms of profits, from a quality business, with a lot of very satisfied customers and, I hope, still a long way ahead of our competitors.'

Banking is a serious business. It hasn't been too long since the collapse of BCCI and Barings. To be able to say First Direct is part of Midland and, indeed, part of HSBC, is very important. It is reassuring to customers. That positioning works very well for both Kevin Newman and Richard Orgill.

First Direct is a young business; the average age of its staff is twenty-nine. That said though, it is not age *per se* that is the issue, it is attitude. Kevin Newman wants people whose mind set is one of continuing questioning. 'This is a better way of doing it, why don't we do it this way?' He says, 'One of our challenges towards 2000 is managing all the creative ideas we have and keeping people motivated, because we cannot implement them all overnight. A lot of those ideas will be about changing the computer systems and, inevitably our resources. Success breeds success and it helps that we have a lot of new people coming into the business all the time. We will be taking on 500 people this year, against the general industry norm of shedding jobs.'

Kevin Newman confesses First Direct has probably got more than a sprinkling of zealots. 'We do need to find a way of institutionalizing our values. We have people who work too hard. There is a very strong work-hard, play-hard culture. A lot of the managers work sixty, seventy hours a week, and we have to find ways of easing off. That will take another year or two. Until we turn in substantial profits, the pressure will still be on us from the main bank. We need to translate an attractive business into one making substantial profits.'

'We would like people to recognize there is a choice; they can change banks, it is not a question of staying with the same bank all your life. People are looking right across the spectrum now and the concept of loyalty, in the customer base of the main banks is rapidly diminishing. It is increasingly becoming a business relationship. "This is the service I expect. This is what I am prepared to pay for it." End of story. It is two-way commitment. We are absolutely committed to our customers. We would hope our customers are committed to us.'

I think there will continue to be changes in society, particularly with people moving around more, who say, "Well, I don't particularly feel part of the community. I go to the supermarket, I am com-

121

mitted to the supermarket as long as the supermarket is committed to me. If they provide the service, fine. If somebody else does a better job I am going to go there." As those changes happen in terms of people's attitudes and behaviour, and they look at banking as a service they buy like any other, then I think people will start to move around.'

Obviously First Direct would be one of the beneficiaries of that movement. 'Our business,' says Kevin Newman, 'is based on a firm belief in the future of personal banking. We based our launch on our idea of the year 2010. We are well on the way to confirming our vision of the future.'

GRANADA GROUP PLC

Turnover (1994)	£2,098 million
Operating profit	£299 million
Profit before tax	£265 million
Employees	45,000
Full time	35,000
Part time	10,000

A leading UK leisure and media company in three divisions: television; rental and computer services; leisure and services.

Gerry Robinson – Chairman

In his early career Gerry Robinson progressed through various accounting and financial roles in Lesney Products (Matchbox Toys), Lex Service Group and Grand Metropolitan. In 1983 he was appointed Managing Director of GrandMet's International Services business, and went on to become Chief Executive of the whole Contract Services Division. In 1987 he led the then largest management buy-out in the UK with the £163m purchase of the division, which was subsequently renamed the Compass Group and floated on the stock market.

He joined Granada in 1991 as Chief Executive and is now Chairman.

Other appointments:
Chairman of BSkyB PLC and ITN. Non-executive director of Caradon PLC.

The Granada group divisions are:

Television

Operates two Channel 3 licences (Granada in north-west England and LWT in London) and is the biggest UK programme producer outside the BBC. Also has shareholdings in BSkyB, Yorkshire Tyne Tees and ITN.

Rental and Computer Services

Through 600 showrooms, Granada rents over 2 million televisions and video recorders and retails televisions, video recorders and other electronic equipment. A full service back-up is provided and a comprehensive computer maintenance and service business is one of Europe's leading operators.

Leisure and Services

Roadside Services is the UK's leading motorway service area operator with 29 sites and also 9 trunk road sites.

Sutcliffe provides contract catering services to clients on 2,400 sites.

Leisure Development incorporates a number of businesses including bowling, travel, theme parks and hotels.

Spring Grove is one of the UK's leading textile rental companies.

Granada Group PLC
Gerry Robinson,
Chairman

1994 marked the sixtieth anniversary of Granada's foundation. Today, Granada companies have high levels of profitability, the potential for significant growth and there is no doubt it is a highly successful organization.

An appropriate measure by which to judge the financial strength of any service company is to consider its interest cover, which for Granada, rose to 8.9 times, for its last financial year, up 24 per cent from 7.2 times on the previous year. It has a strong cash flow – in its last financial year it reduced its net debt by a staggering £110 million, to give year end gearing of 58 per cent. Cash flow before acquisitions exceeded £170 million, even after taking into account increased capital expenditure invested for the future. As that strong cash flow surplus enables Granada to reduce its debt further, interest cover will continue to improve. All this has been achieved despite the major acquisition of LWT, which was financed by cash consideration of £101 million, and the issue of 110.6 million new Ordinary Shares.

A streamlined Granada head office with precise lines of communication in the things that are important – and no lines of communication in the things that aren't – is the way Granada runs. Gerry Robinson, chairman, also chairman of ITN and BSkyB, explains: 'We have a very small head office leaving a lot of power in our divisional bases, but with strict standards in overall targets. If you have some key rules established in a very tightly managed, small organization, you don't spend twenty-four hours a day talking about this or that subtlety. There are just some very simple things that one needs to achieve, and the more clearly people see that, the easier they find it is to get on and do it. That's a hugely important part of efficient business organization.'

When Gerry Robinson first arrived at Granada, one of the things that struck him was that many ridiculous ideas kept coming up to his office through the system. 'It's astonishing in a way. It took three weeks for people to realize, "There's no point in bringing that up to Gerry. He's just going to pass it back and say, make up your own mind on it." Very quickly clarity comes into play. Equally, there's no point in coming to me with really duff ideas. Often people will pass things up even though they know "this is really stupid, you know we shouldn't be doing that". I return it to them and say, "Well, if you are really serious about this, you make a decision on it, you make it live or die." It quickly goes away. The things that are patently nonsense, you just don't get involved with.

'Whatever we do must be well done, in that the Granada name has come to mean quality and getting things right. Our activities must obviously meet certain profit cash objectives but, more important than almost anything else, in any area we must do what we say we are going to do! Yes, it's very simple! In Granada you can't casually explain something away in the hope that it won't be noticed. We have a very good review procedure and any agreed budget, any agreed actions, indeed anything which is to be followed up, gets followed up. That could be seen as threatening but in truth there is nothing worse than doing a good job that nobody notices. So being noticed is a vital part of that process.'

Gerry Robinson is adamant on two issues, one is, the Board does not run Granada, the other is total empowerment. 'Our Board is a controlling one in the sense of ensuring that everything is in order and works well but the company needs to be run at the appropriate level. That is why, if you talk to the chief executive who runs Leisure and Services division, he will not give you a whole series of stuff that came down from me or Granada on high. His brief is very straightforward: to run Motorways, to run it extremely well, to have the best delivery mechanism in the country, to give the customer what the customer wants, and to make the most money out of it that we sensibly can. We have an open philosophy that if *anyone* finds something that doesn't work, it gets reported back appropriately, both to the person on the site and back through the organization. There is an openness and courage in that, which is neither secretive nor negative. I do not have a manual for the chief executive of any division saying, "Look, this is how you run a Granada company, this is how you run a motorway operation." It isn't like that.'

Granada have a strong policy of trying to get people internally to come through and work their way up. They have been successful in doing that. 'I think it is good to see people moved up within an organization and, preferably, in a way which is beyond their expectations, because then you are looking at someone who is keen to show that the move or promotion was a good choice. You get real commitment.'

When you review Granada Group they make more margin out of almost everything they do than their competitors. Why? Is it to do with the style of management outlined by Gerry Robinson? 'It's because we set out to do it. If you believe it can't be done it doesn't happen. I know that's terribly simplistic, and unsophisticated, but if you want to do something and you are passionate about wanting to do it, that is 90 per cent of the battle. Clearly alongside that there must be realism applied to what can and cannot be done.

'What is right in Motorways may often be different from what is right in our other operations: television programme production, TV rental, Sutcliffe catering, or computer maintenance, but there are common objectives of customer service and of preserving Granada's reputation for quality. The customer has recognized the Granada name stands for service, for excellence, and that's the key.'

Granada must have that *consistency* of service excellence right across its businesses. 'We have in TV rental and computer maintenance a business that is about an individual customer where the key is service on engineering and in the shop network. It's a business that is quite different from anything else that we do. It has no link with motorways or with television production but you will find there very good measurements of customer service, good follow up to complaints, good systems of motivating the staff at a local level. We need that kind of attention to get it right in all of our businesses.'

Granada has been growing dramatically over the past three years and now employs around 45,000 people. To Gerry Robinson that's one of the important parameters of success. What he will not do, however, is hold on to people when there is no job: 'I think it is an artificial and harmful idea, that people are owed employment if it means holding on to them just for the sake of it. At some point the whole thing will fall off the edge. The company will never work. If you know you have a business that three years down the road is going to have a smaller customer base, you can cut down slowly and sensibly and everybody knows, that's fine. It may not be the way you want it, but it is important to know where you are going in each part of the business.' TV rentals, for example, is a difficult business to grow, because it is in a well-established and declining market, whereas television production and Granada's contract catering business, Sutcliffe, are growing. 'There are quite different growth characteristics in these three businesses and that calls for different managerial approaches,' says Gerry Robinson. 'Managing a business which is in a mature or declining market is very demanding and is more difficult than managing something which has real growth potential. Growth has all the pleasant characteristics attached to it: taking on more people, the management team feeling good with the whole thing moving forward in a progressive way. If you are managing the run down of a business, that isn't easy. Keeping staff motivation going is hard.'

Granada could, of course, redeploy staff within the company. 'Quite often, however, it's not as clean as that,' admits Gerry Robinson. 'A TV engineer, for example, can probably man our computer side, which is growing and be trained for that; but there are practical limitations to what people can do. Would we be right to try and keep someone who has been paid £30,000 to do a job at £12,000? In practice you are better saying to him in good time, "Look, you'd better be out looking for a job, because there isn't going to be one here in a year's time." That's much easier and more humane.'

Granada's Leisure division is also growing and has acquired Pavilion, the motorway hotels operation. 'It's a short cut to expansion,' says Gerry Robinson, 'an obvious area where we do have expertise and can bring it to bear very quickly. It is a business that requires substantial ongoing capital. To run it well you need to keep it fresh, adding new rooms or facilities as volume grows. You need to be prepared to refurbish restaurants, to introduce Burger King, to introduce new services and attractions. I think a lot of spending can be unnecessary, but there are times, as in this case, when spending is absolutely crucial to get the thing right. With a customer-facing business, one must have it right, it must feel right, and therefore it requires constant reinvestment.'

Robinson is absolutely certain that strong competition is the healthiest environment for industry. 'Whether one likes it or not, where that competition does not exist, be it in the Health Service, the utility companies, even the telephone companies before privatization, it does not work. There are of course complications attached to competitiveness but in the end it produces a better product. That's just reality.'

Competing in television for programme making is where Granada shines through. 'We know that we have to be good to be where we are and to stay there. We make 40 per cent of original programmes for ITV. The reason we do that is that we do it better than anyone else. I have no doubt about that at all.'

Good news for Granada Group is that the number of TV outlets is going to grow. There will be many, many, more channels in the UK. Gerry Robinson can take two approaches to that: 'You can either bury your head in the sand and hope it will all go away, or you can realize it is going to change and you had better be aware of it, take part in it, and make sure you fight your corner. Towards 2000 it's going to be much, much more competitive than it's ever been, but frankly that's much more exciting.

Almost uniquely in the UK, people in television separate the need to establish what the market place is from the artistic quality of making programmes. Gerry Robinson agrees. 'Some wonderful stuff is made but it doesn't meet any kind of audience need. One of the things we have got under way in a positive sense in Granada is that of course we want to make the best programmes on television in every sense, but including being the most popular. There used to be the idea that something which is popular could not have artistic merit – this is utter nonsense. The whole approach now is one of making absolutely certain we know what the audience is, for any particular programme we make, and even more specifically than that, we know who will buy which programmes if we choose to make them. Just that connection alone has made our programme making grow – it has doubled in the past three years. Very simple, uncomplicated stuff, and, I can assure you, in no way has that involved letting up on quality. If anything it has sharpened it up.'

The key ingredient in any programme is the script. Gerry Robinson says, 'If you haven't got an excellent script you are going to be patching and sewing all the way through and you are on a hiding to nothing. Throw it away and pay an excellent scriptwriter, or preferably a group of scriptwriters, to get the quality right. It is not about penny-pinching at all, it's about spending money appropriately. I feel passionate about that. We have all seen beautifully made films, and no doubt everybody had a wonderful time making them, but the script was paper thin. They failed to get the starting point right. Granada's approach has been vindicated by the fact that we now make more programmes and have won more awards than we ever have and we certainly have a much greater capacity to make programmes. There has been no cutting back or stinting on that in any way.'

Gerry Robinson is also chairman at ITN and BSkyB. 'ITN is a classic provider of a service to a small number of buyers – the ITV companies and Channel 4. The quality philosophy applies here too. We don't skimp on reporting, we have a high quality approach with good back-up for instant coverage of events, and well-located offices around the world to provide the service when it is needed. We are there when there's a big event. We don't think about it, we get reporters there, well supported, well backed up, pay for the communications link-ups. There is never a question of resources – but we want paying for it.'

As a philosophy, Gerry Robinson is very comfortable with ITN as it now exists. 'I think in any comparisons with its rivals, ITN gets a higher audience and wins more awards. I genuinely believe that a hugely important measure of the quality of what you do is whether you gain the audience or not. You get nebulous discussions about what quality is but, if you've done a programme like *Panorama* and a million people watch it in prime time television, is that quality? Not to me, it isn't. In documentaries, for example, *World in Action*, made by Granada, is informative and intelligent and we get ten million viewers. That to me is what quality is about. You have seen the awards we have won. I am unconvinced by the argument, "Oh, we did it extremely well, but . . . it only attracted a small audience." Prime time television is about gaining large audiences for a programme they want to watch, which is then well-perceived by people who have watched it.'

British Sky Broadcasting, offering multi-channel subscription TV, where Granada is a shareholder, is a hugely successful company. Why? 'The whole thing is structured to work,' says Gerry Robinson. 'For example, it has the most efficient telephone control mechanism I have ever seen, it's brilliant. At the Sky control centre in Livingston, the phones will be answered within two rings, *every* time. Your query will either be answered on the spot, within a minute, or they will agree to come back to you within the hour, with the answer. And it happens, 99.999 per cent of the time. Why? Because it's set up to do so. It's a very well organized, fast-moving and effective mechanism. With Sky, it's customer service time, giving the customer what he wants, and being able to give him an answer when he needs an answer. People phone up about all kinds of things, like, "My television set's broken down." Absolutely nothing to do with Sky at all. But we will still try to get their problem solved. That is how it works. We are hugely customer-driven.

'Everything that Sky does is first class. If you talk to a sports fan about how cricket is now reported versus the way it used to be done, they will tell you, "It is fantastic." You can be terribly critical about some of the programming on Sky, because a lot of it will not be to your taste, but whatever the genre of programme, it is well delivered. That is why it has been successful. I have never yet come across an accidental success, I really have not. Something is successful because someone has *made* it a success, by knowing what the customer wants, and giving it to them. When you look at businesses that fail, they often fail on this very simple issue of not giving the customer what he wants at a price that he's willing and able to pay.'

Gerry Robinson has strong views on service into the twenty-first century. Not surprising, as his entire Granada value system is built on consistently showing that the provision of high quality services and products in high value businesses, and at value for money prices, is wholly compatible with achieving good profitability. 'We are very self-critical in the UK, but if you travel around the world and compare things, we score hugely well compared to where we were ten years ago. You go to Paris, Charles de Gaulle airport is a nightmare. It's messy and there are never enough people on the passport desks. I think America has declining standards in parts we used to think of as wonderful. Here, our attitudes are changing. People are not prepared to put up with second-grade service. Look at the quality of our shops, clothing, electrical goods. I feel service levels are rising rather than falling.'

If Gerry Robinson had one wish for the millennium it would be that we keep in the UK a deregulated environment within which business can operate. 'The fewer regulations there are the better. There are signs of an increasing desire for that. Let people get on with things and they do a better job of it. The European Union is difficult, because there is a tendency for it to want to regulate. The fact is you have this incredibly uncomfortable alliance of countries. Some, like ourselves and Germany, feel that if you introduce a reg-

131

ulation, you then *have* to follow it through. Then there are those like the French, Italian and Spanish who tend to be willing to allow regulations to come into play but don't intend they should be followed through to the letter of the law in any detailed way! You get a very uncomfortable mis-match between those two temperaments. Whichever way you look at it, more interference, whether it comes from Brussels or central UK government, is unhelpful. That is not a "push off and leave me alone" attitude. It produces the wrong result.'

Despite his reservations on Brussels rules and regulations Gerry Robinson is keen to expand into Europe but only in areas he understands. That, by definition, is quite limiting. 'There is certainly an argument that says, managerial skill is managerial skill, and you can bring it to anything. There is some truth in that, but there is another argument which says you had better just do what you know, because in doing that you are likely not to make as many mistakes as you would going into something new. I largely subscribe to the second philosophy. Therefore, if you are going into a new country, you need to be doing it in a business where you already understand the nuts and bolts. I would like to get into Europe, but only in catering.'

Gerry Robinson never set out in any conscious way to end up running a large company, it just sort of happened. He is quite content and the most likely scenario is he will still be with Granada when he retires. 'I certainly won't be older than fifty-five when I retire, and I'll then go off and enjoy myself, get back to some really basic, important things.' He does not work very long hours, and is insistent on that. 'I can't on the one hand claim to let people get on with it and allow them to make decisions if I am sitting here working twelve hours a day, overseeing everything, and second-guessing. There would be something wrong with the system, something wrong with the people.'

He is highly visible, yet people in his motorway services outlets would probably not have the slightest idea who he is: 'Neither they should. I don't care about that, and I don't think they care about it. The most enlightening thing for me once, was to spend a day with a whole group of people on the catering side, when they hadn't the slightest idea who I was. I got more feel for what life was about, running a canteen operation, as a result of that than anything else. People will relate to what they do in their own section. They may have some vague feeling about what all this senior management stuff is about, and provided that all feels comfortable, there is no problem. The idea that one man can go round and be all powerful, I don't believe in at all. There is good internal PR in having the feeling that the people who run it care, but you had better make it work at a local level, where they're more worried about the site manager coming along than some visit from head office. You kid yourself hugely if you think everyone out there in Granada is worrying about what Gerry Robinson's doing. 95 per cent of them couldn't care less, and why should they? They're worried about whether they are going to get to work or home on time, the kids are ill, or whatever. You need to run a thing, knowing that; not as some kind of grandee. I think you can really overestimate your own importance.'

GRAND METROPOLITAN PLC

Turnover (1994)	£7,780 million
Operating profit	£1,023 million
Profit before tax	£654 million
Total fixed assets	£2,793 million
Employees (average during year)	64,300

One of the world's leading consumer goods companies, specializing in branded food and drinks businesses.

George Bull – Group Chief Executive

George Bull joined International Distillers & Vintners in 1961, rising to the position of Chief Executive in 1984 and Chairman in 1988. In 1992 he left GrandMet's Drinks Sector to become Chairman and Chief Executive of its Food Sector.

In 1985 he was appointed to the Board of GrandMet, which had taken over IDV in 1972. He was appointed Group Chief Executive in December 1993.

Other appointments:
  Non-Executive Director of United Newspapers.
  Director of the British Overseas Trade board.
  Fellow of the Royal Society of Arts.

He has been awarded the distinction of 'Chevalier de l'Ordre National de la Légion d'Honneur' by the French government.

The Company has two sectors:

Food Sector
This includes such well-known brands as Pillsbury, Green Giant, Jus-rol, Erasco, Old El Paso, Brossard, Häagen Dazs and Burger King, the world's second largest hamburger chain. Pearle Vision, the retail eye-care group, is also included in this sector, with some 900 outlets in North America and Europe.

Drinks Sector
This includes more than 150 brands, including five of the world's top 20 spirits brands. GrandMet develops, produces, markets and distributes around 100 million cases a year, more than any other drinks company, with operations in over 55 countries. Brands include Smirnoff, J&B, Gilbey, Croft, Piat, Baileys, Malibu and Cinzano, with licences or agencies for Stolichnaya, Jack Daniel's, Southern Comfort and Jose Cuervo.

GrandMet also has an active community relations programme. It spends approximately 1.5 per cent of worldwide trading profit less interest costs – some £16 million – on community involvement each year. Support is in the form of employee volunteering, donations in kind, sponsorships and support, as well as cash donations.

Grand Metropolitan PLC
George Bull, Group Chief
Executive

Grand Metropolitan [GrandMet] is one of the world's leading consumer goods companies, specializing in branded food and drinks businesses. It is a market oriented organization with particular skills in brand marketing and the management of worldwide operations.

The group operates across a small spread of businesses which possess complementary features, thereby ensuring it adds value to the individual parts. It is known as an innovative company which thrives on change and challenge, not always necessarily understood by city commentators or investors.

The French have that wonderful expression, *plus ça change, plus c'est la même chose*, and it is true the more things change, the more the fundamentals actually remain very much the same. In looking at GrandMet today, it is a highly focused, branded food and drink business, and it has to keep focused on the fundamentals of its businesses, which is the marketing of brands. That is the game George Bull, its chief executive, has been personally involved in for over thirty years now. As he says, 'Although we get much more sophisticated with the use of computers and access to information which improve the speed with which we can react and respond, and give greater detail with which we can take decisions, these are but refinements. They do not alter the basics which are that you need to relate directly with the customers. Find out what it is that they want or aspire to, and fulfil that need in a manner which can generate profit, and also increase the business and the scope of it.'

The challenge for GrandMet is to keep itself ahead of the market. Its competitors are also gaining that same information very much faster, and they are using it much more slickly than they ever did before. The need for good management, good training and good systems backing up the organization is ever more apparent. The need to become more global is a further requirement if GrandMet is really going to continue to grow on the scale it is achieving today. It cannot any longer sustain such growth on this little island. Therefore it needs to look for new markets to develop into, and also ways in which it can actually create new brands and products, whilst developing those it already owns.

Says George Bull, 'Yes, business has changed, and we see periods of recession, followed by periods of boom, and then bust again. In the area of brand ownership we saw this extraordinary period in the late 1980s, when the economies grew very strongly, and people were prepared to spend huge sums of money buying almost anything with a brand name on it. This gave rise to a period of extraordinary growth. That came to a sudden thumping end. It was replaced by recession, which had a depth to it which previous ones perhaps had not reached. This gave rise to a period where consumers became much more questioning about brands, and the value-for-money relationship became the new thing that we the brand owners really had to contend with. It was not that the brands were no longer something people aspired to having, it was just that they were not prepared to pay over the top for them. We had to find a new relationship for the brand with its consumer. The good marketers have found that, know what the premiums are that can be charged and do not exceed those levels. The brand owners have to work harder than they ever did in terms of differentiating their brand from the run-of-the-mill, more commodity type product. So we have seen a change happening, but it only causes better marketing to take place as a result.'

It was interesting to look back at a marketing plan written in 1986 by the GrandMet board under chairman Sir Allen Sheppard (now Lord Sheppard). That vision said that GrandMet would need to focus the business down; the day of the conglomerate, in the board's view, was passing, and it needed more specialization. It should select the businesses it most wanted to be in. 'In this context,' says George Bull, 'we selected the drinks business, because it was pre-eminent and growing, and would continue growing. We then looked at the rest of our businesses and decided that we would actually, in the words of Allen Sheppard, declutter GrandMet. This would mean removing a tremendous number of the other businesses that we were in, and would increase our focus on a small number of core sectors.'

Amongst the changes, it was decided to get out of the original business, hotels, which had been the start point for GrandMet under Sir Max Joseph. In 1989 it sold all its hotel interests and bought into food, through its acquisition of Pillsbury. 'From then on,' says George Bull, 'we had reached the point at which we would specialize further, and we would free ourselves of everything other than food and drink. We have now nearly completed that programme. We still have an interest in pubs, which is a residual part of our one-time ownership of breweries, which we got out of some years ago. We also still own Pearle Vision, the retail eye-care business in America, which may not fit our long-term strategy. But aside from that, we are now absolutely down to what we want to be, which is a branded food and drink business.'

Food and drink are joined together by the fact that they both appeal to the same consumer, you and me, everybody who eats and drinks. According to George Bull, 'All the management members in our group now are focused on the same problems: how do you motivate a value-conscious consumer to buy a branded food or a branded drink, preferably from our stable? It means that everybody is now thinking on business issues from the same perspective. It gives us this incredible sense of togetherness that we now have within GrandMet. We have shed the conglomerate bit of history, and are now absolutely focused on providing that same consumer with branded food and branded drink choices.'

GrandMet's drink business includes the world's leading vodka brand, Smirnoff, and five of the top twenty global spirit brands such as J&B and Baileys Irish Cream. Its food business is across many different types, from Jus-rol frozen pastry to pizzas, Green Giant vegetables to Mexican tacos, Häagen-Dazs ice cream to Burger King fast food. What may appear to be many different types of food are not so different from a branding or marketing viewpoint. As George Bull explains, 'Häagen-Dazs ice cream is bought by the almost identical consumer in many of the same outlets as one buys a bottle of Baileys Irish Cream. Indeed, we have launched a new product, Häagen-Dazs Baileys ice cream, which is highly successful. But the point is that actually the differences are not really that great. We specialize in the food area, essentially in things that are derived from a flour base, wheat or corn, or indeed rice. Similarly with vegetables, because of our Green Giant brands and business. We do not, though, really get much involved with meat or dairy production. So in effect we are specializing in the areas of our food manufacture. When we are actually dealing with pizzas, they are not so terribly different from dealing with a cookie or a biscuit product or something like that.'

Managing a large enterprise in the nineties is, in George Bull's view, about deciding what core business you are in and sticking to it. 'I'm tremendously strong about that, even to a fault. My view is that the more we concentrate our resource in terms of where our strengths lie, the better we will be placed for the longer term into the twenty-first century.' The question is, how tight does GrandMet set those parameters? 'If you get too stupid about it, and say, "We are only in the production of horse carriages," then when the car comes in you are never going to be in business. You have got to move your edge to take care of what the market needs at any given time. You must move with the market trends, and also be flexible enough that whenever the edge actually falls within the parameter of your reasonable expertise, you can accommodate it. It should not, therefore, be impossible to say that you can define what your knitting is, and stick with it, and still grow the business very substantially. That is exactly what we do.'

George Bull, therefore, does not go off with flights of fancy and buy some wonderful shirt manufacturing business in Sri Lanka because GrandMet could make a lot of money out of it. It knows nothing about making shirts, nor the shirt market, therefore it will not entertain it. 'We will buy businesses that fit the mould of the expertise we have, which is very wide. Take alcoholic beverages – not beer, we decided we are not in beer – but we are in wines and spirits. That gives us wide future scope, all around the world. In food, we are largely in, but not totally, the area of flour or vegetable base, and all combinations of that. Therefore, we are able to expand ourselves from our base level of expertise of production technology, in order to be able to build businesses in the markets as they develop round the world.'

What GrandMet has also done is to take a lot of the costs out of its business, making it better positioned and fitter to face the millennium. It has taken two restructuring charges for GrandMet, totalling some £455m, in the past two years. 'The first one we did,' says George Bull, 'largely took the costs out of our food side, mainly in America, through rationalizing plants and offices. We have then used the majority of the funds that we saved to increase advertising and marketing expenditure. We have more recently done the same

138

exercise on drinks. In our view, this is the right way to go. We are taking cost out and reinvesting it in marketing expenditure, mostly advertising, as we are pushing the long-term franchise between the brand and the consumer. That will in turn increase the sales of those brands through increased consumer offtake, and thereby propel the business forward and increase the profits. We will increase the cash flow generated by our businesses, from which we will pay down debt, make add-on acquisitions and further increase sales. This is the very clear cut philosophy that we have – brands are the life-blood of our business, and to regenerate the brands we have to build them.'

There are four ways GrandMet will grow its business into the twenty-first century. The first is by growing its existing brands in existing markets. That is happening by continuing to improve quality and enhance the packaging of the brands themselves, and improving the distribution and range of GrandMet brands where the company already has a presence. The second way is through the development of new brands, both in food and drink. For example the Häagen-Dazs Baileys ice cream is a case in point. There are all types of new drink brands, such as the company's recent 'Black Label' Smirnoff vodka, and new food brands coming off the production lines all the time. Pillsbury produces approaching 100 new products every year. The constant innovation in producing new brands that appeal to consumers is a vital area of growth for GrandMet and its life-blood.

The third way ahead is for GrandMet to develop new markets. Says George Bull, 'The consumption of all spirits brands in Europe, Japan and North America has been gently falling for a few years now, and is scheduled to continue. However, there are new developing markets in Russia, China, India, Latin America and Eastern Europe which potentially can more than replace the loss from the mature markets. Towards 2000 and beyond, the overall level of spirit consumption will actually increase, and this is already taking place to a considerable extent.'

The new developing markets hold huge potential. 'They are not actually new, to the extent that people are suddenly saying, "Hey what is this, a bottle of some spirit to drink?" They are markets that are already perfectly mature in terms of consumers' drinking, but have never been previously accessible to Western companies. Those are the markets that need to be developed, and because they have only recently become accessible to us, we are in the early stages of establishing our brands there. We have a presence in Eastern Europe, in Russia, China, and now in India, and are rapidly building our brands and businesses in those countries. It is a huge opportunity for the future. We are doing it with our drinks business and increasingly moving our food business in as well. We now market Burger King in fifty-six different countries around the world. Our packaged food business is in rather fewer countries, but it has certainly now spread to twenty-five or so. Our drinks business has operations in some fifty-eight countries round the world. We are already established in most of the principal world markets, and in a position now to grow those businesses considerably for the future.'

The fourth area in which GrandMet will expand its business is through add-on acquisitions, but continuing to stick to their knitting and building in the areas in which they have strength. The aim will be to acquire good fit businesses that can be quickly merged into existing operations and can make an immediate return.

George Bull believes one of the things the British are really quite good at doing is getting off our island, and actually creating a business around the world, and managing that business rather well. 'We have had a lot of practice at this! We sit on a tiny island and unless we get off it, we are stifled. We have done it for hundreds of years, and have built an ethos of management thinking around the process of how you get overseas and start the business. We are good at it. Now my view is that although we are pretty good at doing that, we also need to "go local" as soon as we possibly can. This means leaving our businesses abroad under local management. We are also very keen to bring other nationalities of management over here. If you walk the corridors of our head office in London, you will hear many different accents and see different nationalities. At the moment there are a lot of American accents around here, American management from our many US businesses, while some of our British management is in America. The next step is to become regarded as an Anglo-American corporation, because most of our business is either here or in the USA. We are also very anxious now to expand beyond this Anglo-American unit and become truly international. We are already doing that, and wherever we possibly can, we get local management on board as fast as we can, build them up and let the business then be run locally.' Training is very much part of George Bull's local management philosophy. 'They need training,' he says, 'so that they understand where GrandMet comes from, and understand the manner in which we operate, but as soon as that can be done they carry on with the business. It works pretty well.'

George Bull confesses his organization is not as flat as it might be. 'We all talk about it getting flatter,' he says, 'however I think it is awfully hard to run what is a major corporation with a totally flat structure. There has to be some degree of hierarchy, because decisions actually have to be taken. Even I, occasionally, have to take a decision! It runs across the business, and decisions always have the nasty habit of pleasing some and displeasing probably an awful lot more. If you don't have effective management able to take decisions to run the business, then you do get stifled. Consensus is all very well, it has its place, but at the end of the day you need management able to take a decision.

'We do really try to flatten the structure. We empower management down the line to take decisions. Now that's a bit different from saying there is no hierarchy. It is the process by which you actually use the line management. If you empower them to take more and more decisions within their own province of activity, then you get really good results because the management knows that when it is responsible it can take decisions in the interest of the business and be measured on the overall effectiveness of what it does, rather than on each individual decision. This is a process that we have developed very well. We also use a lot of team working, which cuts across boundaries of management, boundaries of culture, boundaries even between the businesses of food and drinks. Because we have this common consumer and customer, we are able to share knowledge, share best practice. We can put people together in teams, to work on problems and issues. This enables them to come up with solutions which we can all buy into.'

One of the things George Bull did when he became group chief executive was to focus on some core management principles; to 'empower' management, develop team work more, and reduce committees. 'We have actually done that. We have taken out six directive committees; we just demolished them. We have replaced them by teams of people further down, that is, the management on the ground. What we do is take a team of production people, basically from food and drink, who will look at issues together. They will meet often with nobody from head office present. They will give us a report on what they have found and what action they are proposing to take. They get on and do it. This will even cover issues like the environment. There are people who are so much closer to environmental issues than any of us sitting here in head office – we regard the environment as critically important. In the past our structure was too bureaucratic with regular committees of dozens of people meeting here. Now we implement this empowerment process, team working, and getting rid of stifling head office committees. Everybody loves it!'

As George Bull readily agrees, there are extremely well qualified managers or directors of businesses further down the company who are well trained, well geared to run their part of the operation, who have previously felt overwhelmed by the great central committee. 'Matters are usually better handled at an operational level, by the operators who know, understand and live with the decisions they have to take and who get on and do it. All we ensure is that they meet and that we are copied in on the decisions. To that extent, we steer a little bit, making sure it happens, but we do not actually have to participate, let alone dictate what the findings or the answers should be. People have really taken to that. It has not been hard – that has been one of my easiest decisions, because people actually want to participate more. They not only *feel* they are running the businesses but they *really* are.'

George Bull says that as people are different they will bring different talents to bear. 'The difference is that individuals will have different ways of expressing their form of leadership, very seldom will they be the same. You can be made into a better public speaker than you were, by being taught, but I don't think that is necessarily the case with leadership. I don't think you can teach leadership as such. That probably comes from instinct of some sort. If you teach everything else, leaders will emerge simply through sheer merit, ability to grasp detail, and all the rest of it; they will have a style which they will create around their own ability. So I do not think there is any real merit in feeling there is a rule that says, person "A" will be a leader and person "B" will not. Life is not like that. Life is a progression. It is an evolving situation, and you need, therefore, to play to your own strengths.'

The concerns George Bull has currently as CEO are largely to do with issues such as the economies of the principal markets in which GrandMet is operating and the currency situations of the moment which impart on the company tremendously. As he says, 'We make a lot of money in America, but the pound is running much too strong, for my liking, against the dollar at the moment. It translates very badly because, with the pound as strong as it is, it appears on the balance sheet as if we are being hit very hard. It's not necessarily true, but that's the way it appears.

'There is also concern about GATT – the General Agreement on Tarrifs and Trade. We do not really want power blocks – Europe versus America, versus Japan, versus the Pacific rim, versus whatever. These things become tremendously isolating. We are an international trading corporation and we need that international element as we develop new markets. There are huge opportunities out there, but I have some concerns. Will Russia and China be totally stable? Will India actually be able to maintain its current thrust of opening its doors to western companies? Will Latin America's broadly improved financial status, particularly in Brazil and Argentina, be maintained or not? Will Africa actually open its doors, following South Africa and all the breaking down of those rigid boundaries? Will that continue? All of these are concerns which are boringly obvious, but which may get in the way of our development in those markets.'

Bull's philosophy is that some of the above will come to pass. 'There will be problems, it is not going to be a nice smooth progression in Russia, China, and India, you know. There are going to be bumps. It is very unlikely they will all hit a tremendous lurch at exactly the same time, but it is equally very unlikely they will all progress in a nice straight line upwards. We have to be ready for turbulence as we go along. We also need to be prepared so that we can provide the management resource that is needed to feed these new markets and to be on top of these world developments. We have to be really smart in terms of our ability to put management where it is needed. And also to put systems in place quickly, so we make use of information, and learn from it, and actually feed it through to the marketplace ahead of the competition.'

Many of these are standard issues affecting any CEO running a large international business. Do they keep him awake at nights? 'No. The answer is we have a very good management. We will get caught by the odd surprise, but by the same token, I am absolutely convinced that we are in the right kind of businesses. There is no problem with brands. Well-managed brands live on, only bad brand managers die, is an expression I often use. It is highly descriptive, because the fact is, my wife would like to have a Cartier watch, a Christian Dior scarf, or indeed a Häagen-Dazs ice cream. The point is that people do aspire to brands. That's the way life is. And we, as brand managers, must make sure we deliver the quality, the differentiation, the communication. It must be really crisp and good – and the price that we charge must be dead right, so that people recognize the added quality, but also do not get frightened away by a price differential that is too far removed from reality. As long as you get those points right and manage and support the brand well, that is the way you grow.'

What George Bull wants by the year 2003 is that GrandMet is seen as the best branded food and drinks business of the world. 'That would be measured by customer satisfaction, on the one scale, and by shareholder value on the other. The shareholders will have been properly rewarded by staying with their investment in our company, and the customer will be fully satisfied by the provision of our fine range of brands for their requirements. That seems to me to be a goal that is quite attainable by 2003. I am not in any way discouraged by anything I see out there at the moment.'

GrandMet has had something of a chequered relationship with the City and its investors in recent years. One of the reasons, Bull believes, is they do not understand what GrandMet is doing. Having once been a conglomerate organization, it is now a branded food and drink business. The problem has been that the process of decluttering, from being a conglomerate to becoming highly focused, has taken GrandMet about eight years. What it has led to has been this extraordinary level of change, so that people say, 'Dammit. GrandMet is restless, can't stand still. Every six months there's a new shift. Why can't it stop it? Just stand still!'

In 1986 it had thirty-two disparate businesses all around the world. Today, it is down to just two sectors, food and drink. As George Bull reminds us, 'To change meant selling off well-known businesses, including InterContinental Hotels, Watney Mann breweries, Mecca and William Hill and Express Dairies. Yet it isn't just a bout of selling, because obviously in the process we have also wanted to build up the shape of the business. So we bought Pillsbury, and then subsequently bought Pet Inc. in the US, because they fit the shape of our business. We have had to both buy and sell businesses. It has always been done with a view to what shape we should be in for the longer term. Now we really are in that shape, but we have lost the City somewhere along the track. But if you see what we have done, it all fits exactly this predetermined mould we are shaping. The things we have sold were all pieces that did not fit.

'Growing the shareholder value will enable us to come back to the top, where we can further refine our branded food and drinks. We are like a sculptor with a clay model. We have got our model, it is nicely shaped, but as we go on modelling it, we decide to shave off a bit here, or add some there. That is a moulding process that we will constantly be involved in. We will go on shaving off cost in order to make ourselves more cost-effective, to increase the effort behind brands, to grow them by the four methods I have described, thereby delivering increased shareholder value. We will continue telling the City, this is the process we are involved in – increasing investment in and growing the brands. We have done it on our food side for eighteen months and the drinks side for six months. Food is growing fantastically as a result of the extra investment we are putting behind it. That in turn is going to grow the shareholder value. The shareholders will get more comfortable, and on the back of that the share price will rise, and the circle regenerates itself.'

This is a story GrandMet must take round the City and explain. Bull agrees. 'We must tell them how we have been reshaping ourselves from this old conglomerate into our new focus. If we can explain that message to everybody, then I believe people will be able to understand that we are really working this business to a process. If you look at it, all the changes we have made fit this philosophy, and our strategy, and people will actually realize that we have a great process under way.'

Although Europe is an important market and will remain so, the fact is GrandMet's business is today largely in North America – some 67 plus per cent of its profits come from there now. The indications are however that the newly developing and growing markets are outside both North America and Europe and these will contribute an increasing proportion of GrandMet's business as it goes forward to the millennium and beyond. The element that is Europe will, George Bull believes, provide a smaller proportion of group turnover in the future. Although he admits GrandMet can live with or without a single European currency, and from his perspective it is not a burning issue, Brussels he considers is now as important, or more important than Westminster. 'The business that we now have in the UK is quite small. Only 7 or 8 per cent of our business is located here and therefore Brussels is increasingly important because we trade with the whole of Europe. It is still our second biggest trading zone after North America. Also, the impact that Brussels has on such issues as GATT affects our overall trading situation. Many facets of our business are impacted by Brussels legislation and that does affect us, and we are intimately bound into that. We are very much involved, and we take steps to make sure that our voice is heard as appropriate. But it is not an issue for us. We ride the punches!'

GrandMet is very strong on corporate community involvement, not just here in the UK and in the USA but increasingly in its other main markets. The aim is to make a significant contribution to local communities in the areas in which it operates. 'We really try and do that as a part of our philosophy all around the world,' says George Bull. 'It is a straightforward issue. Being close to the market is the bedrock of our business. It means being close to our consumers. It is necessary that we understand and work with them, and one of the ways we can achieve this is by contributing to their communities. The way we tend to do it is by helping young people to develop, particularly people who have perhaps failed in formal education terms, or need an opportunity, a second chance in life, which the current education systems do not readily provide.'

George Bull adores the business that he is in. He started life in an advertising agency, and then as a salesman. That is why he went into marketing. He has come up through the sales and marketing tree. 'That still is what fascinates me. I like being out and about to meet our people, and also to meet our customers. I enjoy going over to America and being out with the retailers and sales people, meeting and talking with them. I try and get out into the marketplace wherever I go, and see how business is progressing. I really do like to get as near to the sharp end as I can, that is the bit of the business that interests me most.'

He believes they have in GrandMet a business that is really, in spite of its size, quite neat and tidy. 'It is actually a very manageable business. It has a huge range of brands, but they are essentially aimed at the same consumer, and how we tickle that consumer's motivation to go and buy is always the thing that fascinates me. I really enjoy it. My motivation is entirely to do with brand and marketing success, but the greatest success of all, I think, would be if we could eventually persuade our friends in the City, to understand and believe in what we are doing. My target is to get our message understood, and it needs two things. One is me and my colleagues talking it through with the City, but more, much more important than that, is the proof that at each of these various stages I have discussed, I am able to demonstrate the action that we have taken – the results of what we have done, where we have spent the money – has increased the business. The proof of the pudding is in the eating. Once we have actually shown it works, then at that point we have answered the doubting Thomases. That is the challenge.'

George Bull's view is that right will out, and that sooner or later, people will recognize and appreciate GrandMet's new-found position. It is working to a very careful plan and agreed strategy into the twenty-first century. As he says, 'We have our own vision of what we are trying to achieve and we are well on course to achieving our objectives. I would like to be remembered as a person who genuinely believed in the marketplace. I'd like to leave behind the thought that "He genuinely believed in the customer, the marketplace and in a market oriented business, a business that really did become genuinely motivated by supplying that customer need."'

He preaches brands. 'If our audiences see that brands actually do deliver the end product, which is to improve profits and thereby enhance the shareholder value of the business, then if I can hot gospel (which I do) the philosophy about brands, and persuade GrandMet people not only to believe me, but to believe in it as a means by which you can really run a business, then I will die happy.'

George Bull feels there are many people who play at this 'brands' game, but who do not actually believe it. 'I have spent nearly forty years believing that the primacy of brands and fulfilling that customer need, is the key. If one gets a corporation genuinely around to believing that it is the marketplace that actually drives the whole philosophy and strategy of the corporation, and makes it work to that end, it will succeed. Then I will feel I have contributed to that success by leaving this business a truly market oriented business.'

As GrandMet's food and drinks businesses march forward into new frontiers of opportunity – India, China, South America, the former Soviet Union and Eastern Europe – I suspect George Bull will be at its helm into 2000 and beyond, booming 'brands, brands, brands'. He acknowledges this, but reminds me, 'I don't rate me, I rate the corporation. The company is the hero. I am simply a tool to try to help it. If the company is the hero, then it lives on, and I can then go and play golf, which is what I really want to get on and do!'

With effect from 1 March 1996, George Bull will become Chairman of Grand Metropolitan.

HALIFAX BUILDING SOCIETY

Pre-tax profits of combined parts of the new Halifax (Leeds and Halifax) (year to 31 January 1995)	over £1.2 billion
Combined assets	£93 billion
Combined reserves	£5.5 billion

Number of
Savings and investment accounts	approx 15 million
Borrowers	approx 2.5 million
Branch offices	over 1,100
Staff	over 28,000

Personal finance business.

Mike Blackburn – Director and Chief Executive

Mike Blackburn joined the Society as a Director in June 1993 and took over as Chief Executive in August 1993. He is also Chairman of Halifax Estate Agencies Ltd, Halifax Financial Services (Holdings) Ltd, Halifax Life Ltd and a director of other companies in the group. His 21-year banking career was spent in East Anglia, the Home Counties, London and Yorkshire. Previous appointments include Director and Chief Executive of Leeds Permanent Building Society (1987-93) and seconded from Lloyds Bank as Director and Chief Executive of the Joint Credit Card Company Ltd (Access) (1983-87).

He is also a member of the court of Leeds University.

The Business

The Halifax is the most successful personal finance business in the UK. The Building Society is the UK's largest holder of personal savings, the largest provider of home mortgages and one of the largest lenders to housing associations. Almost half of Britain's households have a savings or a borrowing relationship with the Halifax.

Other activities include
- Halifax Financial Services, providing life assurance, pensions and unit trust investments
- Halifax Property Services, with some 600 offices throughout the country
- Colleys Professional Services, one of the largest firms of professional valuers
- a recently-formed retail bank in Spain.

Its merger with Leeds Permanent Society became effective on 1 August 1995. The next step is for it to obtain members' approval for conversion to PLC status. If approved, conversion is likely to take place within about two years.

The Halifax Building Society
Mike Blackburn,
Chief Executive

Yorkshire has become the home of a new, world-class financial institution since the Halifax and Leeds Permanent Building Societies merged in 1995. Conversion will give the Halifax bank status and represent the largest single extension of share ownership in British history.

The Halifax is a strong and successful organization that already enjoys relationships with over 15 million customers, served by more than 27,000 staff. The Halifax represents some 20 per cent of net lending in the UK housing market and looks after more people's savings than any other UK organization. Apart from being Britain's biggest mortgage lender, it also provides personal banking, insurance and property services and the merger with the Leeds has helped it to build the foundations for the millennium.

The Halifax has set itself various goals:

- to be the UK's biggest mortgage lender and biggest holder of private savings
- to be the personal finance business that is best rated for customer satisfaction
- to build a group of complementary businesses that achieve genuine synergy by meeting a broad spectrum of related customer needs.
- to do all this by capitalizing on the established values that are its traditional strength.

Its millennium wish is not just to be the biggest personal finance business in the UK but also to be the best. Chief Executive Mike Blackburn believes it has the potential to become *the* organization that everyone naturally thinks of first when it comes to personal finance.

Before joining the Halifax he was Chief Executive of Leeds Permanent Building Society. Under his guidance, two strong building societies have been brought together, giving customers access to the most substantial network of branches ever offered by any UK building society.

When he joined the Halifax in 1993, one of the things he wanted to do was scrawl graffiti on the walls! 'I'd have scrawled a series of initials; IBM, GM, BSA – big companies that had market dominance but which had lost sight of what was actually happening in their environment and to their customers.'

That was not going to happen at the Halifax. 'The board and the senior executives in a big, dynamic company must have split vision. One eye must be on what's happening in the company on a day-to-day basis, the other has to be viewing what is going to happen tomorrow and how the organization is to be positioned to deal with that future. Our board goes away regularly – off-site and out of sight – for a couple of days to take the time to do just that. To see what is happening in the world. Not just the financial services world, but the world in the broader sense.'

He is passionate about customers and providing them with a quality of product and service that has them exclusively in mind. 'We don't want our customers getting their personal financial requirements satisfied by anybody else. We want to be able to do it, and we want to be able to do it in a lifetime sense.'

The Halifax is dealing with more people's financial affairs than any other institution, in a relationship based on trust. 'The Halifax has enormous market presence,' says Mike Blackburn, 'and such a reputation for safety and solidity. "If your money is in the Halifax you can't go wrong," is the position we hold. Every member of our organization is aware of the responsibility they have to maintain our standards. Now we are with the Leeds we have to ensure that what were two strong organizations in their own right become an even better provider of services for our customers.'

The difference between the Halifax and the Leeds position in the marketplace was to do with size, he says. 'The function of size was really underscored at the Halifax by its position as a price maker in the housing finance market, rather than a price taker. At the Leeds one had to wait until the Halifax moved rates and then respond.'

Halifax is engaged in something unique. No two large organizations can I recall in this country have undergone a merger and then a conversion to PLC. Will there be culture compatibility?

Mike Blackburn has worked in four organizations, each with its distinctive culture. 'One never underestimates the importance of an organization's culture and how it affects its way of working. It is its invisible glue. Culture in a business is an accumulation of historic practice and thinking. But organizations are living things. It is people that make changes, make culture, influence behaviours, set standards. Obviously I have had a unique perspective, having worked for one and now working for the other. I am totally confident that the cultural similarities will mesh.'

The Halifax has consistently improved its pre-tax profit even through the recession, which hit the housing market especially hard. Yet the Halifax managed to drive forward its pre-tax profits despite having had to make some very heavy provisions for bad debt; it has an unimpeachable record in that respect. Says Mike Blackburn, 'I don't think there is another society that has managed to progress in that way. It certainly reacted very quickly to the recession. It pulled back on 100 per cent lending, tightening its criteria quickly. It put in place processes to deal with those in trouble and who were going to get out of it, and those who clearly never would.'

Despite the elusiveness of the 'feel-good factor' he doesn't think owner-occupation will go away. 'Interestingly, despite the length and depth of the recession in the housing market, it is – by a long, long way – the preferred housing tenure that people want. There is still a strong aspiration to own one's own home. Home ownership is around 67 per cent at the moment, and we think there is actually scope for that to increase a little.'

Over the last few years the Halifax has built unique market-leading expertise in loans to housing associations and is the biggest lender into that market of any building society, with a 20 per cent plus market share. 'The competition there, which is increasing quite rapidly, is still few in number. We have a billion pounds committed to that market, which is continuing to grow because more municipally-owned properties are being released into specially formed housing associations. Looking towards the millennium, housing association activity will grow. First-time buyers are getting older, and are either still living at home or in rented accommodation, which could be in the social housing sector or in the private sector. Wherever they are, there are opportunities for us in financing the roofs over their heads.

'That is quite different from ten years ago when, under

151

Thatcherism, housing policy was synonymous with home owner-ship. The right-to-buy policy, which resulted in 1.5 million council homes moving into the private sector, was one of the consistent threads of the 1980s. Now that has all but come to an end.'

A core concept for the Halifax is to provide lifetime peace of mind for ordinary people in their financial affairs. Says Mike Blackburn, 'The population is ageing. People in their fifties have quite big investment power. We see a lot of growth towards 2000 on the sav-ings side of our business.' The lending side at the Halifax is certainly going to be maintained and grow. On the investment side, it is mov-ing from being historically a home for short-end savings, instant sav-ings, to providing a portfolio of savings products, including unit trusts, PEPS, single premium investment bonds and so on. 'There is a lot of scope to spread the savings portfolio, and to do it in such a way that we have control over product development and manage-ment as well as the distribution channels.'

This is one of the reasons why the Halifax stopped selling the life and unit trust products of another company and set up its own com-panies providing those products to their customers. Mike Blackburn says, 'There is no substitute to having total control. We now have people within the Halifax Group who can create products for our customers which meet their needs in a way which is distinctive to us. The Standard Life products that we used to sell were the same as those being sold in the independent financial adviser marketplace. In that sense, we were just another distribution channel for Standard Life.'

The business climate and changing employment patterns will impact on the Halifax core business towards 2000. Blackburn explains 'When I joined Lloyds Bank in the early sixties I expected to work forty years with the bank. It came as a bit of a shock to me when I chose not to do so! People starting work in 1995 will be shocked if in forty years time they are still working for the same orga-nization. That employment change will force a change in our busi-ness. One of the key questions is how you underwrite home ownership for somebody who might be on a short-term contract and who, therefore, might have six, seven or eight such contracts during the course of their employment lifetime.'

What about overseas expansion? Until recently the Halifax had not gone offshore. Now it has set up a bank currently with two branches in Spain offering both a range of savings products and residential mortgages for private individuals. Says Mike Blackburn, 'There is an opportunity for us to expand our presence in Spain, and particularly into the "ex-pat" market, where the name of the Halifax is known and trusted.'

Are there differences between the housing markets here and overseas as the Halifax considers its way forward? Mike Blackburn thinks markets are local. 'Most customers use just one branch. It may be a terrific comfort for them to know if they are in Inverness, or Penzance, and they happen to live in the Home Counties, that there is one of our offices they can go into. But essentially our customers are concerned with their locality. Just looking at the European dimension, the housing markets in continental countries have their own individual characteristics. In Germany a much higher percentage of people rent and people get into home ownership at different ages than in the UK. There are individual markets rather than a common market in that sense. The maintenance and enhancement of our position in the UK must have the pre-eminent focus for many, many years to come. Our activities in Spain are really part of a year 2020 strategy. They will be of much more interest to my successor's successor than they will to me.'

What about regulation? Blackburn considers that de-regulation has been a real misnomer. It has been common parlance to talk about de-regulation of financial services. What has actually happened is *re*-regulation. We are much more constrained now by regulation than we were ten years ago. The Financial Services Act of 1986 has had a very significant impact on the way in which investment products are sold. Ten years ago our branch manager might have done two or three mortgage interviews at lunchtime. Now, the regulation process makes that impossible. The number one requirement for getting a mortgage now is having stamina!' He cites the way in which mortgages are advertised. 'We have to carry a "health warning" like the tobacco companies. "If you don't keep up your mortgage payment you'll be thrown out of house and home" is the sort of thing you now see. So regulation in that sense is a problem.'

Does he want less regulation? Should there not be an external referee? Will players not take short cuts and commit a few fouls on the field if there is no referee to blow a whistle? 'The Bank of England, the Building Societies Commission, the Personal Investment Authority, each has a very valid role to play. Obviously I want financial services organizations to operate with particular standards of behaviour. People are investing, after all, life savings as well as trust. Anything which causes distrust has an impact, not just on one's own business, but on the industry as well.'

He believes that on balance his industry will become more regulated, because there is now a European legislative dimension alongside the national dimension. 'It is the job of politicians to legislate. That is what they are there for, and we have more of them now!'

He agrees consumer expectations are constantly changing and today people want greater access to more services, more conveniently around the clock. Even though more of their business will probably be direct delivered, i.e. not via a branch, it will still be a matter of picking the phone up to somebody. 'Of course we want to be there to help, on demand, whenever it suits our customers. That is the driving force behind our telephone-based services. Those services, notably in banking and insurance, have certainly become a market force to be reckoned with – as your book will show with First Direct, and indeed Kwik-Fit! They are offering customers convenience and competitive prices. There may be automatic voice response information to your query, but there will be a human being available at the end of the phone. By the year 2000 you could be discussing complex financial affairs at 10 o'clock at night face-to-face with one of our people on a TV screen or via your PC.'

He agrees that it is difficult to envisage financial services with no human interaction. 'Our customer is looking for advice and reassurance. He or she wants to have trust in the individual to whom they are talking. They want trust in the organization too, so all the attributes that make up the Halifax brand remain ever so important. Part of those attributes are the staff and their capability, expertise, their experience and the quality of the relationship they establish with the customer. The recruitment, training and development of staff is going to be as important as it has ever been. Indeed, more so, because part of that differentiation which will set us aside from everyone else operating in our market will be "that really expert and nice person" at the Halifax. It will be technically possible to do all of the transactions over the screen, but people do like to talk to other people face-to-face.'

The quality of Halifax staff and management will therefore be one of the key differentiators for the millennium. Mike Blackburn believes they have to combine control with spark. 'I want our customers, and those who are not yet our customers, to have a perception based on reality of the individual they are going to deal with when they cross our threshold. Whether that threshold is in the high street, over the phone, the screen or wherever.'

As they grow bigger into the millennium they must get better, they can only do this by holding true to the values on which the Halifax has built its strong and durable customer relationships. These are:

- commitment and integrity
- meeting or exceeding Halifax customers' expectations
- being passionate about quality and efficiency
- being justly proud of their personal contribution
- valuing and respecting one another.

'That last point is absolute crucial,' says Blackburn. 'We have enormous financial assets, but our people really are an even greater asset. This is what I try to build into the philosophy of the way we do things.'

The UK does not perform badly in terms of producing good leaders for commerce. 'There are many international and multinational companies based here in the UK. There are many international and multinational companies led by British executives. We are afraid to laud success, even in a sporting environment. If we win, it is because the other side is weak this year, so it was not such a great thing to beat them. There appear to be other, less inhibited societies where success is applauded. Here we downplay success or have to find reasons to justify it.'

His millennium 'wish' is for a high standard of behaviour and for people to applaud success, 'where we get away from building people up and then chopping them down. The media love to build people up and then demolish them. They cannot wait to get a hero's head on the tray.' He also feels there must be more passion within some of the financial services. 'Bankers have to be passionate about customers, have to be passionate about people, on both sides of the counter. I have to be passionate in wanting our customers to have the best. I have to be passionate about having staff of whom I am proud and who I want to be fulfilled in their work with the Halifax.'

He thinks recognition is extremely important. 'We don't use two particular words enough in this country, "thank you". I am sure there are lots of businesses where people are not thanked enough for what they have done. The fact of the matter is that more than 99 per cent of our staff come to the office every day intent on doing an excellent job. They need to be thanked. It doesn't matter who it is, whether it is the manager, the regional manager, the cashier. One of the five published core values I described earlier is valuing and respecting each other.'

To Mike Blackburn there is no substitute for being consistent in thumping messages and expectations home. This is what he believes it means to be part of the Halifax towards 2000. 'I hope I am meeting those five values, just as I hope the newest part-time cashier is meeting them. I want our customers to see that the Halifax stands for something; those values are public. I am very conscious that the Halifax has been around since 1853, and that the business has been taken forward by each of my predecessors onto new heights. In due course I would like my successor to look back and say, "Blackburn did take the organization on, he took it to new heights." Obviously what we are doing now, with the Leeds, is a major development. In terms of the parable of the talents, I hope it will be shown that I did not bury Halifax talents; I invested them, and the whole organization increased their worth.'

HANSON PLC

Turnover (1994)	£11.2 billion
Profit on ordinary activities before tax	£1.346 billion
Employees (worldwide)	60,000

A diversified British/American industrial management company with major investments in basic industries, including energy (coal, electricity), chemicals, propane, building materials, forest products, tobacco and material handling. Originally called Wiles Group, it was renamed Hanson Trust in 1969 and Hanson PLC in 1987.

The Company

Hanson PLC owns major international companies located principally in the UK and USA, producing a wide variety of high quality industrial products, many with worldwide sales. By market capitalization, Hanson PLC is in the top dozen British companies, and in sales, standing on its own, the US arm of Hanson PLC is in the top one-hundred US companies.

Lord Hanson – Chairman

James Hanson (as he then was) started out in the transport business in the UK and Canada. In 1964 he was chairman of Oswald Tillotson Ltd, a publicly quoted UK commercial vehicle sales company, when it was taken over by Wiles Group Ltd. In 1965 Lord Hanson became chairman, and together with the late Gordon (later Lord) White and Derek Rosling he transformed it into Hanson PLC.

Knighted in 1976, he was elevated to the Peerage in 1983. He is a Freeman of the City of London, a Fellow of the Royal Society of Arts and a Companion of The (British) Institute of Management. He is a former chairman of Trident Television and former director of Lloyds Bank PLC.

Derek Rosling CBE – Co-Founder and former Vice-Chairman

Derek Rosling joined Lord Hanson and Lord White in the transformation of Wiles Group into Hanson PLC. He was Vice-Chairman from 1973 to 1993 and retired from the board in 1994. From 1987-94 he worked principally from Hanson's New York and Californian offices. He was closely involved in the overall strategic planning for the company, acquisitions and divestments, financings and shareholder relations.

Derek Bonham – Deputy Chairman and Chief Executive

After experience as a chartered accountant with a major European accounting firm, Derek Bonham joined Hanson in 1971. In 1981 he was appointed finance director and in 1992 chief executive, becoming deputy chairman in 1993. He is also a non-executive director of Glaxo Wellcome PLC.

Hanson PLC
Lord Hanson, Chairman
Derek Rosling, Co-Founder and former Vice-Chairman
Derek Bonham, Deputy Chairman and Chief Executive

Some thirty years ago James Hanson got together with the late Gordon White and Derek Rosling to become involved in the transformation of a business known as Wiles Group – a tiny operation making £100,000 in 1964. Lord Hanson well remembers the first meeting he had in the Station Hotel in Hull, where he became chairman: 'At that first meeting,' says Lord Hanson, 'I said whatever we did must be fun. This is very important. It's important for young people to remember that when you get up in the morning and go to work it must be enjoyable. You must have in your sights enjoyment in what you're going to do. If you have that, you don't take it too seriously, have a joke and a bit of fun out of life.'

Lord Hanson came from a background of transport distribution and trucking. He recalls conversations with the drivers from that family business. 'They had to leave home about 4.30am to walk to work. They didn't have cars and there were no buses running. Nevertheless, they would go to work expecting to enjoy that day. I think that it has always been very encouraging for the owner or leader of a business to think that way.'

It was Henry Wheeler Shaw (1818–1885) who said, 'Laughter is the sensation of feeling good all over and showing it principally in one place.' Nowhere does that feel more appropriate than at Hanson's London headquarters. Today, Hanson PLC is a diversified management company employing over 60,000 people worldwide with the main operating subsidiaries in the UK and USA. Its major investments in basic industries range through bricks to energy, tobacco to timber. They also include chemicals and aggregates.

159

At its epicentre, Hanson is very small. There are only 100 people in London and another eighty in the USA headquarters in New Jersey. There is very little hierarchy, no long-established framework. It does not have a central personnel department, pensions, properties, insurances or marketing departments. All those functions are devolved to the individual companies.

Quite simply, the key to Hanson is its approach to management. Derek Rosling, co-founder and until recently vice-chairman of Hanson PLC, explains: 'Originally there were three of us – James Hanson, Gordon White and me, plus a couple of secretaries. We haven't changed the philosophy or management style since day one. It works for this company and there are no plans to change it. We believe it is the right basic principle on which to run a company now and beyond 2000. We at the centre do not know much about coal, timber or aggregates. We learn a bit, of course, as we understand what managers are doing, but we are not experts, we do not tell them what to do and we never have done. If they are in trouble we want to know about it and then we try to help.'

He means that if they foresee a problem, *that* is the time Hanson PLC wants to know about it, not when it is a disaster. Over the years, as a result of this safeguard, Hanson has rarely had disasters. It knows its problems in good time and has the resolve to act if necessary, never allowing a situation to drift. Says Lord Hanson, 'We in head office exist to help them. Occasionally we may have to haul them over the coals and say they haven't done that right. This is what we want to achieve in that particular area.'

Hanson PLC is seen therefore as a streamlined but very dedicated and disciplined organization. Explains Derek Bonham, 'We are major players on the world stage in most of the industrial sectors we are now in: chemicals, coal, building materials, cranes, tobacco, forest products and electricity. We are concentrating now on our major businesses, but not exclusively. If an opportunity arose tomorrow to go into a major enterprise we would do it. Equally, if it became right to divest ourselves of one of the existing ones, we would do it. There is nothing rigid about the company. We are not a traditional industry company, unlike some of the major banks or even a chemical or an oil company. We are different in concept because we are not industry people. We have not grown up through the chemical, timber or aggregates business.'

When Derek Bonham refers to 'we' he means the twenty senior

executives who comprise the Hanson PLC core central management team. 'Our job is to deal with the financing, the public and shareholder relations, which are very important and have become increasingly so. We ourselves do not mine coal or harvest timber. We are very interested in what those companies are doing and we are keen to ensure the right people are in place. We monitor what they are doing daily, weekly, monthly, whatever is appropriate. Bank balances are looked at every week, for instance. All capital expenditure is reviewed by me.'

Hanson PLC is run along prudent and precise financial lines. The centre controls the purse strings. Because it is simple, people understand it, can respond to it, work within it and succeed. Although there are critical controls at the centre, there is total autonomy and empowerment to the Hanson divisions. Lord Hanson says they learned very early on that you must put your trust in the people who are running the local business. 'We call it "the men at the sharp end", so, be it Hanson Brick, Peabody Coal or Quantum, they are all run by their own management. All they need us for, effectively, is encouragement and the financial backing to do their thing. They are owned by our shareholders and therefore their results come through to our shareholders, but apart from that, they run their own businesses. I think the best way to run a business is to put your trust in people. If they let you down, you can make changes.'

In the operating divisions the yardstick Hanson PLC uses above all else to ascertain where the companies are going, is the return on capital employed. They define *profit* as profit before interest and tax, so it is the operating profit, expressed as a percentage of the capital employed, and the manager's capital employed is the total value of his capital, excluding cash or debt. Says Bonham, 'We compare pre-interest profit with fixed assets, stocks, debtors, less creditors. That is the actual capital that man is using and we encourage managers to understand they have got X million or billion pounds or dollars of shareholders' funds locked into their chemical plant, or standing in their timber, or in the coal in the ground. We expect them to make an improving return on that capital.'

Industries vary however. Although you have to have these yardsticks, do you not need to understand the individual industries? Derek Bonham: 'By understanding a man's budget, you come to understand something of the problems of the industry and why he is saying his return on capital is going to be down next year compared with last year. The bonuses for that man are partly based on improving return on capital. The profit obviously can go up or down, but if the profit is going down, maybe we have to accept that. If he is making less profit, he ought to be employing less capital, so must reduce his capital. Because he is doing less business, a manager can actually make a very substantial bonus on lower profit if he manages his capital, squeezes his assets, reduces debtors and stock. We are always prepared to take the cash back, represented by that reduction of debtors and stock, into the centre and redeploy it somewhere else. Fixed assets by definition are obviously rather more fixed than stock or debtors, but if there is a dramatic reduction in business and he has three factories, maybe he should only be in two. This concept makes him want to reduce to two, where it is economic to do so.'

What the Hanson manager understands is the concept of using shareholders' funds to the best advantage. If he can't use them this year as well as he could last, or this year as well as he did five years ago, he is made to understand that he should reduce his capital and he is incentivized to do it. That sounds shockingly short-term. 'The record shows that we are not,' says Bonham. 'He is not going to be too short-term because if that man wants a job the year after next he is not going to cut his own throat. He becomes a realist.'

Lord Hanson says, 'There are three simple things to remember about running a business. One, encourage youth. Certainly the great thing we have always believed in is giving youth, or managers, or people down the line the opportunity to run the business. That is the single most important thing we have ever done. Two, give them responsibility as soon as you can and they will seldom let you down. Three, you must show an interest in what they are doing and have them report to you frequently on a fairly informal basis. Not in person, necessarily, but in the form of a monthly, weekly or quarterly report. In addition to that you must have very strong financial controls. Not to tell people how to run their businesses, but to make absolutely sure that nothing is going wrong, so I can sleep at night!'

When Hanson bought London Brick, for instance, there was a lot of resistance amongst brickwork managers to the information Hanson insisted was produced, which told them what was happening in their brickworks. 'After about twelve months,' says Derek Bonham, 'one of the brickwork managers admitted he hadn't known how the brickworks had run before "you guys came along." All he did before was make bricks. It didn't matter what the quality was, nor the colour. He just churned out bricks. Under our system, he had to make bricks that could sell at a full margin, to give them a proper profit, then expressed as a return on his capital. So he was suddenly concerned with waste. He didn't want to be producing a lot of seconds.'

Many other organizations have groups, committees, meetings and heavy administration departments, but Hanson people have been prepared, as individuals, to get on with the job, make decisions and be counted on the results. Bonham admits, 'Our mistakes have been of omission, things we did not do, that with hindsight perhaps we should have done. We didn't bid enough for a particular company, for example, or we were too mean. We let something slip through our fingers. You are never judged by that, you see. You get away with that one, because nobody else knows. But *we* know. We are all accountable. There's no attempt to shelter behind committees, or a lot of people sitting round and deferring it, or putting it to another group, which is what I think goes on in many companies. Tobacco may have management groups, or Peabody may have groups of people who meet on a regular or irregular basis. That is up to the chief executive of that business. We do not interfere with that. He runs it as he and his colleagues find most effective, to meet their objectives, which we have endorsed. They have their objectives that we are educated to understand, approve and accept.'

All of this must work, because Hanson PLC held its operating profit at around the £1 billion level through the worst recession since the thirties. Says Lord Hanson, 'That is now behind us and our businesses are expanding, so we are in a "grow-and-prosper" phase. Now is the time to invest rather than consolidate. Further recession will undoubtedly come again – the usual economic cycles - and when it comes I know we will approach it with realism and be prepared to get through it well.'

For Hanson PLC this has meant realistic preparation for the downturn and for future prospects, combined with speed in decision-making and resolution in execution: 'Having the right management in place and giving them the responsibility – coupled with incentive mentioned earlier to get on with the job.' One keeps coming back to this minimum interference from the centre.

According to Derek Bonham, those people at the centre responsible for the interface with a constituent company go to its managers direct. 'They would be at the sharp end with the managers, understanding the business, understanding the problems, talking about the budget. Typically, a financial man from here would go with one of the chief operating officers – let's say, to Imperial Tobacco – for perhaps two or three days at budget time and sit down with the various managers and understand the marketing plan, production costs and go through every facet of the budget and have it explained to them. It is not that they will change it, or that they will necessarily have any pearls of wisdom to impart. But the fact they are coming as representatives of the chief executive and the board of Hanson, sharpens the local manager's attention to detail. It is a discipline. At the end of the day, the manager knows that he will not receive cash for his pet project for that year unless he makes his case.'

Hanson PLC has been accused of being cold, clinical and predatory. I ask Derek Bonham if he agrees. 'We were made very aware of that perception in the public mind ten or twelve years ago. We addressed it through our corporate advertising campaign. It is an understandable criticism, but it is not justifiable, in that we are not a hire and fire organization. Most of the people who are at the top of any of the divisions were there before we bought those companies. All we have done is to change the environment, the climate in which they work.

'Generally speaking, working in the Hanson climate is regarded as much more attractive than previous experiences, because there is no interference from head office. They have our link man who comes to be educated. They really do have a very free hand. Of course, it is more free while they are being successful than it is if they become less successful. If they are very unsuccessful they may find there is a fairly steely hand inside the glove. However, that has only happened maybe three, four times in thirty years, because people respond to the challenge, to the opportunity.'

Interestingly, Hanson believes that a senior manager does not necessarily need experience in an industry to manage effectively in that industry. According to both Lord Hanson and Derek Bonham, a general manager is a general manager and ought to succeed in producing motor cars or producing coal. He must have a good technical team working with him, but his job, to some extent like their centre, is to co-ordinate the activities of his executives, who are the technicians within whatever the industry is.

Derek Bonham says, 'A good manager is likely to be a reasonable leader as well, but they are not synonymous. If you were to ask James

Hanson what he sees himself as, he would say a manager. That is how we have all developed our thinking and essentially, what we are all doing, either at the centre or in a division, is managing people to the best advantage. Recruiting, appointing, trying to put round pegs in round holes, which is very important and having done that, not necessarily moving them later into what for them is a square hole. The classic mistake is the very good sales director becoming a very poor chief executive. A good salesman who can manage other good salesmen in his organization is not necessarily a rounded general manager suitable for a chief executive officer's position. We always try to be careful with the recruitment selection and appointment of people, to get the right people for the job.'

Derek Rosling was the first person James Hanson ever recruited. He was in professional accountancy practice in Huddersfield, with the Hanson family as clients, and James Hanson and Gordon White asked him to join them in 1964. 'James, and great credit to him, has great ability to select intuitively, to know that a person is right, to put people at their ease. He is a man of great charm, instils confidence and is, I would say, a born leader. Leaders are born. They may not all develop, there may be more leaders born than we see, because they may not have the opportunity. James was born with those qualities and through his family business had the opportunity to develop them, went off and ran a business in Canada, where he had to be on his own with his brother. He is a very dynamic man, with enormously high standards and has led, cajoled, bullied all of us in different circumstances, on different occasions, to share those high standards from appearance and cleanliness of offices to everything else. I had no difficulty in aspiring to those standards. Other people's habits are different and they may have to try harder to fall in line.'

As you might expect, Lord Hanson has his own views on leadership. 'I think the style of management is something that you enforce, or, if you are a leader, your leadership will drift down to everybody. You may make certain rules about style, style of management and ethics and the way of dealing with things. We are very particular, and hard on people who don't operate by our ethical standards, which are very high. They get higher the more you become in the public domain. In a major corporation, you have to think ahead. I am aware of the need to watch the shareholders' interest and that is all that matters when it's a public company. You can't have your own private thoughts on whether it is going to affect your livelihood, or anything like that.'

To maintain, retain and sustain this power-house demands leadership skills. Lord Hanson is the first to admit that any future leadership style for Hanson PLC will continue the authoritarian approach, whilst encouraging the team input of different skills and experience. 'Obviously, skills can be acquired academically or by experience, but the central determination comes from within. We have never gone in for textbook or "mumbo-jumboist" structures - inverted triangles or *kaizen*. We have the right organization in place, I believe, towards 2000 to meet current and future challenges. It certainly won't be rigid and if "matrix responsibility" means being responsible to different people at the same time, we won't have that either. I do know that in order to make our corporate and organizational achievements hold into the next millennium will mean having the right team in place.

'Leadership is something that soon shows. In a company like ours, we can't know the intricacies of every individual business. We have to say, "we must leave it to you." You rely on your smallest common denominator – or you should. I was in the army for seven years and the people on whom you rely are not the generals, brigadiers, colonels or battalion commanders. You rely on the platoon. I suppose it is the same in the police force. The chief of police will count on his men in any particular area. His inspector, with his team of men, must know what style is needed. It's not much fun to get a whole bunch of paper from up above telling you how to live, whether you are in business, the army or anything else. That was the worst thing about the army and I suspect about the police. All those – I think they were called ACIs – Army Council Instructions – found their way rapidly into the bin. Sadly, I didn't have a shredder in those days.'

On its American side of the business Hanson has not put British managers in to run things. Several banks came unstuck because they bought banks in America and then put British bankers in to run them. Hanson's simple view of it is that they just got the management wrong. 'They put Brits in and they were out of their depth. They didn't understand the totally different philosophy of American bankers. Hanson did not do that. We have no Brits running American companies. We have applied for very few green cards. The American businesses are run by Americans and the British businesses by Brits.'

According to Lord Hanson, the worst thing that you can do is to let somebody go from England to America and taint the American system. 'The first thing the British do when they go there is say, well, this is how we do it in England, or Scotland, or wherever you want to pick. They'll nod politely and say, that's very interesting but what do you know about it? When I went to live in Canada I was told, "You've got to listen to them, because the conditions are different." We took British trucks out there because it suited our Board of Trade, as it then was, to get exports. But the trucks were no good. They let in the cold Canadian air, they simply weren't designed for that climate. I have seen the drivers buying their own heaters, taping up the doors – because a little bit of fresh air in England coming through the doors is OK, not so bad, but not in Canada. You must listen to your local people.'

Gordon White, having spent a lot of time in America, believed that the American motorbike dealers wanted a certain type of motorbike. Lord Hanson remembers the head of BSA saying to White, 'We'll give them what we think they should have. We know all about motorcycles. Let them have the little Japanese and Italian ones, that doesn't matter to us. We'll sell the big ones.' 'They never bothered to find out what the market was. That's why the Japanese cars are so successful in America, because they send them out with what the customer wants, not what the dealer or the manufacturer needs. They send the cars out with the telephones built into the steering wheel, so you press a button and you get ten phone calls coming up one after the other, without your having to lift the head set. All sorts of innovations like that.'

So where do we go wrong? Lord Hanson says immediately, 'We are too arrogant, we don't study the market sufficiently well. We don't go charging out there like the Germans or the Americans do and research the market sufficiently well. I do try to pick the best of both. We're not perfect in all respects, but there are a lot of things that we do better, quicker, particularly in the financial side. I think the answer is the UK do better in terms of the direct deals, the way that the Brits do it, very quickly; and I think we could do better in terms of researching the market the way the Americans and the Japanese and others do it.'

As he mentioned earlier, there has always been a strong belief within Hanson PLC in youth. 'Everybody was once young and ambitious,' says Lord Hanson. 'The experience versus youth argument is something to be considered and has always been taken into account by us. There's nothing to beat youth. They don't need to be told.'

Derek Bonham adds, 'We always advertise under our own name for any appointments we are making and we are swamped with high quality applicants. There is no difficulty at all for a successful company to pick and choose from very capable, well-qualified candidates for any appointment they wish to make. We do not have any formal training process. We do not run a residential school. The school that we run is the school of day-to-day practice. Employees join us, or they are there when we acquire a company and over twelve months they come to understand the way that Hanson runs.'

Lord Hanson endorses this 'school of knocks' approach. 'We do not believe in training colleges and inter-company cross-fertilization – and other "fashionable" consumers of people's time. There is an open atmosphere at Hanson and managers learn fast on the job. The best ones are promoted and have to keep learning all the way through. It's fine if you can go in and improve your mind at the age of about thirty and be given the time off to take some further education. But you can do all of that at home, you certainly do not need to do an MBA, not in work time. The worst thing in the world is to take an MBA direct from Harvard or London. Some people think it is very important to have post-graduate education, MBAs and management schools. I think it's helpful to have had it, but you need it when you've got some solid experience under your belt. Otherwise you come to expect too much and you don't want to be the tea-boy or doing whatever else we all had to do when we started.'

As far as Lord Hanson is concerned, business is likely to get more competitive rather than less. 'The key to meeting future challenges will be good people and strong resources. Market share in itself is not everything. It is, for example, possible to increase market share, but at an unacceptable cost. Customers will require better products and service and there is no doubt that our company's greatest asset is our people and its fire-power. Net assets of £4 billion and profits in excess of £1 billion – this combination enables us to throw very considerable resources into meeting challenges in developing our future. The "customers" are the key to our future, as with no customers there is no business. Similarly without shareholders you are nothing.'

Bonham concurs. 'It is more difficult to manage in today's climate because the world is more competitive, more demanding. Customers are more demanding, quite rightly, as to quality, price and service.

That is a trend that will go on increasing. So the basic concept of management has not changed. You just have to be sharper and quicker off the mark, increasingly so and continuously. Increasingly, it is the survival of the fittest, or the fittest two or three. If you're not in that area, you will go to the wall. You can't stand still.'

Hanson still thinks it is not competitive enough. It will probably never feel it is competitive enough. Derek Bonham says this is because 'we set such high standards and have such high ideals we would never say what we were doing was adequate. We don't think that way. We try to encourage everybody in the organization to do better. However good you are, you can still do it better.'

Lord Hanson says that operating a major enterprise into the twenty-first century will require swifter responses, constant research and preparation. 'Sales methods may change, but managing people will follow the same principles. Technology will develop and improvements in availability of information will lead us to significant and helpful changes. Markets and consumer requirements are changing. It is now the time to develop and give responsibility to the "young entry". They will find adjustment to future needs much easier to handle.'

Hanson will continue towards the millennium to develop by acquisition and organic growth both at home and overseas. Lord Hanson says, 'The primary countries for further development are the UK and USA and those in the Pacific Basin, which has excellent prospects, rather than Europe – a tidying-up operation for years.' China is gaining in importance too. Lord Hanson believes it is 'too early to gauge the significance of Eastern Europe and Africa in 2000 plus'.

In 1995 Hanson cleared the way for a multi-billion pound takeover by demerging thirty-four of its non-core American businesses in a move which it describes as giving it more financial muscle to acquire major new businesses. The classic deal which followed was the agreed £2.5 billion bid for Eastern Group, the regional electricity company. Perhaps Hanson PLC sees its move into this sector as a useful development towards a global energy business.

Europe concerns both Derek Bonham and Lord Hanson personally. 'Corporately, we are cautious of Europe,' says Derek Bonham. 'Historically, we have not expanded there. We have looked at any number of opportunities over the last twenty years, but always found something at least as good, if not better, either in the UK, like

169

Eastern Electric, or in the US. Again, we are very conscious of factors like language and culture; there are greater differences between the UK and Italy or Spain, or Greece or anywhere else in Europe, than between the UK and the US. It's for those simple reasons, if for no other, we tend to concentrate in the UK and the US. We already have an office in Hong Kong and towards 2000 China could be an important area for the future. We are aggressively looking at the Pacific Rim now, with a manager out there who is actively looking to see if there could be a major expansion for us in that area. But we are not green field venture people. We would rather buy existing businesses, with an existing market share and a proven record, with the management in place, than starting something, because that's where you lose your shirt if you're not careful.'

One thing Hanson PLC does is change people round frequently. Lord Hanson says they do it just for the sake of change and before they're ready. 'They will say to me, "I thought I was going to be in this job for five years, you're moving me." I say, "That's right. But we need you somewhere else." And of course, that's all you have to say! We move people all the time and it's important to do that. Reinvigoration.'

What disappointments does he have? 'I'm always very disappointed with the academic world – and I don't mind being quoted on that. One of the advantages of the MBAs is they are all absolutely aimed at providing young talent for business. However, it's a little disappointing that so often they go into the companies that provide management advice as consultants. If they then go and work as a manager in business, that's good. While it's lovely to have the beautiful minds coming at you from the universities and a wonderful experience to talk to people like them, there are very few who have applied anything practically.'

The group's experience is that the bureaucracy of Brussels which epitomizes Europe is increasing. 'We do not need another layer of government,' says Lord Hanson. 'We've got enough government in this country, without having another superpower of government in Brussels, or anywhere else, for that matter. In the area in which we operate, the area of takeovers and so on, there have been all kinds of edicts from Brussels. Brussels has increasingly been putting its finger into the areas in which we like to have the maximum freedom to operate, all within the law, but let it be UK law rather than something influenced by practice and law of Italy, Greece or Turkey or somewhere else. I both personally and on behalf of the company, fear the federalism, which I think is the right word. It works in the States because they all started together. It won't work here in Europe, because we all have one or two thousand years of history, all different. European government has increased its influence materially in recent years. This appears set to continue, but there is a backlash in this country developing against excessive EC federalism.'

Hanson PLC has concerns about a single currency. Derek Bonham says, 'It doesn't really interfere with trade, to have multi-currencies and if it is a step towards federalism, then that alone is enough to kill it. Changing foreign currency into sterling isn't really a problem. There is an awful lot of paperwork to be got rid of before it is necessary to have a single currency, in order to have efficient international trade.

'I don't want to lose any aspect of our nationalism. I am proud of being British and I don't want to become European. I don't think, in my lifetime – I don't know about my kids' lifetime – it is necessary. By all means let's have a trading relationship. The EC is fine and let's do away with lots of restrictions, taxes and cross-border tariffs and have a free trade area. We have to do everything we can to encourage growth of the industrial sector and the actual wealth it produces. So many people are not actually producing wealth. They are living off the wealth that other people produce and it's important to encourage and give the maximum freedom to the actual workers – the guys who are making the widgets in Widnes. We do not need to become a federal Europe to achieve that. I cannot understand the politicians; if there were a referendum it would be thrown out.'

Lord Hanson was keen to mention non-executive directors. 'There is so much garbage spoken about non-executive directors. I think it's very difficult to get the right ones. I don't have any non-executive directorships at all. I have only had one, to speak of, and that was Lloyds Bank, and I had possibly another in the form of Trident Television, but then I was a big investor in Yorkshire Television to start with, so it just naturally happened. I didn't go on the board for a long time. If you can get non-executives interested enough they're so helpful. If they make an effort to see the business, the people will be glad to see them and they have a great deal to offer. But don't load them up with too much paperwork. We do a summary for our non-executive directors. Any additional information is available if they want it. We appoint a different full-time executive director as a link to each non-executive. So at any time you can call that link and say, "What the hell does this mean?" or "I saw something in the paper. Tell me about it." And you'll get an explanation.

'We only meet once a quarter, but we are in close and constant touch with them on certain points that we deal with. They are very, very helpful indeed, but they should be there to help, not because they're watching the others and checking on them. I don't believe, for example, in having a separate report from the non-executive directors in the annual report. I don't think that's right. It is very helpful if you can get non-executive directors to join and I think they should be well paid. They should be able to travel as they wish, to see any part of the business, but I don't believe they should report separately. The chairman is paid by the shareholders to be responsible for their interests and as such he asks the auditors, he asks this committee or that, he asks others, but in the end he takes the responsibility. He's the man you have to shoot at. You can't have two sets of people running the business. This is all a very personal opinion, but it has worked for us.'

For both Lord Hanson and Derek Bonham, flexibility has always been important and speed of decision making. 'Speed of implementing those decisions. These have all been things that we are known and respected for. It is not unconnected with what I said about the structure. We get on with the job, three or four of us and then someone sees where there might be an opportunity – we're opportunists. When there is an opportunity we are ready tomorrow to take it, tonight perhaps. Even if something cropped up now, we could make a bid tonight at five o'clock. We could put the finance in place and get on with it. We wouldn't wait – unless it involves more than £100 million, in which case we would convene a board meeting. Or we would have a telephone board meeting at three o'clock this afternoon, if it had to be done by five o'clock tonight. The attitude of mind is what I want to get over to you. "Let's do it," and not say, "Oh, we can't do it, because we don't have a board meeting till next week."'

What about succession planning for Lord Hanson? He says 'You have to think in terms of saying, "Do you want the job?" That's the first thing. Do you want to become finance director, do you want to become CEO of Hanson Industries? If you want it, we'll give you the opportunity. But I think you have to bring people into it gradually. What you mustn't do is change them. Everybody will do it differently. Some people will have a huge personality like Lord King and others will have the calm, quiet personality of Sir Colin Marshall of British Airways. They are different, but they bring to the job that essential part of business success which is change, change of people, change of ideas. It's wrong to say you fill somebody's shoes. You should never do that. You bring your own shoes along and make them march around the job in the way that they should do.'

Hanson PLC's employment strategy now and for the future, according to Lord Hanson, 'is to look after our people well and create a climate which allows them to deliver their best. We will always meet the highest level of social responsibility requirements of the day – it's good business practice. One thing I insist on is to have some form of central incentive plan, so that if the company is doing well then the people can benefit. You have to pay the right money for the job, otherwise you get the monkeys and peanuts syndrome. But also there's nothing better than knowing my secretary and everybody else this year got a 28 per cent bonus because the company went 28 per cent over its profit forecast. It's terrific, that's more than a quarter of your salary. Next year, it may be nothing. We don't take it away, they just don't get a bonus if they don't reach the forecast. But if they exceed it, I'll pay for that every time. Then, of course, individually in the companies, they are all on their own particular schemes, the salesmen and others. Keep offering them that carrot! We give them enough stick as it is!'

If Lord Hanson could have one millennium wish for his company, what would it be? 'A continuation of future opportunities for Hanson to grab. Certainly not all my ambitions have been realized. I want Hanson to continue to go from strength to strength – and for my successors to keep up the good work. One thing that makes me tick is an openness to new ideas and ways of doing things, coupled with a desire to do things better every day; a refusal to accept anything other than the highest possible standards from oneself and others. I would like to be remembered as someone who played his part in building up a large and enduring company!'

Before I leave Lord Hanson's office I ask him: 'What would you like on your headstone?' and the answer is simply: 'Businessman and horseman.'

HILTON INTERNATIONAL

Turnover (1994)	£1.7 billion
Operating profit	£126.8 million
Property and leases asset value	£1.6 billion

Over 160 hotels in almost 50 countries
- 56 owned or partly owned
- 19 leased
- 87 operated under management contract or other profit-sharing arrangements
- 30 projects in development

Over 53,000 bedrooms
Over 57,000 employees

International hotel brand, universally recognized for the quality of its service, locations, and facilities.

John Wilson – Executive Vice-President and Chief Operating Officer

Having joined the Ladbroke Group in 1972, John Wilson was appointed an executive vice-president of Hilton International in 1990 and chief operating officer in 1991. His responsibility covers Hilton International's operations worldwide.

He is also vice-president of London Welsh Rugby Football Club.

The Company

Hilton International is 100 per cent owned by Ladbroke Group PLC, one of the UK's top 100 companies. In addition to Hilton International, which is its largest division, Ladbroke Group operates betting and gaming businesses internationally.

Hilton International's strategy for global growth is to continue its expansion into prime city centre and resort locations and develop clusters of hotel properties serving individual countries or regions. This strategy is being achieved principally through securing management contracts to operate existing or new hotels and the establishment of joint ventures of partnerships with regional hotel-owning companies.

Hilton International Group
John Wilson
Executive Vice-President and
Chief Operating Officer

Hilton International (HI) operates over 160 hotels in forty-eight countries, with more than 53,000 bedrooms worldwide. It was acquired by the Ladbroke Group PLC, in 1987. There are two Hiltons – Hilton Hotels Corporation is the USA operation. From the UK, HI have the right to the name Hilton anywhere in the world outside mainland USA. Hilton National is a part of HI, and is a cluster of twenty-five hotels all based in the UK.

Hilton is possibly the best recognized brand name in hospitality, and its reputation for excellence in hotel management was confirmed when it received seven major industry awards in 1994, including 'Best Worldwide Hotel Group'.

It has clearly identified its position in the marketplace – not in the luxury hotel category, but primarily as First Class hotels, with the majority of its customer base in the corporate area. This enables HI to focus clearly on the type of product and facility it wishes to deliver within its 160 properties worldwide. There are in addition a small number of resort properties, many of them in the Caribbean. Even these have a good corporate customer base, because they are ideal destinations for incentives and large meetings.

The group's positioning *vis-à-vis* the competition varies, depending upon the geographic location in which HI operates. For example, in the Far East, HI competes against local companies such as Shangrila and Marriotts, as well as the internationally known hotel companies such as Hyatt. In the UK, Forte is a major competitor, along with Holiday Inn.

One important point is that none of its operations is franchised. It either owns, partially owns, leases, or directly manages on behalf of other owners, all the named properties, and this makes it directly accountable for the levels of quality and service within those operations. In other words, says the chief operating officer worldwide, John Wilson, 'We are masters of our own destiny. Where we would say we are different, would be in the clearly demonstrable operational skills we have within HI. Of the major international hotel companies, we are the oldest. We started in 1946 in Puerto Rico. Because of this longevity, we have built a tremendous skill base within the organization. We were able, before others, to offer aspiring young people international careers within our industry, and we deliberately encourage global careers. We are great believers in exposing our management to all manner of different cultural and economic challenges.'

John Wilson says staffing the management of their hotels worldwide with Europeans will not continue for ever. 'I and my colleagues firmly believe we have a responsibility within those parts of the world in which we are operating, to put back into the community. Because of that, we are deliberately encouraging a policy towards 2000 of developing nationals within those countries in which we operate. In Egypt for instance we have a number of Egyptian managers and the senior vice-president for that part of the world is an Egyptian. In Malaysia we have appointed the first Malaysian general manager of our Hilton, we have a Chinese general manager of the Taipei Hilton and Turkish nationals managing in Turkey. It is absolutely right we do this and more and more.'

HI operates in a highly competitive environment. In certain parts of the world the economies and the market size are growing at a faster pace than in others, but everywhere it is up against some serious players in the industry, and has to concentrate on its marketing and sales activities. 'I don't think it has changed fundamentally, but it has become much more focused,' says John Wilson. 'Let's look no farther than the UK. One of the fastest growing segments of our business is unquestionably the small meetings market: meetings of around thirty people requiring a major meeting room plus break-out rooms. We invented, after consultation with our customers – I am very loath to embark upon anything unless I have talked to my customers – a product called Meeting 2000. This is a facility which caters directly to the conference requirement of the conference organizer. We have "8-hour" chairs, which means you can sit in them comfortably without feeling as though you want to go to sleep, and remain alert enough to focus on what is happening. We have all the latest audio-visual technology. There is a trained engineer on hand. The facility is manned with an adjacent business centre, so all the modern-day requirements of meetings are catered for. You have the normal fax and telecoms systems built into this one centre, and these rooms are never used for banqueting. This is a pure meeting facility dedicated to that market. That's an example of our new focusing.'

Consulting with customers is part of HI strategy. They are the key element in the basic components HI have to satisfy in business: share-holders, employees and customers. 'Increasingly we keep in contact on a regular basis. Through our senior vice-president of human resources we are currently undertaking a complete review of internal communications. Since we operate in forty-eight countries, clarity of message and purpose is not as easy in our industry as in some. We are looking at how best to communicate using video technology and the printed word. That is a major exercise.'

To maintain the Hilton style around the world, HI has to evolve a *consistency* of style, the Hilton way of doing things. This is done by numbers, explains John Wilson. 'First, I organize the world into five distinct regions. Each region is headed by a senior operator and we meet five or six times a year to review the business, look at the pri-orities, decide what short-term actions we are going to take. They are involved also in the formulation of the longer-term strategy for the company because they have years of experience and are where it is happening every day. My own philosophy is: whatever we decide, or plan or attempt to execute from a corporate office, the place where it is happening is in the hotel, and everything we do has to add value to the hotel. The regional heads work closely in a team, and I am a great believer in team concepts.'

Underpinning this is the approach and philosophy towards staff education. Hilton has been acknowledged throughout the industry as a foremost player in the training and development of its people. It runs a training institution known as the Career Development Institute [CDI]. All heads of department and junior management attend programmes through that facility. 'We are now re-instituting that regional organization in a slightly more sophisticated way, on a regional basis, where our young people will be able to focus on issues such as the commercial side of management, as well as the technical aspects of food and beverage, future concepts, etc. This works won-ders for creating the Hilton benchmark. It is excellent in bringing our teams of people together with a sense of belonging, so they feel and touch what it is the company is trying to achieve.'

Towards 2000 HI is expanding its CDI and developing regional training centres. For example, there will be a European training centre, an Asian and a North American one for certain levels of employee. Says John Wilson, 'We have been to them ourselves as guinea pigs to test the programme and to give our input and evaluation, and they will be focusing on shaping the business for tomorrow. One of the key areas is how people actually work together. I am not suggesting that our industry is more or less difficult than others, but we have a wide variety of cultures, and it is creating a common understanding and appreciation of those various cultures – how we mould and weld teams together from varying backgrounds – which is a great challenge to us.'

The key individual in any hotel is the general manager, says John Wilson. 'The GM not only communicates with his heads of department on a daily team basis, he also takes time to put a newsletter together which goes to all the employees in the hotel, so they are all fully aware and understand what is going on. That is one way of doing it. But each of our major properties, and that means at least two thirds of the group, will have its own personnel manager with individual training and development programmes for all the staff. One of the main planks of our strategy is unquestionably the implementation of an excellence in the area of customer service. We put together a small group of people who focus on the quality programme for HI. This is being headed by a senior operator, and the exercise we are currently undertaking is the measurement of quality. We do not see any point in doing this kind of thing just because it's a current whim or a fancy. We have to be able to measure, from a customer point of view, what it is we are doing. If we can exceed a customer's expectations, I am a very happy man.'

HI also manages properties. 'Whilst I am not saying the quality of the fixtures, furnishings, fittings and ambience is the be all and end all – it is not, because you still have to rely upon the employee to deliver the quality of service – it helps, because it creates the atmosphere and is highly motivational for people to be working in a quality environment. Singapore is a good example: an investment of US$20 million has transformed the property, and it's investments like this which we have to be very concerned about because we are talking vast sums of money worldwide – excluding new builds, for example, it is not unusual to be spending over US$100 million a year on the properties.'

Keeping these HI properties up to a certain standard is very demanding. 'We are fortunate,' says John Wilson. 'We employ a team of excellent property and technical experts within the company, our own architects, designers, project leaders and managers. They have a vital contribution to make to the business. Every property will have an ongoing three-year rolling practical improvement programme, so we can take a snapshot today, and know what our commitments are likely to be towards year 2000, in terms of keeping the properties up to shape.'

Most of the legislation within the hotel industry is enlightened. Certainly in terms of kitchen hygiene or health and safety, for example, you will never find any argument with John Wilson. 'I suppose we are fortunate we have not as yet been affected by what I call the petty bureaucracies of law makers. Most of what has been attempted has been to the benefit of the customer *and* the employee and from that perspective I am very happy. Our view is we should always be a step ahead of any impending legislation. In Third World countries – I do not like using the phrase but it is in common vogue – we provide our own health and medical facilities for our employees, and in certain parts of the world we even go so far as to employ full-time nutritionists who are providing balanced diets for a thousand employees. That exhibits a caring attitude which is not patronizing, but it is something which we believe is for the well-being of not just the employees but the business as a whole, because it is keeping people in a family orientation.'

About five years ago HI realized the importance of the impending Japanese travelling market. 'The Japanese now equal the Americans in terms of our customer base by volume. We are the biggest "foreign" hotel operator in Japan, with four properties – Tokyo, Tokyo Bay which is at the Disney resort, Osaka and Nagoya.

'If you look at our old food and beverage concepts (note I say "old") – basically in every Hilton there would be a Grill Room, because that was what the travelling American expected to find, and we were happy to deliver it. Now times have changed. We decided the Japanese required not exactly special treatment but had to be considered differently in terms of service. We talked to over a hundred major Japanese corporations and carried out some 1,000 face-to-face interviews with customers and booking agents. What does the travelling Japanese executive or businessman want when he is away from home – apart from green tea, which is very important?

179

First, they wanted to be able to communicate with Japanese-speaking staff, even when not in Japan. Second, they wanted particular aspects of Japanese lifestyle: in a bathroom, they wanted a hand shower and a Japanese dressing-gown. They wanted Japanese newspapers. In fact, not unlike the Americans and other international travellers, they wanted to feel, at least partially, at home when away from home. This was the basis for putting together a focused programme for the Japanese market, which we know as *Wa No Kutsurogi* – comfort and service the Japanese way. Essentially, where over 3 per cent of our customers were Japanese, we introduced this programme and we provided the facilities and amenities the Japanese were looking for.'

Wherever HI introduced the programme, the local Japanese companies were asked to validate the programme and give it the seal of Japanese excellence. 'This was recognition by the local Japanese community that our company was trying to deliver the service the Japanese expect. One result is that our Japanese business now equals our American market. There is another benefit. Because the Japanese-speaking employees are usually Japanese, they are being brought over from Japan, placed in hotels around the world for a period of time, and learn the experiences of the "western world". Then they return. It's become part of our global training curriculum.'

HI has around thirty hotels in the pipeline, either under construction or where agreement has been assigned to construct. 'We are focused on the Pacific rim,' says John Wilson. 'The Far East is still an emerging market. We are very strong in Indonesia and have a joint venture agreement with a local Indonesian company. We currently manage properties which they own, and have come closer together through this to acquire more properties in Indonesia, which the joint venture company will manage. For example, in Indonesia we currently manage three properties, and the joint venture company will then develop three more, looking at resort islands and provincial cities.'

He has an agreement to manage the Atrium Hotel in Prague, with 800 bedrooms, and is opening in Bucharest and Sofia. Would John Wilson develop in the former Soviet Union? 'Like a shot, under the right terms and conditions. We have been discussing opportunities in Moscow and St Petersburg with a number of interested parties, but it is terribly slow. Its bureaucracy is appalling. We'll get there, not too sure if by the millennium! You have to be patient in this business. It would be extremely foolish of me, or anyone else, to close their eyes to the Soviet Union, but let me say I am cautious.'

The biggest influence on the financial performance of the hotel industry is the local economy in which it is operating. When there is a downturn in the economy, HI experiences a corresponding downturn in the level of its business. 'What's different in the past few years is there has been an almost complete international downturn, aggravated by situations such as the Gulf War. As the economies improve and come out of recession, our business follows. I'm a great believer in cyclicality.'

When you are in recession with the market actually shrinking, rate cutting is an obvious temptation. John Wilson agrees. 'On the other hand, it may be described as "responding to market influences", because corporations – and we are not alone in this, when in such a period – will look at the level of expense being generated through their business. Clearly, travel and hotel costs are a significant expenditure for major corporations who are our customers and they come to the table and ask for better deals. My experience is that as we pull out of recession, I'm not saying that companies take their eye off that ball, but the pressure is less. Hoteliers have to temper their pricing strategy relative to the marketplace. The heady days of charging whatever we felt like are long gone. Not that we ever did! All of which puts increasing pressure on ability to operate with tighter margins, and that is what good operations are all about, the ability to control your margin. I am quite prepared to examine any possible area of saving, but there are more positive ways of doing it. We have a huge purchasing facility within this organization. We can be much better at the way we negotiate with our suppliers, just as our customers are better at negotiating with us. Equally, whatever we do in terms of maintaining good ratios, I cannot afford to allow the level of service quality the customer experiences to be reduced as a consequence of cost cutting, because that would be cutting my own throat.'

So there is a limit. There are economies HI can take in terms of utilities management, services management, there are more sophisticated ways of food preparation, and so on. HI, a while ago, took its eye off this but re-examination has been forced upon it. 'We have always paid a great deal of concern to the level of expense which has gone through our business. One of the ratios all of my people look at it is what we call the gross operating profit ratio. That is the key measurement as far as our operators are concerned. One of the biggest challenges that I, and all of our people face, is delivering a good quality of service at an affordable expense – getting the balance right all the way down the line.'

HI has various segments of customers, who demand more and more value for less and less outlay. Says John Wilson, 'It does not matter whether one segment is paying £50 and another £150, it does not enter my thinking that the £50 customer should receive a lower quality of service. If we start down that route, we will be running hotels within hotels and we will alienate all groups. We have to deliver a consistent level of service, irrespective of who the customer is. For example, airlines are very important to us in terms of airline contract business and crew. They account for a substantial part of our business worldwide. We took the time and the trouble to develop what we call our "Touchdown" product, which is specifically geared to airline crew. They receive rapid check-in and their rooms are ready. We give them a special facility in many of our hotels: for example, in Brazil, they have their own club room where they can meet; we provide them with free soft drinks, and they can always get a snack at any time, day or night. This is exactly what that group wants. They are not a high income group on a *per capita* basis, but they are still important customers to me.'

As the year 2000 approaches, HI is facing the challenge of how sophisticated information technology (IT) can be used to help the hotel industry, which is still in the infancy of technological development. 'The airlines have left us behind, but we are catching up with our reservations systems, our global distribution systems and the ability to acquire, on an easily accessible database, information about what customers like and don't like, where they were last, where they are going next, which room they prefer, and more. The use of IT will enable us to interface directly with customers. The human element is so critical here.

'Just think of the experiences you have in a hotel. Your first experience is when you go to the check-in desk. That is make or break. How much better for the receptionist to know who you are, how many times you have stayed with us before, whether it is your first time, what newspaper you prefer or whatever. This is fundamental customer recognition. We all love to be called by our names. These are basic things, simple things, but we have to have the technical support to be able to deliver it. We are investing right across the company in a new sophisticated front office system and also in research into reservation systems. We are quite prepared to take this problem by the scruff of the neck and recognize the key importance it has to play, not just in the way we run our business but, most importantly, in the way we communicate with our customers, what we know about them and how we can talk to them.

'The service relationships within a hotel are interdependent. When you're checking in, you would love to be greeted, "Hello Miss King Taylor, nice to have you back again. Are you still reading the *Independent, Scotsman, Herald Tribune* . . .?" We must also give exactly the same level of recognition in the restaurant as we do at the hotel reception. We have to get it throughout the whole operation. We need the technological support to enable us to deliver it, not as something in its own right, but as something which is going to enhance the customers' experience when they stay in the hotel. Otherwise don't do it.'

HI's business will grow both by acquisition and through organic growth, because although the latter is still available to it, particularly where both markets and gross national product are growing, the quickest delivery of profits will be through acquisition. Through its corporate development plan HI will be targeting either one-offs or especially clusters of hotels, which HI likes to operate: having more than one hotel in a country provides the benefits of scale. Globally the group is well represented in Australia, but South Africa is an obvious place to be targeted towards 2000, and there is an agreement for a presence in Johannesburg, Durban and Cape Town. A major agreement has also been signed for India. HI is still not to be found in major cities such as Buenos Aires, Santiago or Lima, so South America is an obvious target too.

Is it going to be easier or more difficult for HI to retain market share? 'That's entirely up to us,' says John Wilson. 'Our destiny is in our own hands in that respect, with the provision that we do not endure what the USA experienced in the late eighties – a considerable over-supply of capacity. We have found this has happened in a number of cities: Barcelona is an excellent example, where with the advent of the Olympics, a major building boom took place, and there are now far more hotels than the city needs. The same thing happened in Sydney.'

A style of leadership for the new century? 'I think you have an instinct towards leadership which can be cultivated in a positive way. There are various styles of leadership, as we know. Some of the most effective leaders are some of our quietest, in that they command a great deal of respect and loyalty through the teams in which they are working. Ours, however, is an up-front business, a highly person-to-person business, we're visible to the customer twenty-four hours a day, and quite frankly, leadership, in whatever sense you define it, is king.

'Practical skills can be taught. When I started out, my financial skills required a great deal of development. Now I'm pretty comfortable with any set of numbers! But the intuitive skills, the interpersonal skills, you have to keep working on that. In the people business in which we operate it is so important to get the best out of each other. We have a combination of great assets. First of all, we have the human asset. Our management is top quality. The most important resource is certainly the people in its broadest sense, and by that I mean the fact we have 57,000 employees worldwide, to all of whom we have a responsibility. Our business, in a nutshell, is channelling our responsibility with their efforts to meet the customers' expectations.'

The HI organizational model is the matrix, which, says John Wilson, 'is an excellent expression of team work. The inverted triangle means a real focus on the delivery of service to the customers. Autocracy, no. This industry has a legacy of pecking order, the king in his fiefdom. Fortunately, that is changing and must do. Open leadership style is essential. With 57,000 employees it is the only way, on a team-based concept. I applaud consultation, I am less than happy with consensus. One of the requirements of leadership is to persuade, and then to implement in a positive fashion. Consensus strikes me as almost all things to all men.'

Will the customer be a stakeholder? 'Very much so. What are we in business for, in a local sense, if not to satisfy the requirements of existing customers and broaden the customer base? As well as the customer being an influence in our business, so too is the local community. Very often, in parts of the world where we operate, we are highly visible. Can you imagine the influence of the Hilton International Hotel in Khartoum, in Addis Ababa? We are the focus of the community. We have to build up very strong, powerful relationships with the local community and provide a sense of community well-being to ensure we are not an isolated edifice.'

184

Towards 2000 John Wilson would like HI to be recognized as the largest, most respected hotel company in the whole world. 'My ambition is: "know no bounds". Time is my biggest enemy, there is no doubt about that. I just don't have enough of it. I would like to spend even more time than I do now out with my people in the hotels worldwide. I do love that part of my job. I enjoy being out there, influencing what is happening locally, and I like face-to-face communication. I find it a lot easier to listen to somebody than to read what they have to say. I travel almost half a million miles a year. I certainly get round 30 per cent of our hotels in any one year. Whenever I visit a hotel, as a matter of course, I bring all the heads of department, and assistant heads of department together. We will have a cocktail. I will bring them up to date on what is going on in the company and explain things as I see them from my perspective. I will listen to what they have to say about their own property and their own environment. I think that we are pretty good at that. My only regret is that I cannot do it more often.'

John Wilson knows from his consumer research, that when people say, 'Take me to . . .' and are asked to add the name of a hotel, 86 per cent say 'The Hilton'. 'That is something built over time, and needs to be reinforced in the quality process. Because the key of a Hilton is to ensure that a continuous circle of improvement is maintained from the customer to the level of service, to the employees and back to the customers. We have to find methodology and techniques to recognize individuals, to improve the service to that individual. If it is done for a different reason, I call it bribing. I understand we all need to have additional benefits beyond the one we pay for. The tendency of the consumer to look for more has been developed over thirty years or so with trading stamps, for example, so they expect something else, which is nothing to do with what they are buying: Air Miles to fly on aeroplanes perhaps. It's nothing to do with the product they are buying. I think the future is going to be for us to build on the strength of the brand and the product that we provide, rather than giving the customer a £5 tape recorder when he spends £30 with us. We have to find a lot of added value closer to the specific products and service that we provide rather than far away from it.'

Towards 2000, John Wilson's hope is that Hilton will be the largest, most respected and most customer-sensitive hotel company in the world. 'Everyone in the hotels feels they run a house for guests.

No matter where you are, they all feel it and there is a tradition, I think, that is part of the successful hotel operation. A light bulb can go out. When the engineer knows that, he has to react *quickly* to replace the bulb. The question is not the event, the question is the reaction to the event. It's as simple as that.'

A final millennium wish? Says John Wilson, 'All kinds of things, come to mind, but I suppose I would say, "Please enjoy yourselves."'

JOHN LAING PLC

Turnover (1994)	£1,171.7 million
Operating profit	£12.2 million
Profit before tax	£23.8 million
Total fixed assets (inc. investments)	£96.9 million
Employees	8,475
Staff	4,000
Operatives	4,475

One of the UK's leading construction, mechanical and civil engineering groups, with operations in a growing number of overseas markets and an increasing involvement in investment-led projects.

Martin Laing CBE – Chairman

Appointed deputy chairman 1984, chairman 1985.

Other appointments:
Chairman of the CBI Overseas Committee and member of CBI President's Committee. Board member of Business in the Community. Chairman of Construction Industry Employers Council. Chairman of World Wide Fund for Nature – UK. Member of the World Business Council for Sustainable Development.

The business is in the following divisions:

John Laing Construction Ltd	Traditional building business throughout the UK.
Laing Civil Engineering	Responsible for bridges, roads and rail schemes.
John Laing International	Overseas division working in the Far East, the Middle East and Europe.
Laing Management Ltd	Management contracting offering a preferred form of procurement for many large clients.
Laing Homes Ltd	Home building in the UK and USA.
Laing Technology Group	Includes computers, high-tech designs etc.
Laing Engineering	Off-shore work and other areas such as cable TV.

Major projects include the Second Severn Crossing; Sizewell B Nuclear Power Station; Ashford International Passenger Station, Kent; Midland Metro Line 1 (joint venture); Glaxo Group Research Campus, Reading (joint venture); the tunnel link between Denmark and Sweden (part of international consortium); Ashgabat Airport (joint venture); 12 hospitals in Malaysia (joint venture).

John Laing PLC
Martin Laing CBE, Chairman

John Laing is one of the UK's leading international construction groups, with firm foundations in long-held traditions of quality and care for employees, the community and the environment. As the UK starts its slow climb out of the recession, John Laing Construction has been involved in some outstanding projects, keeping faith with traditional skill and high standards. These include the refurbishment of the Mansion House in London, the new Severn River Crossing, the Eurohub International Airport in Birmingham, the new British Consulate-General in Hong Kong, the Saigon Centre in Ho-Chi-Minh City and the new Inland Revenue offices at Nottingham. It has firmly established an unparalleled reputation for the successful completion of privately financed major projects as well as the provision of public housing and revitalizing the UK's infrastructure such as the transformation of Manchester. Laing is also this country's top hospital builder, its projects ranging from the £177m Chelsea and Westminster Hospital to twelve nucleus hospitals in Malaysia. Increased concentration on finance-led projects, ventures in social housing, expertise in facility management and expansion into new geographic areas are all keys to this company's success and prosperity.

Martin Laing is the eldest grandson of Sir John Laing, under whose direction the company became a national organization, and has been chairman of the Laing Group since 1985, having joined Laing some twenty years earlier. 'Our core business is construction and house-building and the former is a pretty big map. We are in every part of construction. We do nuclear power stations – such as Sizewell B – shopping centres, office blocks, motorways, recreation facilities, hotels and resort facilities, hospitals and clinics, schools, colleges, libraries, railways, bridges, airports.'

189

One of the major areas Laing is involved with at the current time is the private investment arena where the private sector partners public infrastructure projects. 'Since the construction of this country's first motorway from London to Birmingham in the late 1950s we have been continually involved with the improvement of the UK infrastructure. By the very nature of its content this primarily involves our civil engineering side and this is at the forefront of the private finance initiative being promoted by the government. We've been involved in public–private partnership for around thirty years, first getting involved in Spain with some toll roads. We are shareholders, together with several Spanish banks and Ferrovial, and we have 19.9 per cent of the publicly quoted concessions company, Europistas. This company owns and operates 180 km of a motorway running along the north coast of Spain.'

Having gained that experience, Laing then looked for other areas where it could do this in the UK, and obviously the government were very keen on getting the private sector to participate in construction. The first foray was Birmingham Air Terminal, which is used by British Airways [BA]. Laing is a shareholder in this £41m scheme along with National Carparks, Alpha PLC, BA and the Birmingham Council. The funding was a mix of EIB loans and equity, of which the Laing £5m equity investment was key to the successful implementation of the project. To this day the Eurohub Terminal at Birmingham's airport is one of the few in Europe developed and financed by a public and private joint venture.

One of Laing's other activities is replacing gas pipes and water mains. That has allowed it to get involved with cable television. Says Martin Laing, 'We are a shareholder in a cable company in Leicester and are also at the heart of Manchester's renaissance. There we are masterminding construction of some of the city's most important civic and commercial buildings including the concert hall, which will be a new home for the Hallé orchestra, also the Crown Courts and office developments. We are certainly helping to change that cityscape. Our yellow cranes are presently into the sky but they will be replaced well before the millennium by the buildings of Manchester's future.'

The private finance initiative is developing a new partnership between the public and private sectors for the benefit of both. The British government has put the private financing of infrastructure projects at the top of its agenda, and this is a development which is becoming more common in the international arena towards the millennium. Laing wholeheartedly supports this initiative and enjoys being able to invest in the future. Even before the government gave its unequivocal backing to private financing Laing was putting public-private partnership schemes into action. Laing strategy encompasses investment in a range of projects to give a broad and prestigious portfolio, including the design, construction and operation of important schemes such as motorways, airport terminals, river crossings and hospitals. There is no doubt that Laing has firmly established an unparalleled reputation for the successful completion of privately-financed major projects. Martin Laing says, 'It's our commitment capability and ungeared balance sheet which give funders, sponsors or co-promoters throughout the world the confidence to back Laing schemes. The Laing understanding of the way these projects should be structured, and the willingness to always back our commitment with an equity investment makes us an ideal partner to promote private finance initiatives.'

Laing has an increasing involvement in investment-led projects, and with their successful and flexible blend of services, skills and products they won, together with GTM Entrepose, one of Europe's largest and most exciting engineering projects, the Second Severn Crossing, which employs a complete mix of expertise. Says Martin Laing, 'Severn River Crossing PLC bought the old bridge and, in addition to £500m of cash from the international capital markets, we are using the tolls from the existing bridge in the financing of the second Severn bridge. The Concession Company, Severn River Crossing PLC (SRC), will then basically own the two bridges. SRC is made up of ourselves and a number of other interests, including BZW and Bank of America. The cost of the bridge is around £300m and it will be completed in April 1996. SRC will be responsible for its maintenance and specialist teams will constantly test and repair all the components on the bridge to ensure the long-term integrity of its structure. It's technically very complex. The second bridge has a different design from the original – the new crossing consists of a 1km long cable-stayed bridge and two approach viaducts each in excess of 2km long. It is demanding in management of resources, but exciting and challenging.'

Laing is completing the international railway station on the channel tunnel rail link at Ashford and is also working on the light railway from Birmingham to Wolverhampton. 'Our roads and railways are the arteries of our modern economy along which all commerce flows. Since the earliest days of the motor car we have been a leader in the development of highways. Our civil engineering activity has suffered from a market which is adversely affected by a reduction in public sector spending on infrastructure. However, our strategy towards the millennium is to pursue privately funded infrastructure opportunities. Basically, we have taken our skills as contractors and put them together with the other strong skill we have which is financial. We must have the ability to ensure we are going to get paid for any project, and the easiest way to make sure you are going to get paid is to organize the finance yourself! So financial engineering is a key requirement of ours. That is really exciting, and we have a portfolio of investments in projects across the globe.'

Martin Laing explains what he means by the new skill of financial engineering: 'Basically we are not competing just on a construction price at tender. Nowadays we are seeking to become project developers. We have some financial engineers in house but merchant banks also have a role. We have a core of people within Laing and then top it up outside.'

He gives an example: 'In Turkmenistan we were doing the work of Ashgabat Airport. This project was a marketing bridgehead for the Central Asian Republic, with other phases of construction at Ashgabat and in Kazakhstan with Turkish partners Alarko. There were huge logistical problems of getting goods and materials to the site which in itself was costly. The Russians started this project, but when the Turkmenis got their independence they wanted to finish off the airport but hadn't any money. We had to put together a financial package to raise the money to enable the completion of the airport. That's what you would call financial engineering.

'So if you're working in parts of the world where they don't have a great deal of money, you have to go and bend the ear of your bank or the European Bank for Reconstruction or – it depends where you are – it could be the Asian Development Bank or the Overseas Development Agency or the European Community.'

Incidentally, Laing completed the construction of that airport, 6,000 miles from the UK, in less than two years. It is now the most sophisticated airport in the former Soviet Union. This is tremendous given that three years ago it was a partially complete steel and concrete shell.

The Laing strategy has been to invest in the infrastructure in first of all the UK, and then overseas, and third, in the expansion of its home building operations. Part of the core business of Laing is 'Homes'.

Founded as a house-builder, and today one of the leading residential builders in the UK, Laing has also participated in numerous residential developments around the world. Its expertise covers the full spectrum of development and all aspects of design and realization. Laing Homes specialize in the provision of private and public housing, in particular in Scotland, in the south-east of England, and more recently in the Midlands. Seldom are two residential developments the same. From palaces to private housing, from military complexes to modular buildings, each project has different demands according to particular client details. Laing has expanded into the private housing market but also has a considerable number of contracts for social housing. It has monitored the changing requirements of both the public social housing and private sector of the marketplace. 'For example,' says Martin Laing, 'we have been expanding our role in regenerating London's single largest social housing project – Holly Street Estate in Hackney. This was system-built in the early nineties and achieved national notoriety for its multiple social, economic and environmental problems, but it is being transformed with 1,050 new and refurbished homes. We are also involved in projects such as the £6.8m conversion for the Peabody Trust of Bruce House in Covent Garden in London into a new housing and employment project for homeless people.'

The home building business is at the core of Laing's range of activities. But as everyone knows, there has been a significant downturn in the UK housing market. Laing has no doubt it will continue to nurture its home base; however, it has to focus its attention on areas where economic progress is faster and the profit margins and the risks are higher. 'Eighty per cent of our business is in the UK in the way of sales, turnover, and 20 per cent is overseas,' says Martin Laing. 'The whole purpose of our strategy now towards the year 2000 is to have a major push and increase the 20 per cent closer to 50 per cent because we don't actually see the market in the UK going up. But then, overseas you are getting the competition of every other country in the world. Working overseas has its risks. You've got currency risks as well as increased competition. Obviously one way of limiting all this is our approach to developing our own projects – if a country wants a power station we go out and put together a package for the power station. Without a doubt we have been concentrating on the careful development of our overseas contracting business for some time, but it will take an awful lot of overseas work to replace the amount of work that we have in the UK – that 80 per cent.'

I wondered whether Laing had actually foreseen the recession happening as badly as it did. There is no doubt it had a detrimental effect on its construction and home building activities. Martin Laing replies, 'We saw the recession coming at some point, but we didn't react as quickly as we should have. While we knew the housing boom couldn't go on forever, it was good while it lasted. House prices were rising and everyone was feeling great, and we didn't want to be the first to jump off this particular bandwagon which was producing tremendous profits for us. When the cycle stopped, it was just like a train hitting a buffer. Construction was a bit slower to turn down because there were obviously projects lasting two or three years still to be completed, but enquiries for new projects dropped like a stone. Suddenly we had this recession, a falling overall market for construction. We have had to deploy our skills elsewhere. Our response effectively has been two-fold. One is the overseas expansion that we've been discussing and the other one is the public-private partnerships we have also mentioned.'

The profitability of the UK home building activity, Laing feels, has improved significantly. 'Our experience with new sites has demonstrated there is towards 2000 real potential to achieve good sales rates and enhance value from well-chosen locations selling the right product. The market for social housing has been weaker and as a result total sales have reduced in recent years. We are putting a concentration on the higher volume demand for three- and four-bedroom detached properties – this is for the trade-up market and we hope this will counter an expected reduction in the level of sales to first-time buyers. But I should say, on the whole, despite recent interest-rate increases, the prospects for our UK home building activity towards 2000 are encouraging. We build houses in other parts of the world, in the US for example, and their economy is recording another year of recovery and this has been to the benefit of the housing market. Our strategy in California for example is to focus on growth in the provision of affordable housing which proves very popular with first-time buyers.'

It is vital therefore for Laing towards the millennium to maintain both its UK and overseas markets. After a number of successive years of decline in the total value of new orders awarded to the UK construction industry the nadir was reached in 1993. Martin Laing doubts whether even now the state of the UK construction market will allow a return to a satisfactory level of profit for his company. 'We are continually looking for ways to increase our efficiency and improve the service to our clients, and we are certainly committed to the development of our international construction business and to profitable participation in privately funded infrastructure projects. Our financial strength enables us to invest in privately funded infrastructure projects in the UK. However, one has to add that in meeting the challenges imposed on the overall construction industry these requirements mean that the demands on our staff are changing continually. It has been a very rough time for everybody and of course we have had to let as many as 30 per cent of our people go during the difficult economic times. We are doing much more with fewer people. Some of the things we are doing now require different people from the ones we lost. Even so, the new ones will not make up in number terms for the ones which we have had to make redundant.'

Martin Laing still believes that towards the millennium the company will be doing about 2,000 to 2,500 houses in the UK. 'We will be building more detached houses than we did in the past, as that is the way things are changing. But when people are cautious they don't make major capital commitments, especially if they are not secure in the knowledge they have a job or in the interest rate situation. In both these instances we have to watch we don't get ourselves over-exposed with a lot of housing land we can't develop because we can't sell houses already built. It's easy to build houses but can be difficult to sell them, so you have to try and match the demand from your customers with the supply of houses you are building. The housing business is still going to be an important part of our operation but the mix of the houses will be different. We have been doing a lot of flats before and now I see a move towards the year 2000 for more detached and semi-detached houses.'

In the late 1980s, housing was a high-profit-margin business and little risk. Some of the areas Laing is now entering are obviously high profit but also carry very high risk. Martin Laing agrees: 'Construction is a high risk business anyway. There has to be a limit to the amount you can actually do and get involved in. For example, you are asked to invest £5m in a project. Well, if you do twenty projects you have £100m locked away. So there is a limit in the private-public partnership to the amount you can do unless you can then sell your stake in some of the first projects and re-cycle that money to put into new ones. I would say that is one of the prime requirements for an investment of private finance in our industry – you've got to consider your ability to get out of it again. So one would hope that you put your money in, but you'd get it back out again in about five years time. Then you remove your money and put it into another area.'

In comparison with Hanson Industries, also in this book, the figures being bandied around by Martin Laing are not significant amounts of cash. However, in keeping with any housekeeper, the company has to be able to make judgements on whether any particular project is a good thing to invest in. Says Martin Laing, 'It's like anybody investing in anything, you have to make sure you're going to get the best rate of return for your money in this project compared with something else. So we have to be very careful in the evaluation process, we have to agree carefully the amount of money we have allocated to invest in housing, land or private partnerships or whatever else we might find. In the old days we might have invested in property development I suppose. I think towards the millennium owning a share in a motorway is probably better than owning a share in an office block.'

What about their retail sector – would Laing see that as an investment opportunity for the millennium? 'In retail centres and superstores in a way the investment decisions we have to take tomorrow will be very similar to the decisions we used to take when we were looking at investing in property. I believe it is a far more secure income stream than we had when we were dealing with shops or offices. Modern trends in retailing have resulted in profound changes in the sales process. The move from individual shops to the megastores and shopping plazas has resulted in the development of substantial retail sites, whilst the constant drive to attract the customer requires continual revision of the retailing environment. We work throughout the retailing sector, constructing highly serviced, sophisticated shopping complexes, and individual shop units. One of our growth areas towards 2000 I can see is the provision of distribution centres and outlets for use by the wholesale and retail trades. We did a £25m distribution centre for Safeway which is helping to meet that supermarket's fast-track requirements of their customers and we have built out-of-town supermarkets for others such as Tesco and Sainsbury.'

There is no doubt that Laing is having to live with intense competition, slimmer profit margins and lower operating profits than previous years. There is still a high level of surplus capacity in the UK and the volume of new orders across many of the group's sectors has been declining. Therefore, the improving profitability of its overseas business is important to Laing as the continuing low level of profitability in UK construction will not be resolved with any 'quick fix', and strategic moves always take time. 'We shall improve the quality of Laing's earnings by expansion in the Asia Pacific region, and certainly we're placing focus on transportation, power, water and sewage in countries such as Thailand, Vietnam, the Philippines, Indonesia, Myanmar, India and China.'

Martin Laing does see some of the ingredients for a strong housing recovery being evident – low nominal interest rates and a reduced level of unemployment. As a result, he believes, the home building markets in both the UK and the USA are recovering, albeit only very slowly. 'The issue of real interest rates is crucial, and many prospective home buyers delay their decision because of their lack of confidence.' Would all of Laing's situation in the UK improve if there was a change of government? 'Looking at history, the construction industry has always done very well from Labour governments which tend to pour money into the economy. This time, towards 2000, it might be different. I don't know, but we have to put into our scenario planning for any change of government, and I have to take on board other considerations as well. There's the whole area of the environment which is going to have a continuing impact on our business and we have to be in a position to respond to this because our industry is often perceived to be not too environment-friendly. I must also take account of all the political problems of each individual country we operate within. All of this is a challenge, and in a way it is very satisfying to try and look forward and see what the future holds.'

Martin Laing believes that Europe is becoming more and more a factor in his industry. 'Europe has a very well-developed construction industry, so it doesn't actually provide us with a great deal of growth opportunity. For us there is a tendency not to look for opportunities within the EU, rather to consider Eastern Europe and Turkey. However, the influence of Brussels is becoming very significant – health and safety, the social contract, maternity leave, and other legislation. All of these issues are going to affect our business into the year 2000 and beyond, and I think they are in danger of adding to the costs of business rather than making us more competitive as a European Union. With regard to single currency, if it happens it will be OK, but there is no point in it happening until everybody is ready for it. That's not just ready for it emotionally – they've got to be ready for it economically. At the moment it's too soon. Some people have the vision, but I do not think it will be achieved before, say, 2003. It is certainly not something that's going to keep me awake at night!'

And what about Laing and the future of Britain in the year 2000? 'We've got an awful lot going for us. We've obviously got our English language, we have our heritage, we have the amount of money that this country has invested overseas, foreign investment income, we've got our natural inventiveness, our basic skills are pretty good. There are areas where we must be much better, management training, we have to raise the quality of education, we still have to see what we can do to improve the infrastructure of this country. Remember we are competing with countries who are putting in their infrastructure for the first time. We've had an infrastructure for 200, 300, 400 years, and obviously a telephone or electricity distribution or sewage system put in 100 years ago – at least – will be less effective than that of a country which is putting it in in the year 2000. Look at some of the overseas countries and the money they are investing in their educational systems. I mean, it's so tremendous. And their population is very keen and hungry to get down and learn. I don't think we've got that same competitive spirit that we used to have. That must be re-engendered. Overall, I'm optimistic, but it's not going to be an easy row to hoe.'

Why does Martin Laing believe we have lost that competitive spirit – has it vanished entirely or is it just reduced? His response is immediate: 'The welfare state. We went through a period of time when, if anybody had a problem, they had a handout, they didn't actually have to do anything for themselves at all. Perhaps people need to be reminded they have a brain, arms and legs and should be willing and able to use them. I think we should be more concerned about people who haven't got arms and legs, people who are mentally retarded, the elderly, not these young people who just opt out. This regeneration has to come from all quarters. We have to reengender pride in the country, make people proud they're British. Then people have to be reminded that the system does not owe them a living. They have to go out and earn for themselves.'

Having said that, Martin Laing agrees that people have to feel there are opportunities for them. 'There's no shortage of places in this country for people to go and learn. They can learn any raft of skills that can make them highly employable – not just to get a job here but to get a job anywhere. They mustn't limit their working career just to the UK. It's a *laissez-faire* attitude that "well, we can't get a job in Europe because we don't speak French, German or Italian." Theoretically anybody can learn French, German or Italian and go and get a job. We must ask the question why they won't do it.'

Martin Laing is not a moaner. He and his company actually do something about the problems he's raised. 'People are crucial to our business and we have to invest in them. Our programmes of training and development are highly regarded in the industry – school leavers and graduates want to join us because of our training and development standards. They are designed to support both the longer–term business strategy of the company and our more immediate operational needs. This has resulted in a stronger focus on client-related courses in regard to sales and marketing, work-winning presentation skills as well as team building exercises in collaboration with clients and consultants. This is in addition to training for construction staff, focusing on site safety and site management. We continue to support the professional training and development of younger staff, whether through day-release or our close collaboration with a number of universities. We scored a notable "first" when we achieved "Investor in People" status. Our industrial engineering and construction will be the first of our businesses to receive this award, which the Department of Employment makes to companies who support that training and development, and it recognizes the contribution people can make to overall business success. We have a reputation for the training we provide. Then people tend to stay with us longer than many of the other companies, so when we have an AGM we are always presenting people with long-service awards – long service for us is 25 years – just this year 100 people have completed that length of time with this company. That is one of the benefits of being a family business.'

Laing indeed has a strong family involvement. As Martin Laing says, 'We try to ensure that our people are treated properly. It's not just that they are crucial to our business, but John Laing PLC is known to have continuing caring concern for the community, the environment and our own employees and pensioners – Laing has some 4,000 pensioners.'

In faithfulness to its family traditions Laing has a community investment programme which continues to support areas of activity which are both good for the business and beneficial to the community. It has wide-ranging initiatives to help single, homeless people, in fact that has been a key part of its programme. Its charitable trust has supported many activities in the UK, where every effort has been made to link training and employment with accommodation needs. 'We are especially interested in working alongside local community organizations in the inner cities where Laing supports projects aimed at creating a better living and working environment. A lot of these projects are related to young people who are most at risk in today's society and who need help – particularly in the area of training and education, as indicated earlier.'

There are two areas Martin Laing is keen to comment on as the year 2000 approaches. One is the importance of communication and the team. 'We, in the boardroom, know where the company is going. What is important is that everyone out there has to understand what is going on, and the only way that can occur is for us to communicate with them as widely as possible. I would say they - our people – have to be better informed about what we are trying to do for the future of the business. Our communication system has improved a lot but not enough. Further down the organization we do have regular team briefings to discuss not only what is going on in their part of the business but also in the bigger part of construction and John Laing PLC. People need to be told what's happening, otherwise they get annoyed and switch off.'

The second area is training, which has been discussed briefly. However, Martin Laing sees the trend for the future as a move away from the company taking up all the cost of the training. 'We see a move towards the employees themselves having to do much more of their own training. Presently we give training and then we encourage them to do other things themselves – I want people to learn how to speak French or participate in the Open University. However, I feel they may have to do much more of that themselves in the future. There certainly will be a lot more emphasis on the continual learning process. People will not be hireable without basic skills. A continual learning process will take place as people want to better themselves in order to make sure they're up to speed. If people haven't kept themselves up to speed they won't get a job and somebody else will – it's as simple as that.'

Laing is taking on more people with degrees that it would have done in the past. 'We want people now towards 2000 who are much more broadminded than they have been in the past, with a broader range of professional and management skills. We want someone who has other skill capabilities – not just somebody who is an engineer but somebody who has got the ability to think more widely. We will be seeking to hire more innovative people, much more entrepreneurial, self-starting sort of people than previously. Other countries are far ahead of us in the UK on education and I'm not comparing us with Japan, the USA, France or Germany. I'm talking about comparison with Malaysia, the Philippines and places like that. Far Eastern countries are way ahead of us. Obviously we don't sit back, here in the boardroom, and wait for universities to churn out people who are actually no use to us at Laing. We have increasing dialogues with the educational system and we do put people into diploma courses in order to broaden their skill and knowledge base. We go back down the line a bit too, to local schools. Some of our schemes ensure that what kids are being taught today is relevant for tomorrow.'

Laing, because of the business it is in, does experience another difficulty. It needs people with traditional skills, the 'bricky and chippy' end of the market. 'There is a difficulty there. We often find a lack of those skills. Because more people go to college or university, fewer people actually want to work as a bricklayer or a carpenter, so you have to ensure the ones you've got can become more multi-skilled. Whereas before you had a person who was a bricklayer, or a carpenter, or a general labourer, you have now got to have people who can do a variety of things. They must be able to do more than one job. That is beginning to happen, and we are having discussions with the unions to make sure you can now cross boundaries. They are still very protective towards their trades but they know they have to do much more to improve that situation.'

Martin Laing doesn't enjoy looking back. He is much more excited about what's going to happen tomorrow and in 2005. 'I would like to be remembered for achieving something,' he says, 'not for myself, obviously, but I mean for society as a whole. As a family we have a big tradition in charitable giving and I want to keep that side up. I spend a lot of time working with a variety of organizations which are nothing to do with construction, so one hopes that will continue to create opportunities for other people to maximize their own potential as much as anything else. For me there isn't anything more frustrating than seeing people opting out rather than being prepared to do something for themselves – something to help themselves. If the Laing family has created opportunities for people to improve themselves I suppose that's one thing I'd be very proud of into the millennium.'

KUONI TRAVEL (UK) LTD

Turnover (1994)	£230 million
Core business tour operation	£190 million
Independent Business Units for specialist travel activities	£40 million
Profit before tax	£38 million
Employees	310

Britain's most successful long haul tour operator, providing flexible holidays tailored to individual requirements at package tour prices. A fully owned subsidiary of Kuoni Reisen Holding, Zurich, Switzerland.

Peter Diethelm – Chairman and Managing Director

Managing Director since 1974 and Chairman since 1987, Peter Diethelm is the member of the Kuoni Holding Group Management responsible for strategic development of tour operation worldwide.

The UK business is in two divisions:

Core business – tour operation

Kuoni is best known as the UK's leading operator for long haul holidays. For the last 14 consecutive years, travel agents have voted Kuoni 'Britain's Best Long Haul Tour Operator'.

Specialist travel activity

In addition to its core activity, Kuoni is a successful operator in niche market activities such as student travel, trade fairs, sports and incentive travel, as well as handling foreign tourists visiting the UK.

Kuoni
Peter Diethelm, Chairman and Managing Director

The travel industry in the UK has experienced a shake-out during the last five years. The big boom of the eighties finished in early 1990, and was followed by the recession. Then the travel business was hit harder than any other by the Gulf War in 1991 because people just did not want to fly, full stop. Very clearly, that period separated the men from the boys. There were some spectacular failures of several major tour operators and there were others who consolidated and got through. Peter Diethelm, Kuoni's chairman and MD, did not believe that the downturn would last for ever and, instead of withdrawing into a shell and cutting costs, the company actually invested during that period.

Says Peter Diethelm, 'It was quite a brave decision. It stemmed from the confidence that the downturn was a blip and not here to stay. There were two major investments, which were actually intensified during the worst period. One was in people and training, and the other in information technology (IT). One was expensive, and the other one was very time consuming, but instead of sitting back and hoping for better days, we seized the opportunity to really get ourselves ready for a substantial growth at the end of that particular period.'

Kuoni did not really have to wait long. It did not need to wait until the end of the recession, for the end of the Gulf War created a backlog. 'Very few people had travelled for six months,' says Peter Diethelm, 'and afterwards many people wanted to blow it, to forget about it and go on a good holiday. Therefore, our upturn came immediately after mid-1991, and really, during the main year of the recession, as it went through to 1993. Our success lay in the fact that we have invested in and created certain technologies and service approaches, and also, of course, because the market in travel, as a result of the recession, consolidated, with the exit of major players, such as Air Europe and Intasun.'

The long haul market has been earmarked since the mid-eighties as the one with the greatest growth potential, for no other reason than that the absolute figure is relatively small – under 10 per cent of the total package tour market. More to the point, with the way currencies developed, over time long haul became more and more competitive. The gap between the price for two weeks in Tenerife or Greece, and two weeks in Thailand or Kenya shrank all the time. 'Our destinations,' says Peter Diethelm, 'are predominantly in "soft" currencies. It may not be completely accurate to call the dollar a soft currency, but none the less, it devalued and as a result became cheaper; whereas European currencies increased in value. Secondly, because of the recession businesses consolidated, looked at their budgets for travel and entertainment, and reduced those budgets so that the airlines had surplus capacity on their scheduled flights. A jumbo jet cannot shrink, it still remains the same size! We, then, took up the slack at a lower price, and because it was at a lower price we could generate more demand.'

Peter Diethelm is very pleased to know that I think Kuoni is more product led than market led. 'In real terms it is true. We have not deliberately gone out, done market research and said, "OK, what's the next destination, what's the next fashion in travel?" The reason for that, of course, is that we pioneered a great deal. We pioneered destinations like the Maldives, for instance; we now sell over 300 seats a week to go there. If we had conducted market research, asking "Do you want to go to the Maldives?" the clients wouldn't have known where it is, they would have thought that I was talking about the Malvinas, the Falkland Islands, as opposed to the exotic islands in the Indian Ocean. Destinations like Luxor, for example – in the middle of nowhere, in the middle of the desert, which doesn't have the criteria of sand, sun and sea, at least not as a beach holiday – why on earth would people want to go there? It was only known to the seasoned traveller who went up the Nile and spent £2,000. We knew what a fascinating alternative holiday destination it was, and therefore had sufficient confidence to put it to the test, and arrange direct flights to Luxor. It is one of the great centres, the cradle of civilization, and very few people give it credit for what it really offers.'

Kuoni is an impatient and impulsive company. By the nature of its business it cannot wait until the consumer shows the demand. It has to be pro-active, offer a product, and see whether it can make it palatable to the client. It has worked far more often than not. Peter Diethelm says, 'The nature of our business makes it difficult to conduct market research, finding out if the average British client, on long haul, fancies a holiday in Burma, for example. It is for us to put a holiday together, which meets the criteria of health, safety, sunshine, culture or beaches, that we know is required for a successful long haul holiday. Then package it and present it to our client in an attractive manner.' This, as opposed to asking the client, 'Where do you really want to go?' 'Yes,' says Peter Diethelm. 'For the last ten years, when we asked this question, the majority of clients said they wanted to go to Australia. The fact is that only a minute minority ever went. They wanted to go, they had the aspiration to go, but only when Airtours introduced charter flights to Sydney for £499 could many actually start thinking seriously about it.'

Having agreed that my impression of Kuoni of being product led has substance, Peter Diethelm puts a marker. 'Product led, by definition, has a very old-fashioned approach and implies that you do not listen to the consumer. That has never been the case in our organization. We have to be realistic enough to know we must produce something more tangible than a questionnaire to be marketing led. We have to produce the goods and find out from the client whether he wants to buy that specific product at that specific price, as opposed to just having a vision, a dream, an aspiration, with little bearing on reality in his ability to pay.'

Using a product led approach, when Kuoni has a new project which is tested through its brochures, what does it do if it doesn't work? Says Diethelm, 'We pride ourselves on the fact that we do not cancel holidays. We pay the cost. If a project does not produce the 230 clients a week which we need to be viable, then we will pay the difference between the scheduled flight and the charter flight which we costed, for those people who have booked. We will say that what we have learned from this project, has cost us less in producing the product and operating it for those clients who want to book, than if we had undertaken market research. There is a timing difference as well. Take the market research on China. In the late eighties, China opened up – it was the name of the game. It belonged on every traveller's curriculum to visit China. You couldn't go individually, you had to go on a package tour. That alone already gave us the key to it. We knew it had to be a success, as long as we didn't screw it up. We knew the client couldn't go to China himself, and it didn't take great market research to assess the right price for those clients who wanted to go. If you rely on market research alone, and an incident like Tiananmen Square arises, the set of circumstances, the environment could have already changed by the time the market research feeds through. In tourism we are in a very fast-moving world, and we do not have time for two-year market research, because in two years' time that destination may not be on the agenda for political reasons, natural disasters, or whatever.'

Kuoni is versatile, innovative and its world is split into eight different areas. Its people are out there seeing with their own eyes, on the ground, their future marketplace. Is it a buyer's market, or a seller's market? They watch the crucial key ingredients to successful holidays. Is the currency strong? 'Japan is an interesting country to visit,' says Diethelm, 'but nobody goes there, because it is too expensive. You have to watch all parameters. You need to have people on the ground, and operate a quite different decentralized organization. The managers go out, look, see and report back. The organization is very flat. The individual product managers are the experts, who go to the destination, package it, put the price to it and say this is the holiday I can offer at this price. It is really the product director, and myself, who would make a decision and say, yes, let's have a go. We have to move fast, because time is against us, and the goal posts may be moved by the time we have completed great debates and analysis, follow up and researches. We need to seize the opportunity and strike whilst the iron is hot.'

Kuoni will be planning in April its 300-page brochure produced in August, which will sell the holidays for the following winter and summer. That is the framework Kuoni puts together, based on the assumptions made today. 'Of course, those assumptions may prove false,' admits Peter Diethelm, 'even by the time the brochure is out. There may be a revolution in Vietnam and so Vietnam, which has turned into a new destination for us, may be off the agenda. On the other side, if the indications on the brochure show that something which didn't sell very well last year, is selling much better for whatever reason, we then bring out supplementary products. We bring out a safari brochure, or a special India brochure, because there is a segment there which is doing better and which has greater potential.

We zoom in to capitalize off the particular sentiment which rules at the time.'

One of the areas where Kuoni impressed me was its diligence in investing in training during a downturn – usually one of the first areas historically to be cut in UK industry when the going gets tough. 'During the recession, there was little to do except focus on training. First of all, there was not sufficient business to keep everybody occupied. My options were two – either to make people redundant and reduce the workforce, or capitalize on it and do the training for which you so often never have time. We clearly did the latter. A new spirit of flexibility had to be created. The girl on reservations had to do the post room if extra help were needed there. It was, if you like, a trade-in, a quid pro quo – we guarantee you a job, but you must guarantee you help us out where help is needed. At the same time, it could not have been done had there not been a strong self-confidence that this was only a blip. Certainly, ever since we started our business in the UK, there had been a continuous upward curve, and we had survived recessions before. We had these blips but they were invariably followed by a disproportionately high spend, not just a higher spend, but a disproportionate high spend. We knew what our resources were, and there was never any doubt amongst the senior management that the only thing to do was to use the time wisely and concentrate on training which, regrettably, during the period of very heavy growth in the late eighties when we had 50 or 60 per cent year on year growth, we had neglected somewhat. We realized that, and it was a step change in our approach to training. During the most acute period of the recession and the Gulf War, when business was at dismal levels, we captured, and established the base to what has become an integral part of our operation, and we have never looked back since then.'

The training introduced a customer-first programme. Kuoni seized the opportunity to turn itself from a very fast growing company into one with a clear philosophy and structure, where it said, we cannot win on price so we have to win on quality, quality of service. While some of the big operators, which were many times the size of Kuoni, went bust, others became stronger. Those companies would always win if it were purely a straight price for price comparison. Kuoni wanted to establish a product differentiation, and that meant it had to have higher levels of training, of services, than were available from the travel market as a whole.

'Our approach,' says Diethelm, 'has always been value for money, which does not mean cheap at all, but value for money. We do not go to the lowest denominators, in terms of hotels and services. Kuoni's good average price holiday is around £1,000 plus, as opposed to the average holiday price of £300. That allows us to add a little bit more service. A physical transaction for a holiday, booking a flight, having a transfer at your destination, being looked after at the destination, in the hotel and flying back again is not all that different, whether you go to Spain or Bali. Therefore, if you charge £1,000 because it is a totally different package, despite the fact that the relative value is probably greater – if you did it yourself, to Spain, you would pay maybe £20 or £30 more than buying a package, on a long haul holiday you might spend £200 or £300 more if you attempted to do it yourself – there is extra leeway for providing a better service.'

In principle, Kuoni's strength lies in the clearly defined image and brand that it presents as Kuoni long haul. Under the name Kuoni, its promotional activity, effort etc is concentrated on that image – Kuoni and long haul. For the last thirteen consecutive years it has won awards as the best long haul operator. However, when the opportunity presents itself, Kuoni uses its knowledge and infrastructure to go into totally different travel-related products and makes money from them. Explains Peter Diethelm, 'We have a separate building, Little Kuoni House, which is dedicated purely to non-Kuoni core activities – student travel, trade fairs, exhibitions, incentive travel, sports, spectator sports – specialized activities which do not fall into the category of Kuoni long haul travel. Last year, for example we took 1,400 people to the Caribbean to watch the cricket. Obviously, because we are a Caribbean operator in any case, it was easier for our sports division to draw on our resources and combine the buying power of the Kuoni group with a one-off visit. At the present time we have over £50 million pounds worth of business which has nothing to do with Kuoni long haul at all. We do not make a big song and dance about it. We often sell it under quite different brands. Student travel, for example, is under UK Connection. We leave these specialist divisions as stand-alone activities, but they are growing faster than Kuoni. We have targeted them to a total disproportion of growth. They will exceed £100 million in three years, because we have adapted to the market environment, although the market has become very tough. We believe that the growth, the concentration, from the corner shop into the supermarket has only just begun, and we are ready to take specialized small business on board, unlike our bigger brothers, the Thomsons and the Airtours of this world, who would consider it too fiddly, too little.'

The specialist activities Kuoni is interested in are all relatively small – the biggest operator in trade fairs has a turnover of probably £5 or £6 million, while the biggest operator for incentive travel and conferences is probably £30 million. Peter Diethelm maintains that Kuoni can be amongst the best and the biggest, even in these very specialized niche markets, without taking its eye off the ball and without detracting from the core business. That is a big danger.

Kuoni has set up this side of the business as a separate unit with a separate management. In the end it reports back to the same shareholders, to the same MD, but underneath it all, these companies have enormous autonomy. They are little companies within a company. If Kuoni cannot provide the service at a better price than they can obtain themselves, they can go elsewhere. They can actively buy from the competition. Says Peter Diethelm, 'It is the first £5 million of sales which is the most difficult to create in any business. Once you are on the bandwagon, once it is moving, it becomes easier. We have bought over the years two or three companies precisely to get us started in different areas. We do not have the patience to develop a company from scratch over five years until we finally have the five million together so, we buy in a new one. For example, we bought a flight consolidator, for the marketing of discounted tickets. The company is called Far East Travel Centre, which we own 100 per cent, although I would never do this business under the Kuoni name, because it does not fit with Kuoni's image. Indeed it might dilute our name.'

In the non core activities Kuoni has niche areas of the travel industry. 'Within the core activity of long haul it is fair to say we do not remain a niche within the niche. The Kuoni philosophy in the old days was to be in the top end of the market only. It was very much 4 and 5-star hotels and scheduled flights. We broke out of that. We are now an all-round long haul operator, at every level, whether the client wants a rest-house in Sri Lanka or a 5-star hotel in Thailand. We are no longer simply an expensive, up-market operator. We have charter flights, we have scheduled flights. We fly first class, business class, economy class, the full range. Otherwise, we could not be a leader in what is already a niche market, which is only talking to 10 per cent of the British package tour business. So, while some of the old-fashioned travel specialist companies who have been around for twenty years have stayed predominantly specialist, at the upper end of the market, we widened the net.'

Kuoni's external link to its travel agents via its computer system, Kudos, means that every travel agent who is authorized to sell its holidays can talk directly to people in the company. Where it got the winning edge and where it spent the money is in pioneering technology for the main system, explains Peter Diethelm. 'For instance, our system is linked with Galileo, which has access to virtually any airline reservation system in the world. We established the first link in the world between an in-house computer system and a big CRS [computer reservation system] of an airline.'

Kuoni's built-in flexibility for tailored packages is what differentiates it from other travel companies. The sort of person who buys a holiday, as it is presented in the brochure, take it or leave it, is actually a dangerous client because he can go anywhere else and buy the same. 'We become very good when a holiday needs to be tailored,' says Peter Diethelm, 'and encourage the client by saying, listen, "You are no longer just a package holiday maker, you are a traveller. Why don't you do what is right for you, not what is right for us." Maybe his wife has heard of Raffles in Singapore, and really wants to go there because this is a once in a lifetime trip. They cannot afford deluxe hotels for the whole holiday because it is too expensive. However, they can choose to stay at Raffles for a couple of nights in Singapore at £150 a night, by swopping the hotel which is included in the basic package, and paying the difference for the two nights in Singapore only. In Hong Kong if a client wants to be seen to arrive in a private car, it can be arranged. It will only cost an extra £30 on a holiday of over £1,000. With Kuoni there is the flexibility to do it all. Everything can be tailor-made just right for the client, and that is where we try to differentiate from our competitors, who do not possess the mechanism for doing so. The whole IT had to be geared to this philosophy. We could not copy from anybody else because we are offering something different. The only thing we have in common with other travel operators is the destination, and maybe the hotels, but the way we package or unpackage the holiday, that is unique to Kuoni.'

Seven years ago, Kuoni made the decision that the days of reps with cars driving up and down the country, cold calling on the retailers, without any particular mission other than trying to flog a brochure, had no rationale, had no return on investment. It realized there must be something more it could invest the money in, and do something for the industry, as well as doing something for Kuoni. It said let's drop the reps. There is no cold calling any more. Let's embark on an education of the travel trade. It decided to spend the money through its long haul college. The training really falls into two categories. Peter Diethelm explains. 'First, is training in the UK, where we go to all the major cities and centres conducting a seminar-style operation for the travel agents. We do not give specific training on what is in the Kuoni brochure, but give them geography lessons and consumer behaviour lessons, because the worst thing a travel agent can do is to send the wrong client to the wrong place. You do not send somebody who really has no cultural interest to Luxor just because the temperature says it is 90 degrees there, if all he really wants is to lie on a beach. So it is important to try to match the product with the client's aspirations, and the client's mentality, which goes far further than just a brochure selection. It is a training of the trade, of providing a service to the client.' The hope is, of course, that because Kuoni provides that training, the agent would probably think of it when the client wants to book that type of long haul holiday.

Second, Kuoni takes about a thousand travel agents a year to long haul destinations like Bangkok or Bali, for which they pay a very nominal sum, and provides seminars at the destination. 'That is in co-operation with the airlines and hotels that we work with. We do all the organizing and arrange the guest speakers. This method is accepted as being the best type of sales promotion, a soft sell. We may have quite a hard image in terms of our commercial relationship at times, so we are putting something back into that relationship through the training. We also believe that the travel agent will think more of Kuoni if we enable them to learn something about their business as a whole, rather than just constantly highlighting the Kuoni £290 or £499 deals to Thailand.'

The company's recruitment policy, like that of many solid, old-fashioned firms, is based on promotion from within, and there is little doubt that when you start from two people and reach a staff level of 350, there is a great deal of scope within that escalation. In recent years, however, Kuoni has deliberately had to make certain changes. Peter Diethelm says, 'We needed fresh blood, and we have made some external senior managerial appointments, a fuel injection, if you like. We needed a boost from outside, because otherwise we would risk becoming a victim of our own success, cocooned within one set of thinking. It is something which we needed to do, because first, it broke with tradition, and second, although it had a certain downside in that some of the motivation of those people in line for the next jobs up may have suffered, it was necessary to keep in touch with the outside world. It's as simple as that.'

The new managers of Kuoni's future come from a mixture of people from within and outside the travel trade.

In a business fraught with rules and regulations does it not become a hassle for Kuoni? Peter Diethelm, 'When the EU directive came in, at the stage of talking and consultation we were a little worried. We felt: "All we need is another set of rules, created by people who have no idea what they are talking about." Now I think the scare is over, and what we have basically assessed is that our own self-imposed quality control criteria, and customer relationship criteria are far higher than the regulations which are coming through. On balance, with a few exceptions, the regulations are beneficial for the good companies, because they have already met the standards and exceeded them, some time ago. If the regulations are properly policed and implemented, it will be the rogues in the business who will come under scrutiny, and from that point of view, it will concentrate the business into fewer hands. That may be a downside ultimately for the consumer, but it is a fact of life.'

Peter Diethelm does feel that most affected will be those small businesses which have good ideas, add an extra choice, an extra value, and may well not be able to compete any more because of the regulations. 'When the business is a certain size, it is able to organize itself. Many of the regulations are really for customer protection, and the top operators in this group have met all those criteria already, otherwise they would not be in the business or the position they are in. At the moment we have to be vigilant and constantly watch that the bureaucrats do not come up with some crazy new ideas or make some almighty mistake. We have quite a strong lobbying force – the Federation of Tour Operators [FTO] – which is an association of the top fifteen tour operators in this country. What is of some considerable satisfaction to me was the fact that the bureaucrats listened. I didn't think they would listen, but we were actually able to change things. There was a directive which we just recently got shot of –

nothing to do with travellers, but a direct sell directive – which stated that only 25 per cent of the payment should be made prior to departure and the client would pay the rest after he came back from his holiday, unless the travel agent saw him on a one to one basis, and he signed a form. If you buy a car and it is no good, you can give it back. But buy a holiday and you did not like it, you cannot give it back. You rely on the information which is produced. That directive would simply have increased holiday prices. This is not a charity business, someone would have to pay for it. It was a total misunderstanding of the industry and a licence to print money for the professional complainer. Anyhow, travel is excluded now as a result of a great deal of lobbying. A lot of the FTO lobbied through MPs both here and in Brussels, and finally somebody saw sense. Overall, however, legislation has not presented us with a problem.'

The holiday market, by any worldwide research, is a growing business. Demand grows with the increase of far more leisure time and disposable income. Peter Diethelm believes it will have its blips as it always had, but the underlying trend is up. The sorting out of the men from the boys in this country, as well as in Germany, France and the leading mature markets of Europe, is complete. 'If there were any more sorting out there would be problems with the Monopolies and Mergers Commission. The number of leading players in these markets are now here to stay. One may be doing better than the other but generally, it is a sound, healthy, well-financed industry, and the spectacular failures of the travel giants of the past cannot happen now.'

Towards 2000 Kuoni relies on two aspects. One, is to keep pace with and adapt to the new technology, with whatever is on offer – the super-highway, the multimedia and how it communicates through a new distribution network. The second one, in keeping with so many companies in this book, is to maintain the innovation, which is getting progressively more difficult. 'When we began,' says Peter Diethelm, 'we started with two or three countries, where nobody had ever been. Today, any country worth going to is featured in a brochure. Geographically, there is not much more we can do other than change the emphasis from one country to the other, almost like a fashion on a seasonal basis. What we need, of course, are new types of holidays, active holidays, to be able to introduce a new dimension: for example, holidays where you can safely learn scuba diving, or wind-surfing – wearing a wet-suit in muddy waters in this country is just not the same, you have to be a real enthusiast for that. We are able to broaden this culture, to introduce new personal achievements, allow someone to learn something on the holiday. We are adding an extra dimension of personal challenges.'

Should there not also be the opportunity for multi-activity holidays? Does Kuoni's role end with sending the client to the destination? 'Destination management is one of the core issues, where one operator differentiates itself from the other,' admits Diethelm.'What do we offer our people when they get to their destination? We can enhance the enjoyment of the holiday tremendously by zooming in to very individual needs. When our clients go to Sri Lanka or Mombasa, what do they do when they are there? That is the future element where there is great scope for further innovation. As the number of new destinations decreases, you need to create new opportunities of what you can offer the client to do within existing holiday locations.'

Financially, Kuoni had spectacular increases, up to 50 per cent plus, year on year, in the eighties. Then it was cut back to size by the market or by the environment, the recession and the Gulf War. Is a more balanced development the new way forward to the millennium? 'We have reappraised our situation,' says Peter Diethelm. 'We looked backwards and felt that rapid growth of 50 per cent per year is not in the best long-term interests of a long-term company. We are a long-term company. I believe very strongly that around 15 per cent is right for our development. The other thing is, if your growth is disproportionate to the market you have to make a decision whether you sacrifice the profit margins for growth. I think if we have no growth or only average market growth, we would then probably review the situation. But it is not what we are aiming for. We are aiming to grow faster than the market and to hold our position in the specialized niche in which we operate.'

In addition to being chairman and MD, Peter Diethelm is also responsible for the strategic development of the tour operation activity within Kuoni Group, Europe-wide. 'My ambition is a very clear one. That is to export the same success we have been fortunate to develop in the UK, to Italy, France, Austria, Spain and other countries. I consider some of those countries like one of our independent business units. My ambition is to bring those on to a leadership level.'

The most difficult part in any development is to get it off the ground. Isn't it expensive and risky? 'These countries all operate,' says Diethelm, 'it is not a question of just starting afresh. They have not achieved either their critical size or their leadership status in the industry. The focus is on becoming the long haul leader in these countries, both commercially and, in the image, the standing and the quality of the product. That is a big task, and there will be problems, they are different cultures. What you cannot do, we have already learned, is simply export one formula and say, take this, now just do the same in another country. There are different client behaviours, different ways of doing business, in each of these countries. At times we are light years away. Professionally, commercially that is my biggest challenge.'

In this country, Kuoni has made a contribution to making long haul holidays more affordable and more accessible to a much wider range of people. When Peter Diethelm first came to the UK in the late sixties Kuoni clientele consisted of the idle rich, and some of the professional classes. 'The Kuoni client profile, you could read it in Tatler or Country Life. It was so obvious who was the Kuoni client. Well there has been an equalizing over the years, and there is no stereotype profile of the Kuoni client any more. It could be the garage owner, the taxi-driver, it could be the doctor from Harley Street. It shoots across the classes. Of course they need somehow an above average disposable income in order to buy our holiday – but if you think that in those days you needed the annual salary of one of the working classes, that's no longer the case. I mean, I would get you a very good holiday today for £800, and if people wait for the right opportunity, next year it will be less than that. The big companies in this business would never have come into long haul if they had not seen how successful we were. They would not have shown any interest in long haul because they would have linked it with some type of exotic minority business. The fact that our competitors take us seriously means they see a business opportunity and we have widened the market.'

A millennium wish for Peter Diethelm? 'I think if there is one wish it is the total success of the group. It is not an individual profit centre success but the whole Europe-wide growth, as being that fighting force where everybody reckons Kuoni are the ones to beat. We are number one in long haul in the UK, and we want to be number one in Europe.'

Kuoni has the resources to do what is necessary and will do what is necessary to achieve this aim and retain market share. 'We will be delighted if we do,' says Peter Diethelm. 'Nothing is on automatic pilot. We cannot say steady progress will get us there. Europe is a very big target. We are strong in Switzerland, in our niche market, and to a certain degree also in France, but we have a lot of catching up to do in the other countries. Really, there is a lot of excitement into the millennium if we get our act together. We have a head start on everybody else; there is nobody who is in all those countries. There is no European tour operator product – yet!'

KWIK-FIT HOLDINGS PLC

Turnover (1994-95)	£297.6 million
Operating Profit	£26.7 million
Profit before tax	£29.3 million
Net assets	£129.5 million

Europe's largest automotive parts, repair and replacement organization, employing over 5,000 people.

Tom Farmer CBE – Chairman and Chief Executive

Tom Farmer founded the company in 1971.

He is a board member of Scottish Enterprise and Investors in People UK and Chairman of Investors in People, Scotland, and of Scottish Business in the Community

The business is in the following divisions:

Kwik-Fit operates through 730 specialist fitting centres, with 578 in Britain, 140 in Holland and Belgium and 12 in Eire. Open seven days a week, each centre offers a drive-in, while-you-wait service for motorists.

Kwik-Fit Fleet focuses on the special needs of fleet operators, aiming at reducing the costs and administrative burdens of running their fleets of cars and vans. Kwik-Fit Fleet has strong business links with almost all the UK's major fleet operators.

Town & Country Tyre Services is the largest independent mobile tyre fitting service in the UK. Acquired by Kwik-Fit in 1994, it is on target to achieve a nationwide service through 150 specially equipped vehicles, meeting the needs of garages, fleet users, local authorities and the private motorist.

Uitlaatservice Nederlands is the largest importer and wholesale supplier of tyres, exhausts, batteries and shock absorbers in the Netherlands, supplying over 200 independent customers as well as all the Kwik-Fit centres.

Kwik-Fit Insurance is a telephone-based insurance broker run in association with Alexander & Alexander, offering the private motorist the benefit of a 'one-contact' insurance service.

Apples Car Clinics. Kwik-Fit has a 25% stake in this car servicing and MOT test specialist in the North of England which operates through 71 centres.

The Kwik-Fit Group
Tom Farmer CBE, Chief Executive

Tom Farmer is extraordinary. He started his first business when twenty-three, selling tyres at discount prices. In 1968, he merged with Albany, a publicly quoted company and cashed in, deciding to stop working in 1969. He lived in America for a short time and came back in 1970, starting Kwik-Fit in 1971, specializing in exhaust systems. Having been in America Tom Farmer had seen it work and the phenomenal growth of such businesses was just starting. He admits, 'I have actually no embarrassment about identifying other people's "good business ideas": I think sometimes it is much better to be second first – or maybe it is first second – to pick up an idea or concept and do it better with fewer hang-ups than the initial innovator.'

He specialized in replacement exhaust systems, then returned to doing tyres as well. In 1980 he acquired one of Kwik-Fit's competitors, Euro Exhausts, which operated fifty centres mainly south of Manchester. The price paid was £10 million and when combined, the two companies established a chain of 125 centres under the Kwik-Fit name.

Tom Farmer admits the hardest job was to put two companies together. 'They had different cultures. The people in Euro didn't like the fact that we'd bought it out, but we started to work on that. Then, within months, I got an opportunity to acquire the Firestone Tyre & Auto business, which had 180 outlets. Within weeks of acquiring this business, eighty of the outlets were sold to Dunlop for the same price paid for the whole business. With the Firestone deal, Kwik-Fit ended up with just over 220 centres throughout the country.'

Tom Farmer goes on 'When we had fifty centres we were on the crest of the wave. We thought we could rule the world and knew everything about business, but it was such a big expansion, we discovered our inadequacies. The single biggest find was the fact we were not professional managers – professional trained managers as such – and had shortcomings in areas like financial controls, marketing, training, personnel, administration etc. What we were, was very, very good operators, the best operators in the world; there was nobody better than us. But there we were, from seventy-five up to 220 centres in twelve months, and that size of operation needed a more professional team to control it. We went through a period for twelve months of what we call a profit sabbatical. In other words, the profits went from £4 million to £1 million! That was concerning, but we had confidence that with our strengthened team, we would overcome the problem.'

He had a colleague join him who had retired from Marks and Spencer's, and they employed another ex-colleague, David Jenkins, as managing director. They also employed a financial director, who had been a senior partner in Arthur Andersen; a director to take responsibility for marketing and advertising; and a property manager to look after all the centres. The MD's main job was to bring together the three companies and create one culture. It had to be Kwik-Fit culture, and he had to make sure that he implanted it into the Firestone and Euro outlets. Financially Kwik-Fit was a strong company and was not in any difficulties, it was just it was a big business to manage. Bringing that team in enabled Kwik-Fit to concentrate on the operation of the business. Within a year it had pulled it all together, and Kwik-Fit has continued to expand ever since as Europe's leading independent car parts repair and replacement organization.

Tom Farmer admits making mistakes; lessons for many. 'We expanded in France and lost considerable money there. In fact, we made the same mistake twice in France. Twice we tried to expand there and both times we were not successful. Looking back, the reason was simple: we did not do enough forward planning. We didn't really set our stalls out properly, we didn't spend enough time discovering what the market was all about. We thought, because there were 55 million people there, and 20 million cars, and there are 55 million people in the UK and 20 million cars – and it is only twenty-two miles across the Channel – it would not make any difference! The fact we didn't speak French was not important, and the fact they didn't speak English, didn't mean anything either. The fact they had a Latin culture, and we were Anglo-Saxon was something we thought we could overcome! Nobody else has overcome it, but we thought we could because we were better than anybody else. But the truth of the matter was, quite simply, we made a lot of mistakes.'

Regretfully, Tom Farmer and Co. came out of France. Philosophically he recalls, 'It was nice to visit, you know, and sit there on summer evenings having a glass of wine. It was really very pleasant. However, it was not profitable. So we came out and continued to stick to the knitting and grow the business.' That business today is 800 plus centres, 5,000 people, more than 4 million motorists a year through their centres, with turnover of £296.7 million and profits £29.3 million for the year ended 28 February 1995 and growing substantially. Added to that, in 1995 Kwik-Fit joined forces with Alexander & Alexander, one of the world's largest insurance brokers, to provide a new service to motorists – low cost motor insurance cover.

He is certainly an excellent example of how, if you have a 'can do' attitude, if you have single-mindedness, and opportunity, you can achieve a great deal. 'If I am a role model it is only because Kwik-Fit is a big business which is composed of a lot of little businesses. Each centre is a business on its own, and maybe each manager says, "I want to be like Tom, I want to do what Tom has done."'

Tom Farmer likes to lead from the front. 'A lot of things I have found are dependent on creating a perception, rather than the reality. I'm interested in the end result, not necessarily how we got there. That is how the business has been, ever since the first day I started. I decided then that our customers didn't really want to deal with us! Nobody gets up in the morning and says, "Let's buy an exhaust system." What we wanted to do was to identify the company and say to our customers: as it is a people business, you are dealing with people rather than an organization.' His profile therefore has always been right to the forefront – in the adverts, publicity etc. His name is closely associated with the company, a bit like Colonel Sanders and Kentucky Fried Chicken. Everybody then thinks that what Tom Farmer must be doing is fitting every tyre, every exhaust, and nothing ever goes on that he does not know about. 'Well that was true in the early days. I mean, there wasn't anything that went on that I didn't know about in the early stages, up to the 200 outlets. But once you begin to bring in a management team you must let the reins go in some respect. Having a financial director who implemented all the necessary financial controls meant I no longer had to check the suppliers' invoices on a Sunday night at home: having a marketing director meant no longer did I sit on a Saturday night, drawing adverts.'

Other managers were doing the work, but Tom Farmer admits he was still totally involved. 'All the management books tell you about the need to delegate. You have to be realistic about it. You cannot be in a position like myself, develop a business, and then overnight give it all up. The only way you can do that is to pack up and go away. As long as you are there you cannot give it up, it is part of your life. It is a way of living, it is family. I am sure if you look back in the history of Marks and Spencer's, you will find that no matter what happened, the founder's immense interest was always there. Then you realize, if you want the company to prosper and grow, you cannot be there all the time and handcuff people. Then you go down the road of saying, "I'll have to start to delegate," and that is a painful process to learn.'

He confesses it was initially difficult for him. Even when he told people he was delegating responsibility and authority to them, he had nightmares wondering what was going on. 'People don't always tell you what is happening in every detail. Eventually, you ask, "Well, what's happening about that?" Then they say, "Well, you delegated it to me." But you protest, "No, I delegated it, but I want to know about it." And so you learn!

'Often you find out you're abdicating not delegating. That is wrong, because you abdicate, give the situation to people, and it causes all sorts of problems. Then you learn that abdication is not the right thing to do either. The real art of delegation is to be able to give people responsibility, give them authority, but also make them accountable, and ensure there is a very good report-back system to you.'

The essential is that as soon as you have put into place a really good reporting system, it takes away altogether the thought at the back of your mind about what is happening, what is going on? It leaves a person to get on with the job, but they report back to you in a structured manner. Initially, people who have formed a company and built it up with their own effort, never believe that anybody can do the job better, or as well as they can.

Tom Farmer agrees. 'That is the other reason why it is difficult to delegate, and why you are always interfering and wondering what is going on. You end up recognizing that in most matters which you are delegating, if there is a hiccup, providing you have got the right accountability, the correct reporting back system, you pick it up very quickly. Then you have the opportunity to do something about it. As time goes by, you get more relaxed with the people, they get more relaxed with you, and you understand that, well, just because at the end of the day we want to go from Edinburgh to London, and you want to go by train, and I want to go by plane, it doesn't really matter, as long as we both get there for twelve noon. How you get there, provided it is not costing any more, is not going to have any real effect on the business, and it doesn't matter. So one learns to respect people's individuality. You develop systems and procedures within the whole organization that everybody follows – they are not like railway tracks, they are elastic bands, they open and shut, and people are allowed to expand the elastic band. What you have done is create a system which is monitoring the business all the time to ensure the elastic band does not snap; the situation does not develop to harm the business.'

The procedures Kwik-Fit tries to work to are very simple. Everything it does, the success or failure of Kwik-Fit, depends on the centre manager and the Kwik-Fit fitters. As customers, our vision of Kwik-Fit is about what happens when we go into a centre. If it is a dirty old run-down building then that is our total vision of Kwik-Fit in every place, because that is all we know about it. Tom Farmer therefore tries to ensure that every centre, every centre manager, he or she, recognizes, quite simply, the success or failure of their local business is the success or failure of Kwik-Fit as a whole. It is *their* business. 'We tell them,' says Tom Farmer, 'we operate a programme called branchise, not franchise. We work hard on the fact that one centre is a small business on its own, it's operated by a centre "master manager". Anywhere else they would be managers, but in Kwik-Fit they are something special, "master managers". We encourage our master managers to operate that centre as their own business. Every three centres form what we call a partnership. We assemble the operation so effectively we have four master managers for three centres, and one of these master managers is appointed what we call a partner, and he's responsible for the performance of the three centres. The reason for our manager/partner structure is that we are a seven days a week operation. If you don't work in a centre, then the only reason you are employed by Kwik-Fit is to support the people who do. That is all. Everything happens in the centre, and everything else that goes back from there, is part of the support team. Your job is to support the people that are working there. Support them by making sure the stock has been ordered for them, by maintaining the property, by ensuring the advertising works effectively, by having the correct training programmes in place. Support them by making sure the suppliers get paid on time, by controlling costs, because the better the cost control, the more profitable the business will be. Everybody who is not in the centre is part of the Kwik-Fit support team. I am part of the Kwik-Fit support team.'

Kwik-Fit has put in new monitoring systems to identify the level of performance to its customers. Helping it to monitor its service levels, there are independent AA inspections and a mystery shopper programme. Therefore remuneration is on both financial performance and quality service performance. The profit share is paid out on the third Friday of every month. For April's sales and profits, for example, the profit share is paid out on the third Friday in May and everybody gets an income statement so they know exactly where they are. Almost 40 per cent of Kwik-Fit people are shareholders in the company. Last year everybody in the company who met certain criteria on length of service and performance received £500-worth of shares, free of charge. There is also a private health care scheme. 'Everybody came in on a promise that if they had courage in their own ability, and were prepared to join a winning team, we would recognize their input,' says Tom Farmer. 'That is how I worked from the very first day. That is how it will be in 2000. It is not written down but understood. If people start to question what you mean by this reward or that reward, they are not the people for us. You don't let people down.'

I am impressed that in a business such as tyres and exhausts there is so much caring and sharing. 'I suppose we were brought up in an environment where everybody shared. My dad was a shipping agent, and I can remember as a boy, he'd come home sometimes when there had been a ship come in, and he had got some presents from the captain. Mum would be saying, "Oh, the girl down the road is getting married on Saturday. We'll give her the nylons," or, "I'll take two cigarettes up to Mrs Brown and two for Mr Jones." This caring and sharing was just the way you went about your life. You did it without any thought about that's how life should be. Then I began to identify there were possibly tremendous business benefits to it as well. A lot of the people who began in this company are still with me, even though the business now is much more technical and technological. We never milked the business either. The money was ploughed back into it, put back in to develop, develop, develop. Because of that, everybody has tremendous confidence in the company, and is willing to put a lot into it. If they have no confidence in the people who are responsible for making the business, then you have a real hard problem. That is how we operate, everybody is involved – if you are not in the centre you are part of the support team, but through it all the most important people in our organization are our master managers and Kwik-Fit fitters.'

In my experience, most of the time, organizations have a support team trying to mop up what has gone wrong. The real thing is to make the people at the front know what to do, so things don't go wrong in the first place. The fewer things that go wrong, the smaller the support team you have.

Tom Farmer agrees. 'There is one area that we never ever try to cut down on within the support team and that is anything to do with people programmes. All the books stress that the "customer is king". You have to wonder whether that statement is actually factual. I say, that this is the case, maybe the people who provide the service are presidents, the people who satisfy the needs and wishes of the customer. Take a master manager of Kwik-Fit. If he is not highly self-motivated, and isn't in there on Monday morning, opening up the centre at ten minutes to eight, so when the rest of the team come in, he is already on the boil, with everything going, I tell you, no matter how many customers come, no matter how much money we spend on advertising, our sales will be terrible, and the service will be poor. I think at the end of the day, that expression about the "customer is king" is not quite right. the Kwik-Fit fitters and master managers within the organization are the kings. And our customers are the ones who, by keeping us in business by their choice, keep those beings in office!'

For Farmer his people are the most important element of Kwik-Fit. Unless they really make it happen and give good service Kwik-Fit won't have any customers. What about those who say, 'Well, unless you've got customers, you won't have any business.' He states, 'Unless you have people who are highly self-motivated, and really believe in the company, then I tell you, you will not have any business either. If your people just do a job, you end up having a mediocre business. The difference between successful businesses and mediocre businesses is where a potential customer says, "See that company, there is a lot of buzz about it." Go to a tyre or exhaust depot, and, for example, you get two tyres and you drive out again. So what? Go to another and you go in and you come out and feel really good. Why? You've got the same tyres, you paid the same price, they were fitted the same way. The difference was the inter-personal relationship; the way the person spoke to you. Little bit of chat, pass the time of day nicely, so it made the customer feel good. The customer, in turn, also made them feel good, because that is what happens, and that is our success. So we never scrimp on any-thing to do with people programmes.'

The one philosophy Kwik-Fit insists upon is it wants people to earn as much money as possible. Tom Farmer believes that people work mainly for money. 'I have never found anybody yet who went to work happily on a Monday that had not been paid on a Friday. We have to work for money, because we need money to buy the material things that help to improve our quality of life. We need money to educate our children, to clothe ourselves, to pay the mort-gage. So this saying that money is not the most important thing may be true if you are in a monastery, or in a convent or something, but the rest of us are doing it to obtain financial rewards to enable us to improve the material side of our lives. Once the money side is right – and that is why I believe firmly in our profit share, and that people should earn according to their capabilities, and what they put into the job – there is something else you must get right. That is, you have to make sure that people *enjoy* it, that people enjoy working with you and being part of the organization; if they enjoy it, then you have got all of the ingredients right.'

I agree nobody enjoys doing a job if they do not know how to do it, or if they are working in lousy conditions. Nobody enjoys doing the job if they do not like the people they work with, or if the travel arrangements are terrible. Kwik-Fit constantly reviews these issues. 'Sometimes we see cases where a good member of the team is work-ing at a depot miles from home, because that is where the initial opportunity arose. Then the way to make a good team member into a great team member is to have him working in his home town, and take the travel hassle away from him. Simple but so effective.' Most of the staff I have met say they enjoy Kwik-Fit. 'The most important part of that enjoyment is they trust you,' says Tom Farmer.

Business is getting tougher and, yes, Farmer will agree it is more competitive because, quite simply, more and more companies have recognized, at the end of the day, they have got to deliver what the customers actually want. At one time Kwik-Fit used to think their only competitors were people who sold tyres and exhausts. What they now recognize is their competitors are Airtours, Dixons, Currys or M&S. Everybody who's out there is trying to get Kwik-Fit's customers' money. People earn a certain amount of money. If they give too much to Airtours or too much to M&S, they are not going to have enough to give anything to Kwik-Fit. It is just the competitive world we live in. 'If you recognize a competitive world,' said Tom Farmer, 'then try to raise your standards to higher than those of your competitors. What happens then is you have a more efficient business. The more efficient business you have, the easier it is to run that business, and win.

'We advertise Customer Service. We always try to give 100 per cent customer satisfaction/delight. About eight years ago we changed satisfaction and called it *delight*. The reason we did that was quite simply a customer came in and paid us £150, and we said, "Thanks very much, I hope you're satisfied." The customer turned round and said, "Satisfied? I'd better be satisfied, I just paid you £150." So satisfaction was no longer good enough. Customers became better educated about their purchasing power – into the future they'll be even more so – plus the fact that there were other people down the road who were wanting to try and get their money as well. So we changed customer satisfaction to customer *delight*. Our delight is just doing that little bit extra. You've got to do that for your people, and for the customers themselves.'

Tom Farmer does not think customers are any more difficult today than they were when he started. Customers have always had rights. Is it tougher into 2000? Is it changing? The answer is 'Yes, it changes. Some would say it is tougher today than it was ten years ago, but it is different. The levels of everything you do have got to be higher. All of us continue to demand more. If I went to a hairdresser now, and there was hair on the floor. I would be saying to the guy, tell me have you got anybody here who can sweep the floor? If he gave me a hairdressing cape and it was dirty, I would tell him to "get that off". So customers' expectations are rising significantly, mainly through the power of our money.'

There are other pressures says Tom Farmer: 'There are more unfair criticisms about businesses. What's happened is that people jump on and expect everything to be at a level of 100 per cent all of the time.

You can't do that. At the end of the day, when you're in a service industry, when you're dealing with customers, so much of that is interpersonal relationships, and our people will not always perform at 100 per cent level. They will make mistakes, because we all make mistakes. We are not computers or robots. The customer comes in sometimes and doesn't communicate properly either. Things will go wrong. What we try to do at all times is say to people, "Listen, in the type of business we are in, it all depends on people, people make their best judgement, and people try to do the best job. However, there will be times when something is not right, is not to your satisfaction. Let us know, and we will move heaven and earth to put it right. We will guarantee it. If you tell us, we will put it right." We do that not just for the person who drives in with the car, but we also do that for our own guys. Of our 5,000 people some 4,000 get paid every week. Out of that 4,000 someone's wages will be wrong, or they will think they are wrong. And we say to them, "Don't get uptight about it, because the person making up the wages made a mistake, we'll get it put right for you." We work at that all the time.'

Continuing his theme on pressures on business, Farmer is one who believes that if we had never had trade unions, or employment legislation, there would still be boys climbing up chimneys. 'People would have continued to be exploited in many cases. Pressure has brought in certain standards which people work to, and others recognize. Certain legislation such as the trading standards, have helped to ensure the customer, too, is getting a better deal. I agree with all that. There are opportunities to catch the fly boys and do something about them, the industrial tribunals, nothing wrong with that; there should be ombudsmen who you can go to who are there to look at disputes. But the trend is that too often these things come over one-sided, that the company is wrong automatically, and then a company has to spend a lot of time and money in proving that's not the case. There are some people who still think instinctively, or intuitively, that it is a bad thing to be making a profit in a company, or profit-sharing. But that is the type of pressure we face today.'

Ah, Tom Farmer, but if you are operating a pure, perfect service, then you have nothing to fear!

'I have nothing to fear, Lynda. But I haven't got twenty five hours a day, and sometimes the time and effort you put into it is immense. Do you know in health and safety standards alone in the past fifteen years there have been thousands of new regulations. You live with that and handle it, but in Leeds they interpret something one way, and in Liverpool another. It seems today that companies are unpaid tax collectors, we collected £100 million worth of tax for the Government last year. Nobody pays us for that collection. VAT, income tax, the corporation tax, etc.! That's the world we live in. However, if you look after your people they will do anything for you. Look after your customers, they will do anything for you. Running a business today has pressure but there are also opportunities.'

Tom Farmer stands his ground on corporate ethics and social responsibility. He believes firmly in setting up your stall properly. 'You don't allow yourself to be trampled when you know your company is right, you stand up and fight for it. If somebody is going to criticize our company they had better be sure they're right. If not, we will fight it twenty-four hours a day, seven days a week. But if they are right, do you know what we'll do? We'll work with them twenty-four hours a day, seven days a week to put it right, that's all we can do.'

He would like to see statutory laws taken seriously. For example: 'It would be good business if the law specifying the amount of tread on tyres were enforced. There is a law. But it is not enforced. A law that is not enforced, is it a law?'

What about corporate excellence in the year 2000 for Kwik-Fit? He would love to be able to say he has a detailed, well designed and researched business plan, whereby he knows where Kwik-Fit will be in five to ten years time. 'Unfortunately,' he says, 'we haven't got a crystal ball. What I have usually found is with all the planning that you put into a forecast, if it ever comes out to reality, it is often co-incidental! But we all need to have a vision, a few dreams and targets to work to.'

His dream right now is to continue to become a more dominant factor in the car repair industry, not solely in the UK but in other European countries. He is not wanting, nor anticipating to go too far away. Despite being bitten in France Kwik-Fit still has more retail outlets there than any other UK retailer. Not surprisingly France would be low in its priorities as far as Europe is concerned! But Holland and Belgium? 'We are very strong in Holland now, with 140 places,' he says. 'We will look at each country differently. There might be some cases where we have to do partnerships, and work with nationals. Maybe that is the way we would handle France in future.'

LONDON TRANSPORT

Turnover (1994/95)	£1,155 million
Profit before tax	£101 million
Operating profit (before depreciation, renewals and grants)	£40 million
Total Investment Expenditure (including renewals)	£954 million
Government Grants Received	£686 million
Total Fixed Assets (historical cost)	£3,835 million
Employees (at year end)	18,602

London Transport [LT] was established in its present form in 1984. Its remit is to plan, provide or procure services to meet the present and future public transport needs of London, while ensuring that its services are safe, efficient, economic and make provision for all passengers, including those with disabilities.

Peter Ford – Chairman, London Transport

Peter Ford was appointed Chairman in 1994. He is also Chairman of London Underground Ltd, London Transport Buses and London Transport Property.

He was formerly Chairman of P&O Services Group Ltd and before that of P&O European Ferries Ltd and North Sea Ferries.

Denis Tunnicliffe CBE – Managing Director, London Underground Ltd

Denis Tunnicliffe has been Managing Director of London Underground Ltd since 1988. He is also a member of the London Transport Board.

He was previously with British Airways, rising to the position of Chief Executive, International Leisure Group, Aviation Division.

Operations

In 1994/95 LT sold its remaining bus operating companies into the private sector. These and other private bus companies now run services under contract to LT. LT remains responsible for running the Underground and for improving and extending its services.

Nearly 570 trains serve 207 stations and 408 kilometres of route carrying 2.5 million passengers a day, while some 5,000 buses on 600 routes carry 3.6 million passengers a day. LT also provides 35 bus stations, 100 bus stands, 17,000 bus stops and, in conjunction with Adshel, 9,000 bus shelters.

LT works with Railtrack, British Rail, Docklands Light Railway and the private bus companies to plan and co-ordinate London's public transport and to provide integrated ticketing information.

It also operates Victoria Coach Station, providing services to 1,100 destinations in 26 countries in addition to handling over 90 per cent of long-distance domestic coach travel. Some 10 million passengers pass through the station annually.

LT controls the London Transport Museum, attracting a quarter of a million visitors each year.

London Transport Ltd
Peter Ford, Chairman
Denis Tunnicliffe, Managing Director, London Underground

In a book looking towards the year 2000 I want to review a vital part of our infrastructure, and have selected London Transport as operator of one of the largest and most complex urban railways.

Peter Ford, Chairman of London Transport, has always believed in having good transport available to the public. 'If you live in London, you need a way of travelling other than the motor car. There isn't enough road space. You have to remember that London was a collection of villages strung together, a patchwork quilt of streets. Some American cities were designed for the motor car. London was designed for horses. We need a system for getting people around that is quick, effective, safe, clean, and preferably not too expensive. Foreign visitors always talk about the transport system, because most of them use it.

The history of transport in London, in the eighteenth and nineteenth centuries, illustrates incredible changes. The form of ownership and financing has changed dramatically. Whole systems have come and gone; for example, the tram system has now vanished.

There is one especial change, according to Peter Ford. 'We have become more egalitarian. London is truly a world city, in the sense it is incredibly racially mixed. People come here from all over the world. One has got almost a world customer group. Many bring attitudes from other countries, and compare us with them, saying, "Why don't you do this, why don't you do that?" That is a very exciting aspect of the job.'

It is not easy, dealing with six million people a day using the entire transport system. 'Every day I and my colleagues use the system several times, allowing chance conversations with the travelling public. It's not as though we are making some obscure product. They all immediately identify and say, "Oh, do you know what's happened to the Number 73 bus? What the hell's going on? Your information signs in Victoria Station . . ." They've all got views on it. Certainly, by travelling on the system the whole time you can see how people are reacting, and that's good.'

LT does extensive market research, and the London Regional Passengers Committee, a government-established organization, has the statutory duty to represent the interests of transport customers in London and the South-East. Many people write or phone in direct, and Peter Ford deals personally with as many of them as possible. 'Every day I personally deal with between two and ten customer complaints, and take on board what they've said. I always send a personal reply, fully detailed if I have most of the answers. If it is something that concerns part of our organization which I do not know the details of, then I ask the appropriate person to reply and copy me. We maintain a very strict control over complaints. If it is something particularly serious, for example poor standards of behaviour by our staff, then I personally get involved in the investigation.'

Peter Ford remembers being told that you don't need a single original idea to be a successful business person. What you do need is the ability to get out and about, find out what everyone else is doing, pick out the best ideas and you'll have a cracking firm. 'There are some aspects of LT where we are totally original and world leaders, and that's fine. But we don't rely on that. I spend on average two or three days a month, out and about on the system, visiting staff on the trains, operators in the stations, engineering depots, everywhere. I have a regular programme, but I try not to make it too formal. I have regular meetings with the local managers, discovering their viewpoints, then talk to the front line staff, finding out how they think we can improve the service and, indeed, how their own job could be made more agreeable and more rewarding. It's another way of receiving customers' views, because staff tell me what they think the customers think. We have 16,500 employees in the Underground, about 19,000 in total in LT. All have views which are worth listening to.

Peter Ford also reviews the practices in other countries. 'A slight criticism I would make is that LT was, and possibly still is, such a preeminent organization, there was a feeling we know best, we do it best. However, there are a hundred full-scale metro systems in the world, with something like 300 tram and track-type systems, and literally hundreds of thousands of bus systems. There are not many things we have thought of doing that somebody else has not already considered, so it's important for us to get out there, compare notes and see what's going on.'

It is essential for LT to do that with the most comparable systems, Paris and New York. 'We spend time with them on a regular basis, a few days a year, discovering their activities, what feedback they're receiving, how their customers react. Paris is also a highly international city: their public is not so different from ours, very much the same people, certainly as regards tourists. The things that work for them may well work over here and vice versa. We have a lot to gain by discussing infrastructure with other cities. When it comes to tram and bus systems, you find a lot of cracking good ones in Germany and Central Europe. There again, we need to spend some time out there, looking at what they're doing, being very open-minded about it, sharing our information, and then saying "Look, that's a good idea. We'll pick that one up."'

LT's buses were divided up by geographic region into ten bus companies within London, which have all been sold off to the private sector. LT determines the routes, fare structures and frequencies. It also runs and maintains the bus stops and shelters, and the communication and ticketing system.

In the rest of the UK, bus services are completely deregulated, but the government decided it was wiser to maintain some form of regulation in London. LT was the natural organization to do that work. Says Peter Ford, 'It is very important not to become bureaucratic, an obstacle instead of an aid to a better system. The evidence so far is that we can do this job very well. They are even saying that some form of regulation may be needed in other parts of Britain: if they want that done, we are probably the best people to do it.'

Each route is re-tendered every five years, and LT undertakes that process. 'We have a lot of power, but it is wisely used. It is my firm intention we will have the best value for money bus service of any major city in the world, and we will keep it that way. The only way we can achieve that is not by being bureaucratic power maniacs, but by undertaking a systematic programme of getting round all the bus companies. We see them, talk turkey about how we can make the services better, and, if they think our role is an obstacle to that, they have plenty of opportunity to tell us. We must demonstrate that through this particular arrangement, the public in London get a better value for money bus service than they do in other cities. That is the test.'

The proportion of commuters who come into London by car is declining. To some extent it is a question of habit. They either take a car or use public transport. It is difficult for people to shift between one and the other. Car drivers are potential customers for LT, and Peter Ford would like to get their business, persuading them he can offer a good alternative. In most European cities there are stronger regulations than in London against bringing cars into city centres, which makes it easier to run bus services.

An important factor is delivery vehicles. Says Peter Ford, 'In London we are undisciplined about this whole activity. In Hamburg, for example, all deliveries to shops and restaurants must be before 9.30 am. Most of them are made between about 5 am and 9.30. After that none is allowed. They put up with some congestion during those hours, but after that the buses run like magic, because there are no parked vehicles. I challenge you, walk down Victoria Street, first count the number of delivery vehicles, and secondly, look at their parking. They are all over the place, there is very little control. That is a vital area for us to influence.'

Air pollution is increasingly a cause for concern. 'Somebody has to take responsibility for the quality of the air in London. It is not an accident. It happens as a result of policy. I feel we should set stringent standards as to what we think is good quality air, which will not impair people's health, particularly the elderly and young. Towards 2000 we must work back from that, saying, 'What is the maximum amount of traffic of different types we can allow into London if we are going to keep the air quality at that level?' I'm sure that would point to greater use of public transport, as that is one way of achieving that goal. The Underground does cause some pollution from the power stations producing the electricity, but it is far less per capita, and in any case it is geographically removed. The buses may contribute a minute fraction to the pollution emanating from cars and delivery vehicles. The Royal Commission report on the incidence of asthma and bronchitis in London shows that it is rising fast. I don't think we should let that happen. That is a government and public health matter and should be controlled.'

Peter Ford feels there are certain aspects of transport where you need to engage in an activity which is currently unfashionable, namely long-range planning 'I am not advocating it where it is unnecessary, but where you have to build structures which must last a very long time, you can't just leave that for future generations. If we are to build a new Jubilee line extension, as we are currently doing we've got to ensure we take prudent account of what is likely to be happening to people way out into the future. Is this what they are going to want, is this still going to be useful to them? You need to sit down and plan. It needs co-ordinated action across several different parts of the system to make sure it happens together. That planning is essential. We haven't got that at present.'

Let's see what we think is going to happen in fifty years' time. What is going to happen to life, to the key technologies, to micro electronics, power generation, water, air travel? Where is the technology likely to go? What services and products is that likely to lead to? How will they affect people's lives? How will people spend their time? What are they likely to want? Will they want to travel around or sit at home and look at a screen?'

Peter Ford believes LT has a responsible role in leading such discussions, at least within its own are of activity. Co-ordination is cardinal. 'Take Heathrow – the most significant construction in London since World War II. Its impact on London is huge. Over 50,000 people are employed there. But Heathrow has grown up like Topsy, and the transport infrastructure to support it has not. We are left with a ridiculous situation where, even though we do our best and run our Piccadilly line out there, the interconnections between Heathrow and the West End, the City, the developing east side of London and the other airports are not good by any standards. That is something which should have received attention much earlier on. We have to look into the next century and say, "What needs to happen? Longer term, is it going to spread that way? Is it shrinking, expanding? What is going to happen to all these tourists? Is office work as we now know it coming to an end or not? What's going to happen to the theatre and the arts, what's going to happen to medicine, what's going to happen to publishing?"'

Peter Ford acknowledges that although London is an international city, the British as a nation do have certain characteristics. 'We are relatively anarchic, and it is no good trying to force us into something we don't actually fit. On the other hand, maybe in the above area it would be beneficial if we became slightly less anarchic. I would recommend as a minimum we look carefully at the major projects under consideration to see they are being co-ordinated. It requires various people to work together, but it is the government of the day that should finally decide how that happens. We at LT have an important role to play, but we are not the only ones. We try and work with others such as the CBI, London First, the City Corporation and Westminster Council, but the work does need to be co-ordinated. A spirit of good will must prevail, with people sinking their differences and concentrating on issues where there's a joint interest. We are public servants, in that LT is publicly funded, and it is our duty to work with whoever has been elected to power. We ought to be looking 50 years ahead, not just to the millennium.'

Staff attitude is a major challenge for LT. 'It has changed a lot, but it has further to go. We have a lot of people out there, many doing jobs which are difficult. They can find themselves dealing with highly aggressive members of the public behaving in a totally irrational and sometimes even diabolical manner, for instance, on the ticket barriers of Piccadilly Circus at midnight. We need a highly motivated, trained workforce to be able to cope with those conditions. We have made lots of progress, there's a lot of pride amongst a lot of our people, but that area is a continual challenge.

'I think we can do it by getting the message across to them how important they are. We have enthusiastic staff running the different lines. We have to work on that the whole time, really get people on our side.'

LT carries six million passengers a day now, 2.5 million on the Underground, 3.5 million on buses and is currently seeing good growth. 'That may be a short term thing, but I think the better we can get the service, the more people will use it. Eventually, we will reach a point where our main problem is coping with the demand. I can see that happening, because we will have so many people. I like that problem.'

Peter Ford's own objective is not particularly grand in terms the reader might expect. 'LT has some specific goals, such as the Jubilee line extension being built on time. That is a lot more complicated than the Channel Tunnel, as building under the centre of London today is a massive undertaking. However, I would be happy to feel that the public perception of the quality of the service we offer had risen several points during my period of office and beyond. If it continued to rise, and if we continued to drive down costs so we reached the point where we were virtually self-financed, I would be delighted.'

For Peter Ford there are many paths to heaven. 'I don't think one necessarily should go round aping others, but should study what other people do. At the end of the day, we have to find our own way of doing it. LT has a strong history, and the winning formula is to take that historical background and the things that were good about it. We believe in a very high quality of service to the public, which was always there, and build on that. Take that excellent background, and then incorporate modern techniques, modern attitudes, modern equipment and systems in place for the public. That's the winning formula for the millennium.

'A lot of it has been done by my predecessors. It has begun to change. It has begin to feel much more like a managed system, and that is to the credit of those who are reforming it and still here. My job is just to take that process further.'

London Transport owns and operates the Underground system in its totality. It carries nearly 800m passengers a year, 2.5m daily, serving 233 stations up to 20 hours a day and running more than 460 trains at peak times.

Denis Tunnicliffe, the Underground's Managing Director, recalls November 18th, 1987, the day of the tragic fire at King's Cross station which was before he joined the organization. 'That provoked an inquiry. The old management changed. That awful tragedy caused us to have a very simple objective: to recover public confidence in our ability to carry them about safely. The most shocking thing is the way the Underground was being managed immediately before the crisis.'

In many ways everything for which Denis Tunnicliffe is responsible started in 1988. He introduced a new management structure that year, and it has not been radically changed since, although it has evolved, developed and strengthened. He explains. 'The management was initially totally caught up on the issue of safety. It was clear that this needed efforts in two directions, software and hardware, people skills, people structures, and in investment. We spent '89 in this safety phase. We also had a very difficult year in terms of industrial relations. We had 14 one-day strikes. It's not clear to this day why, but perhaps one reason was that the clarity with which we intended to manage the business as opposed to simply letting it drift, was lacking.

'The thrust for safety made the service extremely poor, and during the early part of 1990 it became evident to us we had to do something about quality. By the summer of that year, having tried various initiatives, we set out some fairly simple targets.'

Concurrently with that, the Underground experienced a financial crisis. 'This was caused by a number of factors moving against us. The recession bit and hit our revenue very hard. Peculiarly, the financial year started buoyantly, because we managed to collect more of our revenue by restructuring the ticket gates. We thought it meant that the macro economic situation wasn't as bad as it was. We were also used to contractors not being able to deliver their contracts and we tended to plan on that, whereas as we went into the recession the cash flow caused contractors to become more efficient. Since they became more efficient at delivering contracts, we spent money faster than we expected.'

Because of the financial crisis LT tried to save money quickly, but it is not an industry that can do anything quickly. 'At the back end of 1990, we said we must understand how to run this business better, so that when we want to save money we can. We initiated a programme of internal review, where we had typically teams of six people (and I think we had about 35 teams altogether) examining ourselves. It emerged by the summer of 1991 we did most things badly. We put in hand a series of improvement programmes to take two years, which we called the Company Plan, that tackled everything we did. We initiated a programme to save about 5,000 staff, to improve our internal cash generation by about £120 million yearly, to improve our safety, and to improve our quality, all of which we have done.'

Over the same period LU evolved its management structure so that line general managers (a position created in 1988), took on responsibility for all the assets on their lines and the maintenance of those assets. They became self-sufficient, with a high degree of accountability, and they became very focused on engineering standards.

Says Denis Tunnicliffe, 'Those five years from 1988 were the best five years of my life. You can't spend your whole career trying to become a managing director and then not enjoy it, can you? It is a waste of life, if you do that. From where I stood, we didn't and don't have problems of low morale, because the people I work with, the top 50 people, all tend to have enjoyed promotions during the period I've been here, to have more responsibility, more freedom of action than they have ever dreamed of before, and most of the people who work for me are enjoying themselves. It has really been quite fun.'

Sadly, further down in the system, LU has had problems. 'People have to remember that the events following the King's Cross disaster had less of an impact on people further down. Its impact morale-wise was on the senior management, who effectively and understandably got blamed for it. What the troops felt bad about was when we started managing them. Hitherto it had been very much a self-man-aged workforce. People just turned up, and went home again, they floated through the day. No structure at all. They were shocked when we introduced a corporate management structure, and since then there have been periods of insecurity and uncertainty. I suppose they are worse than for many other people, but not much, because in many ways, sadly, we have been introducing our workers to the level of insecurity which is endemic now in post-Thatcherite England.'

Denis Tunnicliffe admits that LU becomes very anxious about the relatively low morale. 'The lowest point was when we introduced a programme called 'make or buy', which philosophically reviews all our activity and says what do we do, why do we do it, why do we do it ourselves, are we going to do it best ourselves, or could some-body else do it better for us? That programme created uncertainty. We also set about sorting out the problems of our Northern line trains which we are replacing under the Private Finance Initiative. There was an institutionalised insecurity which hit morale. I think we are coming out of that.'

Another thing LU did at that time was to define precisely what it was here for, what its purpose was. 'We call it "the best possible service for all our customers", and then we have a rather technical definition, which is "to maximise the net social benefit within the available terms." That gives us a matrix to measure all our decisions, and to decide whether putting on extra trains is a good or a bad thing, whether to open or close a station early is a good or a bad thing, whether to invest in a particular piece of infrastructure, or train, and so forth. We have been very much involved with getting this matrix right the way through the business and making sure that everybody understands why they are there. In other words, they are there to serve the customer, but against a prosperity criteria, and how we measure the benefit to the customer, and so on. We have that fairly well installed now, and instilled in our management posts. Our man-agers are clear as to what they are there for.'

Before the King's Cross tragedy, LU was being told to save money and given very few other criteria. After King's Cross, management was told to make the Underground safe, deliver a good service and do it cheaply. Denis Tunnicliffe recognizes that there is nothing on which you should spend an infinite amount of resource. Everything has benefits and a cost. The difference between the public sector and the private sector is that in the former there is very little debate. 'In the private sector you deploy output to maximize your return to your shareholders, whereas in the public sector, you are essentially seeking to maximize the benefits you give to your customers. In a sense it is the marketing side, not the production side, which is different.'

The only real problem with the public sector, according to Denis Tunnicliffe, is its owners. 'Owners are funny things. They're remarkably fuzzy thinkers. It has been the tradition in the public sector to ask the owner what he wants – which has not tended to serve the public sector well. Where the public sector has had a clear vision of what it wants to achieve and then put it to the owner, that has been more successful. With respect to transport, one should judge from the owners' actions, and in the past six years these have included the deregulation of buses and the 1993 Railways Act. Both of these policies, broadly speaking, imply that the marketplace will produce a benign result. LU doesn't do that. We have almost gone in the opposite direction. We have said that the benefit we bring to the community will not be capturable at the point of use, in the way that it is useful for the community. So we have to not only put the revenue into the equation, we have to put the benefit that we are bringing to those customers into the equation.'

Broadly speaking, what LU does in making its decisions is to ask what benefit do we bring to our customers, and what does it cost? 'Then we ration out our monies' says Denis Tunnicliffe, 'be they current monies or capital monies, and those which have the best ratios. There is actually no difficulty in comparing cash benefits, cash costs, and non-cash benefits, and sometimes non-cash costs. We have to recognise that there are long-term benefits and measure them.'

LU is an expensive fixed-cost system. It costs a tremendous amount of money just to run it as it is, and it makes sense to run it to maximum capacity. LT wants to increase the level of its services. Its future plans embody a proposal to increase the level of service on the Underground by something like 30%, and to increase the level of services on the buses. Peter Ford says that increasing the level of services improves productivity, because 'the costs rise at nothing like the same rate, as our variable costs are relatively low. There are, of course, areas where we can increase efficiency just by looking harder and longer at every aspect of activity to discover better ways of doing it. Certainly there is scope for cost reduction as well as productivity improvement. We are taking a highly positive view. We want to increase the level of the services. We want to complete the process of correcting the under-investment which took place over a 25-year period between 1960 and 1985. We need a certain level of government support and the funding to do that, but at the end of that period, around 2000, we will reach a point where we become close to self-supporting, in terms of generating profit out of our activities to pay for our own capital programme.'

The fares increases that LT proposes to help achieve these improvements is slightly above the rate of inflation but not hugely so. 'Remember, at the end of that period the service level and frequency will be a lot higher than it is now, a 30 per cent increase. There will be a higher frequency and better quality of service, a more reliable service, fewer breakdowns, fewer signal failures. Also, at the end of that time we can really take our foot off the pedal in terms of price increases and start thinking about getting the prices down. The only factor then would be overcrowding, which already is a problem at certain times, such as at King's Cross in the rush hour. So that would be the limiting factor, but that's a nice problem to have!'

Denis Tunnicliffe admits that there are very few people who actually enter the Underground system in order to enjoy the experience. For most people it is a cost. 'That cost is made up of the fare, but also the investment you make in time, and not only the investment you make in clock time, but the *perceived* time. If you stand seven to a square metre in a train you are physically squashed on all four sides and if you compare that experience with getting on a train where you could sit if you chose to, we reckon that's about a two to one ratio. In other words, a journey seems twice as long when you are crush-loaded as when you are comfortably loaded. If you wait in a ticket queue, it will seem three times as long as if you are walking in an uncrowded area. We have rafts of research that builds up this picture of perceived time. There is also pain in the way you are assaulted by the environment, visually and through your other senses. If LU is dirty, if it feels threatening, if it feels unkempt, visually unpleasant, smelly and so on, I call that pain.

'Then people invest some risk when they board a train – when you do anything you take a risk. Maybe the risk of accident is about 1 in 200 million, compared with an aeroplane where it's about 1 in 2 million, but you have still made that investment. That is what you do to travel.'

Society makes other investments. It currently puts in some subsidy, but it also, according to Denis Tunnicliffe, consumes a part of the environment one way or another, or does some environmental damage. 'When you sum the total transport activity, there is probably a net gain on environmental impact, in the sense we are doing less environmental damage by going on the Underground, than, for instance, going by car. By trying to optimize that total picture, that total cost and bringing it down, you are bringing benefit to the people you serve, which are your customers, but, of course, also the community in which they work. Central London, the City and Westminster are dominated by rail and commuting. Therefore, the employers in those areas are utterly dependent on rail. The effectiveness with which their workforce functions, the price that workforce charges in terms of salary, is a function of their daily travel experience. When we improve the journey for an individual traveller, we are also improving that journey effectively, over a longer period of time, for that person's employer.'

LU customers are not like airline travellers. 'Our customer is, broadly speaking, all-knowing, because the customer is a regular user. We can't deceive customers. They won't do mathematical sums as I have suggested, but if we deliver regular trains, they won't be able to complain about trains. If we don't have major breakdowns, problems or unpleasant-to-look-at environments, or crime or violence, and so on, the customer will appreciate that. It is a pretty but unreal idea that customers will arrive at their desks saying "I was really invigorated by the Tube journey this morning!"'

The objective for Denis Tunnicliffe is to reduce travellers' dissatisfaction to zero. 'The objective of the customer is not to travel, but to get there. Travelling is the price of getting there. If you travel to your aunt in Colchester you may think, I'm looking forward to the drive. I've got my car, my stereo, the sun's out – how nice! I am probably in a good mood by the time I arrive to see my aunt, because of the experience itself. Or you might go InterCity, and say, I'll have breakfast on the way. Very few of our Underground customers are like that. The more the experience is to arrive than to travel, the more the experience will be intrinsically negative, and all you can do is drive down the negativity.'

LU measures the attitudes of tourists and commuters – all the market segments. 'Leisure passengers, with some few exceptions, don't demand capital, because they have the wit to get up after the workers, and travel in a much more random way throughout the day. They do add something to congestion, but they rarely have any significant impact on the morning peak. Tourist and leisure customers merge to some extent. If you go to the theatre by train are you a tourist or a regular customer? If you live in Milton Keynes and you come to London for a day by train, are you a tourist? It's a spectrum. Normally they don't cost us very much. We are now looking at our "floats" during the day. We are backward-looking, because what we have done is reinforce the tradition of public service in a very structured and businesslike way. But we are not in the cost-maximising business, we are in the benefit-maximising business.'

One of the areas LU is looking at is the old traditions of high frequency train services right through the day. 'We are putting frequency up between peaks and at weekends. We are recognizing that Sunday is changing, and becoming a leisure day, not a stop-at-home-and-go-to-church day.

Towards 2000 LU sees its growth centre as leisure and tourism. 'The Jubilee extension opens on March 28th, 1998. We would expect business travel to go up 1 or 2 per cent per annum between now and then, and leisure traffic to go up by more. The opening of the Jubilee Line extension would give us more room for growth but remember that putting up our capacity by 40 per cent is not saying we expect 40 per cent more customers to travel. We're saying we should be providing a better service to some of the passengers who presently travel. For instance, on the Central Line we'll be putting frequencies up in the peak, from twenty-seven trains per hour to thirty-three trains per hour, which is around 20 per cent increase in capacity. That is simply to carry the passengers we carry now more comfortably. Some of these changes are quality improvements.'

The decision making processes LU use are as applicable to the opening hours of a ticket office as they are to renewing a piece of track. The trick is to keep going back to the customer. What is the impact on the customer of their actions? Denis Tunnicliffe says the most important part of the product is the time. 'We can measure what's happening to our infrastructure by what it does to the time people spend travelling.'

What does Denis Tunnicliffe hope to have achieved by the next millennium? 'I hope to have remarkably reduced the dissatisfaction level that accompanies people's daily experience on LU. I want the ambience that people live in to be less negative and to improve what it does to a community. One noticeable area would be an improvement in the workforce, and maybe the attitude of society towards us. The feedback we get is essentially through what politicians, the media and our customers say to us about their experience. In many ways, what we are looking to achieve by 2001 is a satisfactorily refurbished selling machine. It is a machine that should purr, that should be error-free. It should be a machine where people tell a colleague about a delay on the Underground with some surprise, where people think of the other experiences they had that day, not negative thoughts of their LT journey.'

The biggest hassle in achieving that seems likely to be the failure of government support and unnecessary government interference. 'To be fair,' says Tunnicliffe, 'government interference tends to be more irritation than substance, but it creates noise that has to be managed. You know you're in the public sector most severely when you are punished for success. If you make the system run better by getting your people to perform better, government gives you less money. It says, "Well it ran all right didn't it? You don't really need £700 million a year, you're managing quite well." Broadly speaking politicians react to fear, as opposed to any enthusiastic, motivating type of administration. This is very sad. It means they don't tend to take a realistic view of their role. Everything they have done about transport in this country amounts to under 1 per cent of GDP. I think in my career here it has gone down from £8 billion to £4.5 billion across the country. That is absurd.'

The traditional solution, proffered by short-sighted governments without vision, is to set special interest groups against each other. Denis Tunnicliffe agrees. 'If you don't want to spend on the railways you privatize them, because the amount of noise the privatization process produces means you won't notice the fact you've stopped spending money on BR, and BR's infrastructure is decaying at a rate of knots. You are in a virility race up to privatization and you get people to say how little they can run the bits for. In the real world it won't add up, there will be a big hole, and a big mess. Same with setting the roads lobby against the rail lobby. This year, the road programme has been slashed, which is incredibly bad for the economy and the construction industry. Incredibly bad for us all.'

Denis Tunnicliffe hopes and prays a future government would take a more intelligent view. 'It is a national problem, frankly. We are a near-term gratifying nation, we distribute more of our profits than our competitors. We tend to look at the next year's budget. There are very few genuine programmes, either in the industry or in government which have any sense of looking ahead. We've become a nation that looks at its feet, not at the horizon, and until we get our eyes up again, I think we have real problems.'

Should one continue subsidizing? 'Our customer base is quite affluent, and intrinsically it does not need to be subsidised. What needs to be subsidised in the short term is the renewal of the infrastructure system. Once we get that right and the service right, there is no reason why on average, people shouldn't pay what it costs. That's not the same as behaving in a profit-maximising way, where we write off or ignore significant internal costs in running our business. Broadly speaking we ought to be able to pay our way entirely by probably 2001. Hopefully that will give us more freedom.'

Both Denis Tunnicliffe and Peter Ford fervently believe LT is an excellent part of the public sector, because they share common visions about what continuous improvement looks like and how they measure it, making lots and lots of small decisions. Says Denis Tunnicliffe, 'We have 350 capital projects at any one time, and individual managers responsible for doing them. We have major programmes on all nine lines to improve their performance, all centred around the key of the best possible service for all our customers.

'I don't make decisions or do things, I create environments where other people make decisions and do things. It's seeing all these things bubbling together.'

Tunnicliffe thinks the human soul likes to evolve. 'In practice, all any of us can really achieve is improving the processes. But improving processes isn't really exciting, so we have invented a goal. If you want me to describe what a decent modern LT metro would be like in the millennium, I would say it would be basically as good as the best in the world, recognizing the inherited assets. We're not going to make the Tube trains bigger or the platforms longer, because that would simply not be a cost effective thing to do. But given the fact we're going to have small trains and short platforms, there's no reason why we shouldn't run them as well as any metro system in the world from every aspect. That requires a lot of cash and numerous years of continuous improvement programmes with our people. That is the vision but it's not a goal I guess you would ever really get to. As one approached it, one would want to kick out and run beyond it, because the real value to the customer is that this year we do it better than last year, and next year we should be doing it better than this. If you stop doing that you are saying that we've arrived. But arriving is an impossible, unstable position to be at. One is really looking to move, move, move.'

THE MARKS & SPENCER GROUP

Worldwide

Turnover (1994–95)	£6.8 billion
Group profit before tax	£924.3 million
Number of stores	638
Number of franchise shops	73
Number of employees	63,000

Europe's most profitable retailer, with a worldwide reputation for quality, value and service. In 1994–95 the group sold more than £5.3 billion of British-made goods, production of which provided employment for over 100,000 people in the UK.

Sir Richard Greenbury – Chairman

Sir Richard Greenbury joined M&S in 1953 as a junior management trainee. He became a full Director in 1972, and joint Managing Director in 1978. He was appointed Chief Operating Officer in 1986, Chief Executive Officer in 1988 and Chairman in 1991.

Other appointments:
    1992 Non-Executive Director of Imperial Chemical Industries PLC.
    1993 Non-Executive Director of Zeneca Group following demerger of ICI.
    1993 Director of Lloyds Bank PLC.
    Former director of British Gas Corporation and of Metal Box PLC.
    Chairman of CORDA, the heart charity, and patron of the Samaritans.

The Company

Marks & Spencer began in 1884 as a stall in Leeds Market.

Outside the UK it now has wholly-owned stores in France, the Netherlands, Belgium, the Republic of Ireland, Hong Kong and North America as well as franchises in eighteen countries worldwide. Five stores in Spain are run in partnership with Cortefiel, a well-known Spanish retailer. The company has recently announced its intention to open stores in Germany.

In April 1995, the Group won the Queen's Award for Export Achievement for the fourth time.

Marks & Spencer PLC
Sir Richard Greenbury
Chairman

Every week millions of shoppers visit the 711 Marks & Spencer [M&S] stores, subsidiaries and franchise shops around the world. Delivering the M&S shopping experience to customers on three continents is a huge enterprise and the group is presently Europe's most profitable retailer. Developing merchandise of the highest quality, offering outstanding value and providing good customer service, have always been the cornerstone principles of the group's growth and success.

M&S stores and franchise shops are becoming an increasingly familiar sight in leading cities across Europe, North America and the Far East. Last year overseas sales accounted for 14 per cent of the group's total turnover – an excellent result in view of the relatively sluggish levels of consumer demand encountered throughout Europe and North America. Its UK store development programme continues to add to the scale and quality of its property base. Last year some £230 million was invested in 400,000 sq. ft. of new selling area. Over 75 per cent of the UK's population now lives within a 45-minute drive of one of its edge-of-town stores.

Sales of St Michael foods in the UK increased by almost 5 per cent on a like-for-like basis and despite strong competition the company remains streets ahead in several key areas. It is the market leader in hot meat pies, desserts, and one of the world's leading retailers of fresh strawberries. Its Kenyan runner beans reach UK stores within two days of harvest, it is the largest retailer of cut flowers in the UK and one in ten households sits down to an M&S Christmas lunch. Eighty-five million pairs of ladies' briefs are sold every year, one in ten pairs of ladies' shoes in the UK is bought from M&S and 2,500 men's shirts are sold every hour. Last year the company received the

British Fashion Council's award for the top retailer of classic clothing, the first time a chain store has ever been honoured in this way.

In the eyes of its customers M&S is a professionally managed, financially robust and highly profitable business, dynamically but prudently investing in the future. It sticks to a tried and tested retailing formula with its principles of high quality, value-for-money products and good service, developed over more than a hundred years.

Sir Richard Greenbury is the chairman. He has the reputation of being one of the UK's most pugnacious business leaders. You would think, with all Marks & Spencers success, that it was unassailable. Sir Richard, however, knows his company cannot afford to be arrogant. Whatever the St Michael brand guarantees, it cannot take customer loyalty for granted. As he puts it: 'The days when it was easy to make profits are over. Today's consumer wants everything, not just value for money. They want the right products in the right colour.'

As chairman he has guided his company through the worst recession in the post-war years and come through that time with an increase in profits of almost 50 per cent. That is some achievement – will it continue? 'Of course no one knows what retailing will be like in the future,' says Sir Richard. 'I can only speak from my experience of over forty years in the industry and my observations of current trends. Successful retailing depends on anticipating consumer demand and responding effectively. Today things are much tougher and retailers are forced to review their operations to improve efficiency and cut costs.'

The response at M&S at the beginning of the recession was to take a number of steps to safeguard their future: 'We significantly reduced stocks and commitments in order to limit the capital involved in running our business and, more importantly, through faster stockturn to become more responsive to sales trends.'

M&S also vigorously progressed the benefits of its substantial investments in new operating systems and IT, resulting in improved staff productivity, greater efficiency and better consumer service. 'But most importantly' says Sir Richard, 'despite flat trading, we did not lose our nerve and resort, like many traders, to discounting or holding additional sales to stimulate volume growth. We maintained our gross margins and profitability while ensuring our goods, at full price, represented good quality and value to our customers. We succeeded in maintaining our selling-price/value integrity with consumers, which in the long run is fundamental, I believe, for retailing success.' The key to this, Sir Richard believes, was their partnership with their suppliers. 'It is, of course, always in their interests to help us to increase sales, as it means bigger volumes for them. They worked with us to simplify the production of certain lines. We were able to negotiate lower prices on 25 per cent of our lines, while our others remained at the same selling price as the previous year.'

The M&S clothing supply base is 80 per cent British which gives the group the advantage of a short pipeline. This allows them the flexibility to fine-tune their fashion business and control end-of-season reductions more tightly. This same British supply base gave M&S a special advantage when the pound was low against the dollar. Says Sir Richard, 'Those retailers importing heavily from economies based on the dollar – such as those in the Far East – had to choose between cutting their margins or increasing their prices. In this context our prices, which already represented excellent value, looked even keener. We survived the recession in a strong position to build sales. How glad I am that through thick and thin, we have always taken the long-term view, ignored the short-term easy buck and remained loyal to our unique retailer-supplier relationship. At M&S we are good marketers, but we don't make things; so the people that make things for us have to be the best in the world. Our suppliers are.'

Last year M&S made further UK investment in excess of £55m in new information systems and equipment. Sir Richard insists that IT improves efficiency and reduces costs. The point-of-sale and replenishment systems enable the stores to re-order goods faster and more accurately, improving availability of merchandise and thus benefiting the customer. High-tech cash-counting and handling equipment serving clusters of stores has been installed. 'Within our distribution centres, we are rolling out new, virtually paperless administration systems built around barcode scanning and radio communication. These not only improve efficiency and reduce inventory, they release time for stock to be prepared at the distribution centre then taken straight to the sales floor from the delivery vehicle. Space and staff once devoted to stock rooms are therefore released to the sales floor. While the costs of developing systems and purchasing the hardware are substantial, over the years our investment has proved cost-effective, as the initial expenditure is offset by productivity gains throughout the business.'

Sir Richard feels IT is opening up exciting possibilities in retailing. Store and Switch cards already provide convenient ways of paying for goods, and point-of-sale equipment provides continuous accurate information for the retailer. This is only the beginning for the electronic revolution in retailing. 'Hassle-free shopping is coming in which customers walk round the store with hand-held electronic devices enabling them to access information about products that interest them. At the touch of a button they will be able to earmark and pay for goods which will be collected behind the scenes and delivered to the customers' cars or to their homes. If this is done imaginatively, it will provide easy shopping without completely losing the human interaction which is a key element of traditional retailing. All these developments will be taken seriously by us – and whatever else comes along, such as home shopping via the TV screen. They will not all be for us. We will want to be satisfied that these innovations can live up to our customers' expectations of us and offer them a fair deal. For instance, we didn't rush to introduce Switch cards but waited until we had completed trials in our stores and had negotiated a deal with the banks that didn't saddle us with costs that had to be passed on to all customers.'

Today, Sir Richard believes the factors are in place for continuing recovery. 'Inflation is the lowest for twenty-seven years – and steady. Although there is continued uncertainty about interest rates, they are nevertheless low and seem unlikely to rise significantly. Manufacturing output is high. Growth in GDP is the highest it has been for five years. Productivity is rising. Unemployment, although still high, seems to be falling. The only brake on the system is lack of confidence. Customers are wary of spending, which is not really surprising after what they have been through. I am no economist, but I feel sure this wariness will continue towards the millennium and the economic improvement will be gradual.' He thinks replacement expenditure is now the order of the day until some new technology creates demand for a particular new product. 'I believe the spending habits learnt in recession will continue to operate. Consumers will become even more skilled in their purchasing decisions, looking for newness, choice and value for money, insisting on precisely the products they want and making careful judgements of quality, service and value.'

Sir Richard says we are now entering a new phase in retailing. Customers expect shopping to be an enjoyable experience – at least to be quick and trouble-free so we have more time for our leisure pursuits. For these reasons Sir Richard believes the public will become sophisticated shoppers, and this will call for a sophisticated response from retailers. 'With late-evening shopping and some shops staying open round the clock, seven days a week, I believe the UK is now effectively over-shopped. In a climate of restrained spending all retailers must work to survive. To be really successful in these circumstances calls for a high degree of professionalism.'

What about the product – apart from the importance of having the goods the customers want? Sir Richard talks about 'winning with style'. M&S's 'Outstanding Value Campaign' has been continuing since 1992 and remains a key element of the group's strategy towards 2000. The policy of offering high quality goods at constant good value-for-money prices has helped to build sales in nearly all merchandise areas. In 1994, this approach was extended to Continental Europe and particularly France, where turnover responded immediately with significant volume increases. Sir Richard knows that customers increasingly demand fashion and newness: 'Meeting these needs while maintaining high standards is our driving force. The exploitation of IT in both purchasing and stock replenishment coupled with increased responsiveness by our suppliers has allowed us to extend fast-selling lines more quickly and to a greater number of stores. Customer store ordering has been developed further and complements the improved distribution, which better satisfies our customers. In this new age of sophistication the retailer must move quickly, but to do this he needs to work in partnership with his suppliers. M&S with its long established relationships with a world-class supply base has an immense advantage here for the millennium.'

Sir Richard suggests, as we move towards 2000, that retailers will try a variety of ways of increasing sales while trying to protect their profits. Will the battle be fought over price? 'Many retailing developments in the UK originated in the USA, arriving here about ten years later,' he says. 'In the States, discounting is a way of life and you might expect American-style warehouse clubs and factory outlets to make a killing here. But the situation is very different in the two countries. The cost of retail land is higher in the UK and it will be difficult for these operators to obtain the sites they need for stores and car parking and still make a profit. At the same time, manufacturers' brands are dominant in the States while private labels are much stronger here, so discounting is more difficult in this country. Hard discounting has definitely arrived here, however, and will reinforce the value-consciousness of customers but I don't think it will pose a serious threat to the quality end of the retail market – just keep us on our toes!'

Turning now to an obsession of his – property: if the battle is not to be fought over price, does Sir Richard think it may be fought over space? 'The scale of opening stores in the second half of the eighties was amazing: almost thirty million square feet of shopping centre space was opened, 250 retail parks and four regional centres like the Metrocentre in Gateshead. In the last five years, M&S, too, has seen its UK store chain change and evolve. In 1990, M&S had 266 stores and 9.1 million square feet located mainly in high streets and city centres. Today it has 283 mainland stores covering 11 million square feet and is modernizing existing major stores as well as opening new edge-of-town ones. It is also expanding stores in smaller regional centres, especially in areas where the local authority is committed to managing and upgrading the town centre. Says Sir Richard, 'There are tremendous opportunities in this country and the idea that we can't grow our business here is absolutely wrong. As we extend and modernize our stores we are seizing the opportunity to refine and tailor ourselves to local requirements and expectations. This recognizes that most of the customers who shop in our local high street stores each week want everyday and casual clothing, underwear and foods. The tendency in our smaller and medium-sized stores is to show products which are of interest to customers who want to shop as close to home as possible for foods, toiletries, hosiery, basic skirts, jumpers and underwear. Our customers do understand that their local 10,000 sq.ft. store can't possibly have the range available at Marble Arch. When they plan a major purchase therefore, such as a new suit or sofa, they tend to travel to one of our regional centre stores for a larger choice. As part of our extensions and renovations we are ensuring that stores are accessible for all our customers, including elderly people and those with specific needs. All our newer stores have lifts and ramps to assist our disabled customers, and we are working to include similar provisions in our older stores. Baby-changing facilities are now incorporated into our larger stores wherever space permits. We are currently adding new space at a more rapid rate than for many years, and we envisage maintaining our UK development programme at similar levels towards the year 2000.'

Sir Richard believes however that a recent Department of the Environment change of policy will mean that there will be a brake on out-of-town development. 'Businesses in town centres will have to stop complaining about out-of-town complexes and start getting their acts together. Many will realize that they can compete because they can offer comparison shopping not available out-of-town; and they can exploit their heritage to provide leisure trips which combine shopping and eating out with sightseeing. The partnership approach to town centre management is already successfully tackling the problems of access, parking, amenities, cleanliness and security. Some towns will manage to draw people back to the traditional high street. I think, however, the real battle will not be over the price of goods or the position of shops but over service – in the widest sense of the word.'

By 'service' Sir Richard doesn't just mean having friendly, knowledgeable and well-trained staff – vital though this is. As he explains, 'Much good service is unseen by the customer. It's the work that goes on behind the scenes to buy the right goods and make sure the store is not out of stock of what the customers want. The sophisticated retailer will use his IT systems not just to replace purchases accurately and speedily but also to inform buying decisions on a continuous basis. But this is just the beginning. For the future, successful retailers will sharpen their competitive edge by making the shopping experience easier or more pleasant. Out-of-town centres, for instance, will exploit their superior facilities for car-borne shoppers to provide family-oriented, one-stop shopping with children's play areas, restaurants and entertainment. They will add to the existing car-related services like petrol stations and introduce motor accessories, car maintenance or even car sales.'

Sir Richard believes that all retailers will have to take account of the growing number of older people in the population. They will need to build comfort and convenience into their stores – like easier-to-manoeuvre shopping trolleys, lifts and clearer signage – which of course benefits us all, but are essential for the elderly.

He also believes retailers will have to poach other areas of consumer spending – financial services, catering, probably also estate agency, travel agency, hairdressing and post offices. For example: 'The Marks & Spencer Financial Services business is very successful and growing fast and we have in the last year entered two new fields – pensions and life assurance. The key to such diversification is choosing areas which exploit the retailer's reputation and expertise and enhance the retailer's image and over the last ten years or so, we have proved that the M&S principles are just as relevant in financial services as in clothing, home furnishings or food.'

As an increasingly global business, M&S requires an expanding international supply base. It remains the policy wherever possible to support the industries of the countries where it trades. It sold £5.3 billion of British-made goods – nearly 80 per cent of total sales – last year, providing continued employment for well over 100,000 people in the UK. The international factor to M&S is vital towards the year 2000. As Sir Richard says, 'As international travel and global media increasingly shape culture and taste worldwide, the products and colours that sell well in the UK are similarly successful elsewhere. Sophisticated IT systems have been a major factor in enabling us to identify what international markets differ on or have in common. For example, all over the world people are growing taller and heavier but there are still enormous national differences so we are adapting our ranges for world markets where we cater for both the average Dutch woman who stands 5'9" tall and the average Spanish or Asian woman who reaches about 5'2".'

Towards the millennium Marks & Spencer will be adding volume to quality, value and service worldwide. Its objective is to develop a truly mainstream volume retail business in all the countries where it trades, and is clustering stores in metropolitan areas to achieve efficiencies of scale. Sir Richard tantalizing talks about M&S's expansion plans. 'We will build up our biggest UK stores to be "Marks & Spencer department stores", with large clothing departments, food halls, home furnishing shops, garden centres, financial services and, in some cases, restaurants. We see great potential to expand all sizes of unit in the UK, and the bulk of our business will remain here for the foreseeable future, but we have taken the view that for long-term growth in the next century, we must take our tried-and-tested retail formula overseas. We are already well-established abroad but we have plans to expand, particularly on the continent, and are looking at the possibility of going into mainland China. We have a representative office in the People's Republic of China to explore in more depth the potential for development in mainland China. We know what the prizes are, what we're looking at now are the problems. I know we've got what that country wants, but whether we can overcome the problems that far away and make a reasonable profit for shareholders is another matter. That's something we've got to assess.

'We have appointed a divisional director to consider, amongst other issues, how best to manage our growing our international procurement requirements and this will almost certainly be conducted in tandem with many of our long-established UK suppliers who are already active in the Far East. Can I add, the Pacific contains five of our twenty franchise customers, who are rapidly expanding their businesses. There are now franchisees in the Philippines, Singapore, Indonesia, Malaysia and Thailand, operating twenty-three stores selling a comprehensive range of our merchandise. The Far East has to be an enormous opportunity for M&S. You are talking about 2 billion people: they are all going to be consumers one day. Around the world, we're talking about a business which we believe we can build into the millennium.'

I want to include Sir Richard's views on the management and conduct of both the board and the boardroom in UK companies. 'The most important factor governing a successful board meeting is obviously the quality of the board itself. Commitment must head the agenda. If the members of the board are all people with a strong commitment to the company – and a real knowledge and experience of its operations – then constructive discussion will be possible and sound decisions can be reached. The balance of the board is crucial and requires the right number of "heavyweight" non-executive directors to bring in an independent viewpoint and experienced judgement and knowledge not available within the company. They must have a range of skills, complementary to the expertise of those who have made their careers within the business.'

Sir Richard believes board meetings must be well-organized, held at regular points in the calendar with the dates agreed formally six months ahead so that no one misses a meeting other than for exceptional reasons. There should be a clear agenda determined by the chairman and all relevant papers should be circulated in good time in order that everyone comes to the meeting fully prepared. 'Board meetings must not be solemn affairs although they should always be business-like. There is a place for humour in the boardroom which helps one and all to keep a sense of proportion. Everyone should respect the authority of the chairman, but there is no need for every remark to be addressed "through the chair" as this will tend to stifle discussion. In arriving at clear, agreed policy decisions the discussion must be completely free; indeed the more controversial the better, provided it is within the bounds of courtesy.' Once a formal decision is reached, the directors are bound to abide by it. 'It is important they *all* give full and whole-hearted support. Minority views must be forgotten and for this reason every member of the board needs to voice his or her opinion before the final decision, particularly if it is contentious.'

Sir Richard thinks full board meetings should be confined, as far as possible, to taking strategic and policy decisions: 'Short, separate weekly meetings of executive directors can discuss things that would clog up a full board meeting, including the current progress of the business, any topical issues and the day-to-day running of the company.' He says, 'There is no absolute magic formula. Every company has its own culture and metabolism, and different types of business require separate styles of management. Nevertheless, all board meetings have the same objectives and responsibilities towards shareholders, staff and customers, and therefore must be conducted with total integrity as well as efficiency.'

One other area that Sir Richard has strong views is his belief that a healthy business needs a healthy community in which to grow and prosper. Each year M&S invests part of its profits to improve the quality of life for the communities in which it trades. Sir Richard sees this increasing. With the enthusiastic participation of its staff, M&S shares its experience and know-how through secondment, supporting various causes, working to promote health, care for the elderly or the sick, and providing funding for education and the arts. M&S commitment starts at the top with board members hosting several Seeing is Believing visits during the year, which are mentioned in more detail in the chapter on 'Business in the Community'. M&S is a founder member of Business in the Community and these visits take business leaders to see for themselves the needs of charities and the difference the involvement of companies like M&S can make. An example would be the secondment of David Leigh, formerly the manager of M&S's Chelmsford store, to Crime Concern during which he set up the Ealing Community Safety Partnership. The Partnership has identified and begun tackling the safety and security issues that concerned local people. This M&S secondment proved so successful that Ealing has created a permanent position of Manager of the Community Safety Partnership. Another secondee is helping with Youth Works, a partnership between Crime Concern, M&S and Groundwork, supported by the Leopold Muller estate. It aims to reduce crime through environmental projects on housing estates in Blackburn, Hackney, Plymouth and Sunderland.

As Sir Richard puts it, 'Wherever M&S people go around the world they take with them the company's cultures and values, which increasingly means social and environmental involvement. We have always acknowledged corporate responsibility to society and the environment. We are increasingly committed to helping the communities in which we operate, and we support projects which we believe make a positive contribution to the environment. Last year, we donated a quarter of a million pounds to the hospice movement and committed £1 million in resources to education. Towards the year 2000 we will give increasing practical help and advice to organizations which are trying to make our towns and cities attractive and vibrant places, and we will continue to run our business with proper concern for the impact our operations have on the natural environment.'

Increasingly, M&S is minimizing the use of packaging across the business. Over 90 per cent of its transit packaging is now re-used and every year it recycles over 16,000 tonnes of used packaging. Recently it started a scheme to re-use unwanted plastic garment hangers and with the help of the customers it is currently recycling 20 million hangers annually. These are cleaned by a specialist contractor and returned to M&S's suppliers for re-use. M&S expect this programme to double in size in the next year, saving some 1,200 tonnes of plastic.

Sir Richard is committed to continuing investing in people and training. 'With an overwhelmingly female staff, we are concerned to ensure that the talents and abilities of all are recognized to the full. Currently, over 50 per cent of management are women and the proportion of women in senior management is increasing all the time. In recent years, the average trading week has lengthened and many of our stores are now open more than seventy hours a week. This has required greater flexibility in our working patterns which have to be better designed to benefit both our staff, many of whom choose working hours to fit in with their family commitments, and our customers, especially working women who are unable to shop during the standard working day.' With today's long hours in retailing and the growth of Sunday trading it is becoming harder to recruit the calibre of people needed at all levels. Sir Richard appreciates that fewer people stay with a company for any length of time now compared with the seventies and eighties. Has he found it is much more difficult to find dedicated staff at every level than M&S used to? 'Success is a big issue and it attracts people – but it does not necessarily keep them. Of course, you have to pay people well, that is vital. And you have got to give them all the necessary support, such as caring for them if they are away sick. Career progression is important, the belief that into the next century this business will give them opportunities to exercise their talents and make progress.'

Training and development has always been a key business function throughout M&S, and commercial business-based programmes cover store management and head office staff, from new recruits right through to the most senior positions. Sir Richard says that increasingly 'these programmes will incorporate an international dimension as more M&S careers include periods working outside the home countries.'

Sir Richard is fond of quoting Simon Marks, and a favourite is that 'Sales are for vanity. Profits are for sanity.' He hopes this will be the hallmark of his reign. As chairman and chief executive, is there not a suggestion there is a great concentration of power in a single pair of hands? Sir Richard will deny this, insisting, like his hero Harry Truman, on 'surrounding myself with good people and listening to what they say'. His famed directness and his imposing presence with a broad-shouldered 6'2" frame could be alarming to some of those he meets in the stores which he visits every week but, advocating his keenness for listening and open debate, he holds regular monthly meetings with a dozen junior employees, most of them only in their twenties, to hear what they think about the company and how it can be improved. He is at his happiest striding around the shop floors, talking to his sales assistants and the customers, and always spends Fridays and part of Saturdays in the stores. 'We have 14 million customers each week, and they tell you whether you have got it right or wrong. I spend so much time in the store because that is the only place to find out what the customer thinks of you. And at the end of the day the customer is king.' He admits his favourite job was as a shop manager in the Marble Arch store in the late fifties: 'I was near the customers and the goods, and this is the most exciting part of the business.'

Sir Richard is a man who totally knows the business he is in. 'There is no substitute for knowing every part of the business. Good judgement comes with experience and takes time to acquire.' He is very much a hands-on boss; at a one-to-one meeting he is certainly amiable, courteous and even shy. However, Sir Richard is also a man who has never backed away from anything in his life. He will not be frightened off and can be extremely blunt. He admits to being too forthright: 'I upset people sometimes. I don't mean to but it's my nature. I am a Yorkshire man.' Blunt, he may be, but his counsel and care for the company and his employees, and especially his suppliers, plus his customer commitment, are truly one hundred per cent. He is not a corporate Attila.

He is notoriously wary of the press and the City and can be contemptuous of City reactions to his sales figures and profitability. He often believes the press give unfair criticism and there are many bruised souls in the press and the City who know that he reads any criticism they produce of the company as criticism of himself. He prefers to listen to his customers rather than to other commentators.

Even when M&S doesn't get it right, which it sometimes doesn't we, the customers, still come back and visit its shops every week. Why do we do that? It must be because deep down we believe they are honest traders. A stickler for tradition, Sir Richard will steer his company towards the millennium, scrupulously sticking to the very deeply-rooted pioneering principles of M&S – recruiting high-calibre staff, providing a quality product, good service and value for money. Sir Richard's words go ringing in your ears as you leave his company. 'Quality and value; that's what people want.'

And how would Sir Richard like to be remembered? 'I'll quote Harry Truman, when he was sent for to be told he was going to be sworn in as President of America. He said he would do the job to the best of my ability. I hope people will say of me that I did the job to the best of my ability. That's all you can do.'

MIRROR GROUP PLC

Turnover (1994)	£463.0 million
Operating Profit	£116.1 million
Profit before tax	£84.7 million
Total fixed assets (inc. investments)	£1039.5 million
Employees (full-time)	2,785

Leading publisher of popular daily and Sunday newspapers in the UK, with strategic investments in the *Independent* and *Independent on Sunday* (43%) and Scottish Television (20%). Majority shareholder and operator of Live TV, a cable exclusive entertainment channel.

David Montgomery – Chief Executive

Appointed as Chief Executive of Mirror Group Newspapers, London, in October 1992.

Other appointments:
1991 Director of London Live Television Ltd.
1992 Director of Caledonian Newspaper Publishing Ltd.
1992 Non-executive Director or Donohue Inc., Canada.
1994 Director of Newspaper Publishing.
1994 Director of Mirror Television.
1995 Director of Scottish Television PLC
Business in three main areas:

Popular Newspapers:
Daily Mirror, Sunday Mirror, People, Scottish Daily Record, Sunday Mail, Sporting Life.

Broadsheet Newspapers:
43% owner and services provider to *Independent* and *Independent on Sunday*.

Television:
90% owner and operator of Live TV, a nationally distributed cable exclusive entertainment channel; 16% shareholding in STV PLC.

264

Mirror Group PLC
David Montgomery, Chief
Executive

The rise and fall and rise again of Mirror Group Newspapers in the second half of the twentieth century was not only a story of the changing world, revolutionary print processes and distribution systems, it was the extraordinary story of two men. One – responsible for the once great publishing empire, former Member of Parliament, one time bankrupt, one time NCO, one time central European entrepreneur, friend of heads of State – was Robert Maxwell, who used his company pension fund to prop up his ailing company. The other is David Montgomery, who is trying to resurrect the company after Maxwell mysteriously drowned from his private yacht.

Maxwell really did nothing to the newspaper business, either good or bad. That is perhaps the legacy that he would least like to have assigned to him. He interfered a bit, but his corrupt (with a capital C) régime was awkwardly echoed by a corrupt (with a lower case c) approach to the operation of the newspaper as a business. It seemed to us on the outside that it fitted in with the rather carefree lifestyle of the people who were there.

David Montgomery has been chief executive of the Mirror Group since 1992. He filled senior roles on both the *Daily* and *Sunday Mirror* night desks before moving to News International where he was chief sub-editor of the *Sun*. He returned to the Mirror Group as assistant editor of the *People* in 1982, then returned to the *News of the World*. He was editor of the *News of the World* when *The Times* moved to Wapping, and he was both editor and managing director of *Today*. I recall he was running these great businesses with a degree of autonomy which much annoyed Rupert Murdoch. 'He let me get away with it for a number of years,' admits David Montgomery, 'because I was, I suppose, on the fringe, and therefore as I made some progress he did leave me alone. Maxwell offered me jobs, including the *Daily Mirror* editorship which I had previously coveted, but I didn't take any of them. That was not any sort of foresight, they just were not right at the time. The experience I got in an entrepreneurial company was obviously going to be applied at some stage of my career. Then Maxwell died and I was contacted by friends in the City and asked to put together a bid for the *Mirror*. It was as though I had been preparing for the moment for many years. Here I was, in 1992, back in my old company, which I had left in 1980 through sheer frustration.'

David Montgomery believes the Mirror Group had been kept together by a handful of people who were supremely dedicated to the business and got on with it regardless of the corruption, inefficiency and extreme behaviour of some of its free-living inhabitants. Fortunately, it had key directors who were doing their jobs and holding the whole fabric of the company together. Despite what was going on, and had gone on, they were not engaging in any of the excesses of some of their colleagues. Says David Montgomery, 'I suppose if it hadn't been for that core of people then the company really would have collapsed. Everybody was swamped by this culture of what can only be described as more social life than being at work. It suited Maxwell's style perfectly, because, you know, he would buy and sell people. Many of the people who were proclaiming to be serving the cause of socialism through the *Mirror* were, in fact, only using it as an excuse to preserve their own cosy positions. Certainly many of the people who left in the wake of the new management's change did so amid hypocrisy, bitterness and jealousy.'

David Montgomery's arrival and overhaul of the company necessitated redundancies. 'It wasn't particularly skilful,' he says, 'just realizing that there had to be discipline. The fact that we have reformed the company and we've become efficient and more profitable, confirms we are on the way.'

Certainly the last year has been one of considerable progress for the group, in spite of the continuing cut-price activity of the competition. While an unprecedented price war was raging in the newspaper market the Mirror Group had trading margins that actually rose, and the company is now in a healthy shape, able to put the Maxwell years behind it. With an improved financial position the group is expanding. In 1994 it acquired a 43 per cent share in the *Independent* and the *Independent on Sunday*, helping to draw in an upmarket constituency of readers in addition to its narrow tabloid base. It purchased an almost 20 per cent interest in Scottish Television PLC and also in Scotland, where it has market leadership, its newspaper circulation increased substantially as readers warmed positively to editorial reforms and aggressive advertising promotions. With the development of Live TV, the successor to London Live TV, founded in 1991 by David Montgomery, it has announced its intention to progress in the cable TV market towards the millennium. The group's core newspapers – *Sunday Mail, Daily Record*, the *People, Sunday Mirror* and *Daily Mirror* – have all achieved what Sir Robert Clark, the Mirror Group's chairman, calls, in the circumstances of last year 'an outstanding performance'. These circumstances included the cut-price newspaper battleground which occurred in Britain in 1994–1995 and the marketplace also became highly competitive when all other national newspaper groups made a bid to increase their sales by heavy spending on promotions and editorial resources. Despite a price disadvantage in daily markets, all eight titles in the *Mirror* stable actually increased sales year on year in May, June and July 1995.

For David Montgomery, the preparation done in getting the company under control helped in resisting the price war. 'We know that Rupert Murdoch was very surprised we did not buckle under the strain of that competition,' says David Montgomery. 'Indeed I don't believe he understands that the *Independent* has been kept going on a much lower cost base than anything he's been able to do or whether indeed it is possible to produce anything at such a low cost base. There must be surprise at how that newspaper hasn't gone under. It is regrettable, of course, that a lot of the efficiencies we made would have, in normal circumstances, generated huge profit growth. We've been more or less at standstill, but being at standstill in a competitive market and rising newsprint prices of the like not seen in a lifetime, is impressive.'

The effects of newsprint rises are having to be absorbed internally through further cost efficiencies. This has occurred, in part, by completely rehabilitating the newspapers technologically. In the group, productivity is up 30 per cent and staff is down 20 per cent. Says David Montgomery, 'We must always aim for continuous improvement of editorial. The production side is now pretty efficient and is approaching full utilization. The big area that needs to be tackled is the distribution of newspapers. As publishers in a modern interactive age, we need to have closer relationship with the reader.'

What Montgomery has done is to identify individual management to be associated with individual titles. 'Essentially our newspapers were rebuilt around the editor and by staff grouped to work together as a team to give the papers strong individual personalities and develop them. The *People* had dropped a million copies in circulation. In 1970 it had dropped another million copies, it dropped another million copies in the eighties, and it was dropping at 15 per cent a year. Now that paper has been reformed to one which is up substantially year on year. We know what was a 15 per cent decline in 1991 is now a seven or eight per cent increase year on year.'

The *People* has, in fact, increased its market share to just over 16 per cent of the Sunday tabloid market. This revival as a popular Sunday family newspaper with two magazines every week is an example of where improved editorial quality has enhanced the paper's attractiveness to advertisers as well as readers. With an enhanced sports service, consumer features and a core of what David Montgomery calls 'compelling popular journalism' it has reversed the long-term trend of decline. The improvements in the *People*, he believes, should gain recognition in terms of continuing increased revenue and excellence towards the year 2000.

Research has shown that readers have a great sense of loyalty for, and belief in, the group's mass tabloid title, the *Daily Mirror*. As David Montgomery says, readers believe in its credentials as a newspaper that represents them. 'It campaigns and crusades on their behalf with the *Daily Mirror* having the highest home delivery of any UK mass tabloid title – 35 per cent versus the *Sun*'s 26 per cent giving the former a measure of stability.' This has been an impressive showing, maintaining circulation in the fiercest price war the newspaper industry has ever seen. Last year alone the *Daily Mirror* was recognized for its increasing quality by winning awards ranging from the National Newspaper Editor of the Year in the Newspaper Press Awards, to Sports Reporter of the Year at the Sports Council Press Awards, to its industrial editor being voted Industrial Correspondent of the Year in the British Press Awards and its long-term agony columnist, Marje Proops, receiving a British Press Award for her outstanding services to journalism.

The *Daily Record* remains dominant in Scotland's popular daily market, commanding almost 55 per cent of total sales. A staggering one in every two adults in Scotland reads the newspaper daily and such statistics confirm the newspaper's remarkable penetration of the

Scottish population. It has a proud tradition of campaigning, honest and hard-hitting journalism and last year this achievement was recognized in the Bank of Scotland Press Awards with a *Daily Record* team winning the Campaigning Writer of the Year. From the same stable emanates the *Sunday Mail*, commanding a unique position as the leading paper in the Scottish Sunday market. The success of the *Sunday Mail*, according to David Montgomery, derives from its long-standing reputation for consistently delivering quality and for exposing public scandals. Certainly it seems as though the very fabric of Scottish society is bound up in its pages and it is another example of the strength of editorial integrity and individualism being pursued under the audit of Montgomery.

However, great newspapers are not made from one individual. He has rebuilt the *Mirror*, for example, by 'giving it a stronger personality, and the professionalism is better. It has got more of a unique quality and in the middle of that, surprisingly some might say, it's much more commercial. We have a professional operation and are well-focused: all the constituents seem to be right. In the past, it was a sort of club, mainly a boys' club, strangely enough, or maybe not strangely! That sort of attitude has been replaced with a much wider ranging approach to journalism. I suppose it is a particular hobby-horse of mine because I think journalists in the last two decades have been devalued. They have been pigeon-holed in a newspaper structure which allowed people to vegetate in the same job for years and years and didn't promote their careers. So a bunch of bright young people mainly turned into prematurely middle-aged men, not in control of their careers.'

The Mirror Group is putting greater effort into attracting and training new staff. 'We have already recruited a lot of new people who are contributing well but we have to continue the process of upgrading the talent base,' says Montgomery. 'We have re-established a graduate trainee programme, and it is much more pertinent than it was in the past. We have multi-skilled journalists who can write, edit, use video cameras and have onscreen interview abilities.' He believes as you build media companies you must challenge the staff and spread their skills across more products. 'To achieve that therefore you need a higher calibre of very adaptable, flexible, intelligent people. It needs a high calibre of person. It is as simple as that. If you like, as discriminatory as that. The net result is that there will be better paid, higher skilled, more fulfilled journalists putting out a bigger range of products at less cost.'

It was the *Mirror* that broke the story of former Prime Minister Margaret Thatcher's memoirs, which was undoubtedly one of the scoops of last year. Sir David English, of the *Daily Mail*, and possibly the most successful editor in the second half of the twentieth century, made this assessment of the new *Daily Mirror*: 'The Thatcher scoop was symbolic of the new *Mirror*. It is back in business as a serious newspaper after many years in the comic wilderness.' Says David Montgomery, 'It doesn't matter what the subject base is, the *Mirror* does a very professional job. It gets the story. It has helped drive the new Labour Party into being – remember the *Mirror* broke with the past first and challenged the old Labour Party. In doing so we were criticized by hundreds of Labour MPs at the time. We challenged old attitudes and made it in some ways easier for first John Smith, then Tony Blair, to have the confidence to move the Labour Party ahead. We shall continue to be at that leading edge because it makes commercial sense for the *Mirror* to be advancing the cause of modernizing and improving society for the benefit of our increasingly sophisticated readers.'

The political stance of the Mirror Group's titles has remained resolute in spite of considerable efforts by the group's commercial competitors to bring into question its traditional position of broad support for the Labour Party. Montgomery suggests that the *Daily Mirror*, in particular, has improved its political coverage with much more intelligent and thought-provoking news spreading across a wider range of personalities and issues. He says the *Daily Mirror*'s leader writer and political editor have delivered opinion-forming commentary independent of any particular grouping or individual in any party. 'This has kept faith with the paper's traditions but rejected the strident and unthinking abuse which characterized the *Daily Mirror*'s political comment during the Maxwell years. The *Daily Mirror*'s campaign in support of the one-man, one-vote issue within the Labour Party was extremely influential. Our political stance is radical left of centre, as a modernizing force in the country, now best served by getting the new progressive Labour Party into government under Tony Blair.'

Looking ahead to operating the Mirror Group into the twenty-first century, David Montgomery has already touched on some of the areas he thinks will be changed, particularly in the lives of his personnel. 'They'll be more multi-skilled and they'll produce more products. I would hope that the whole organization as an entity would be a bigger company altogether, because we have to have interests spread throughout the media.'

His editorial overhaul had to be carried out against the background of the old-fashioned and restrictive practices of some staff, and indeed executives, but it was essential for the future prosperity and competitive position of the papers that these practices were eliminated and new disciplined standards introduced. David Montgomery says this has now been successfully achieved. As he has indicated, in beginning the process of upgrading the quality of all Mirror Group titles to benefit readers and advertisers, the company embarked upon a programme of major reform and rationalization including the recruitment of talented new management, journalists and staff. It also moved to Canary Wharf in London Docklands, allowing all its national titles, together with the team running its TV interests, to be housed in modern, technologically advanced offices. To David Montgomery the move has been extremely positive for everyone. 'From a cultural point of view it has transformed people's working lives and productivity has certainly improved. There is a gym, a decent staff restaurant and the offices are equipped with the latest technology. There are financial services companies, advertising agencies as well as other newspaper companies, which means that the whole narrow-mindedness of the old Fleet Street culture has been thrown off. People's horizons have broadened, but management must continue to develop staff by providing opportunities to vary and promote the careers of individuals. Only this will prevent stagnation and promote creativity.'

Last year the group had 3,000 employees, and as such is small compared with the multinationals in the business. Three decades ago the group was a large company, producing the same core number of papers but with 13,000 employees. Then the group was considered a giant. 'All that has changed,' says David Montgomery. 'What was big in the past is no longer big today. You know, we are dealing with American companies which are ten, twenty, thirty times our size – they are movers and shakers in our world. We have to get up there, to compete globally. The world is moving much faster than it did twenty-five years ago and particularly among media companies. Today is very exciting, and there are infinite ideas being brought to market in the media; some will work, some will fold. We have gone from having no involvement in television, no involvement outside tabloid newspapers, to having a number of strands which we will continue to develop towards the millennium.'

The Mirror Group is small compared with the multinationals who are able to grasp the opportunities available as the media highway widens to carry more products, whether it is TV, print or information services. Nevertheless, according to David Montgomery, the group has a powerful infrastructure of news, information gathering and production, and is able to leverage this in widening its product base. 'The key strategic thinking is that one product alone, tabloid newspapers, cannot justify a dedicated set of resources. Into the future that set of resources must be spread to produce as many products, newspapers and TV stations as possible. These products should also cross-market each other, just as News International's newspapers have supported the Sky TV channels.' He believes this collegiate approach can be applied to the group's products and also be used in partnership with other organizations. For instance, Live TV has been set up to take advantage of the gap in the market for local television created by the development of cable TV. Mirror Group will provide a national stream of programming which will be customized at the local franchise area. To David Montgomery this will fill the vacuum created by the consolidation of Channel Three as a national station, and the failure of the BBC as a regional provider. 'We have identified partners to help us make a network of city stations viable from an early stage. Cable TV, and in particular Live TV will market very effectively through all our newspapers and those of our partners.'

As indicated, the Mirror Group has a very strong position in Scotland which it believes it has not yet fully exploited. It has purchases a 19.9 per cent interest in Scottish Television PLC, simultaneously with the announcement of its intention to enter the cable TV market with the development of Live TV. David Montgomery believes opportunities for growth are better exploited through combining resources and the partnership approach. For example, in Scotland, 'through combining the resources of Scottish Television [STV] and the *Daily Record* we can better capitalize on our market leadership there; and we have plans to develop cable television in Scotland, which can be done more effectively with STV. The plans we have would benefit both companies and STV sees the logic in that. Our group also has a record in efficiency which, if applied to STV, will enable it to further exploit its monopoly position in the next few years. As with the group, STV will eventually be unable to justify a massive and separate infrastructure duplicating some of what the *Daily Record* does in the same City of Glasgow, only a mile or so apart.' This enlightened view of co-operation is already shared by Midland Independent Newspapers which, together with the group, is co-operating in leveraging their joint resources and marketing power to produce local TV for Birmingham on cable. As David Montgomery adds, 'In the last two years this group has realized huge improvements in internal productivity that keeps us highly profitable in a fiercely competitive environment. In the next few years I think the group's management will be aiming to generate significant productivity through our various alliances and partnerships and this will take place as the media goes through a massive re-shaping in the last years of this century.'

David Montgomery also firmly believes in the collegiate approach when producing newspapers, as it makes far more sense to run more titles from a common set of resources. In the group's first year of ownership of the *Independent* titles it has been able to reduce the cost-base of the *Independent* significantly. 'In addition,' says David Montgomery, 'we want to broaden our base from a total dependence on tabloid newspapers. The *Independent* titles have a young, affluent readership and this has not been exploited. Those papers were losing their sense of direction. As a partnership of shareholders, and with a loyal staff on those newspapers, we have done a lot to improve their appeal. The problem we have with the *Independent* is that it is competing with a broadsheet which is ludicrously under-priced. However, *The Times* has also lost its sense of direction. It is more down-market than before and in fact its current price demeans it. *The Times* is after the *Express* readers. *The Times'* advertisers are definitely not. With the *Independent* we have proved that the collegiate system works well and we will look for further opportunities to improve efficiencies for us and for our other publisher partners.'

The circulation of tabloid newspapers had been in slow decline for a long period until the price-cutting action of News International in the mid-nineties. David Montgomery, however, does not think that newspapers will lose out to television as people's main source of news and information. 'Anyone who thinks newspapers are going out of style is wrong. Look at the *People*. As we said earlier, it was written off as a tired, declining product yet is now putting on sales aggressively. Newspapers relate to the individual more intimately than television and they are more focused. News on TV actually promotes newspaper sales, especially, when there is a major story. The *Daily*

Mirror, particularly, continues to be trusted by people far more than its rivals.'

Last year the Mirror Group managed to push trading margins up again to a record 25 per cent. That has been achieved in a competitive marketplace by emphasizing and reinforcing the quality of its group titles and a continuing focus on improving the cost base. 'The abiding principle of managing Mirror Group,' said David Montgomery, 'is that the newspapers must be enhanced month after month, year after year. For the first time in many years we have made progress by increasing circulation in all our titles. In spite of our significant disadvantage in cover price, we have succeeded in attracting readers through the quality of our newspapers and the more distinctive editorial style. We don't think that investing in price cutting is the best use of the company's money, but effective marketing certainly is.'

Apart from its desire to be more effective in its use of promotional spend the group has also invested heavily in a new printing plant in Scotland because the old one was inadequate for producing quality newspapers. That new plant is now fully operational and the Mirror Group is able to print all its titles, plus the Scottish *Independent*, in Scotland, thus reducing distribution costs. This also gives an important inserting capacity and a greater ability to win additional readers and advertisers.

Initially, any future Mirror Group developments will come in the UK where it has its resources but in time David Montgomery wants to have involvements elsewhere. 'We have been diligent in building contacts in North America and if there's anything that happens in the media world it tends to be the Americans who originate and bring it to market first. So our whole specific and media global ambitions may stem from a springboard beyond the UK.'

Meanwhile at home the Mirror Group is shining. The tight régime within it has raised its trading margins but it is early days to write whether this will also be achieved at the *Independent*, and the venture into cable TV is still an unproven quantity. The effects of the abnormal circumstances which affected the group in 1991 have for the most part substantially been dealt with and the hope is that for the first time since Robert Maxwell's death the group can operate free from the consequences of past events.

The challenge is to live constantly in the future and not the past. His millennium wish for the group is to continue being outward-looking with an ambition to make the Mirror Group a major player. 'Companies such as ours are so much bigger than individuals, much bigger than anyone's role. Towards the millennium our development of a team of individuals will continue, and new talents will emerge because, especially in this country, there are many ambitious people. In my view there will never be a vacuum in a company like ours again. There will always be someone who wants to take Mirror Group on to new things. We have now set those standards – we are attracting the right people and are continuing to hold dynamic, talented people. Once that's engrained in the culture it will continue, I believe, to create a broader and more secure foundation not just for ourselves but for the whole spectrum of our sector as we grow towards the year 2000.'

THE NATIONAL HEALTH SERVICE, ENGLAND

Hospital and Community Health Services
Family Health Services
Central Services } £34 billion
The Drugs Bill
NHS Trusts external financing

Capital Assets £24 billion
1995-96 Capital Programme £2 billion
NHS Supplies £5.9 million
The National Blood Authority £20.2 million

Publicly funded health system, employing 1 million people. Its purpose is to secure through the resources available the greatest possible improvement to the physical and mental health of the people of England by promoting health, preventing ill-health, diagnosing and treating disease and injury, and caring for those with long-term illness and disability: a service available to all on the basis of need, regardless of the ability to pay.

Alan Langlands – Chief Executive

Appointed as Chief Executive in April 1994, having previously been Deputy Chief Executive (1992) and Regional General Manager, North West Thames (1990).

Honorary Fellow of the Faculty of Public Health Medicine
Member of the Institute of Health Services Management
Advisory Board Member for the Centre of Corporate Strategy and Change, University of Warwick.

The Organization

8 Regional Offices
105 Health Authorities
2,603 Fundholding Practices
443 NHS Trusts

276

National Health Service, England
Alan Langlands, Chief Executive

In a book which travels towards and into the twenty-first century I want to review an organization which affects every reader. Health and high fortune have always been the greeting of hope. Juvenal (*c.* AD 60–130) said '*Orandum est ut sit mens sana in corpore sano*', 'You should pray to have a sound mind in a sound body.'

Responsibility for improving the nation's health lies with the National Health Service [NHS]. When it was established in 1948, the NHS represented an international landmark in the provision of healthcare. The principles on which it was founded remain as true today: the NHS provides comprehensive care, everyone in the UK has the right to use it and care is provided according to people's clinical need – not their ability to pay.

The NHS is a unified system and, as such, the biggest single organization in Europe, employing one million people and spending over £100 million per day. Of our GDP 7.1 per cent goes on health compared with say 8.6 per cent in Germany and 14.1 per cent in the States.

On a typical day in England alone, some 700,000 people will visit their doctor, one-and-a-half million items will be dispensed on pharmacy prescription and more than 100,000 people will visit the dentist for a check-up. On the same day, over 90,000 people will be cared for by a hospital outpatient clinic, over 1,700 babies will be delivered, 9,500 people will give blood and 150 patients will receive a hip replacement. The NHS holds the responsibility for providing all these services and has had to evolve to meet the changing needs of Britain's population and find new ways of providing healthcare. The challenge towards the millennium for the NHS is to provide a caring and supportive environment for patients whilst improving quality. Effectiveness and value-for-money remain a constant requirement.

It is worth noting that at the heart of the reforms introduced into the NHS in the early nineties is the principle of separate responsibilities for the funding and provision of healthcare:

Funding and purchasing healthcare

This is mainly the work of the Health Authorities who have a strategic role to improve the health of the residents in their areas by assessing needs, identifying service requirements and purchasing services through contracts with 'providers'. Some general practitioners ('fundholders') also buy services from hospitals.

Providing healthcare

Almost all hospitals, community and ambulance services run themselves as self-governing NHS Trusts. From 1991 this has been carried out according to contracts agreed with 'purchasers' specifying work to be done, standards to be met and money to be allocated.

With a budget of some £40 billion, the NHS provides a comprehensive level of care; *primary care* through family doctors, opticians, dentists and other healthcare professionals, *secondary care* through hospitals and ambulance services, and *tertiary care* through specialist hospitals treating particular types of illness such as cancer. At the same time, the NHS must work in partnership with local social services departments to provide *community care*.

The challenge is simple – to pursue these aims in a way that achieves good quality services and universal coverage.

The Department of Health [DofH] which is a mainstream government department, has three responsibilities. One is running the NHS, and Alan Langlands and his NHS Executive do that. The second role of the DofH is its responsibility to social care, social services in local authorities and the Children's Act. The third facet of the DofH's role is health. The health of the nation. That role mainly involves relationships with other government departments. For example, there are people in the DofH who work with the food industry, who work with the drugs industry, who work across the boundaries with the Departments of the Environment, the

278

Department of Education, and others. The NHS Executive, which bears the main financial responsibility within the DofH, is the part which Alan Langlands is responsible for. He runs the NHS in England – Scotland and N. Ireland have separate arrangements.

The NHS Executive is an integral part of the DofH. As chief executive, Alan Langlands has three jobs. First, he provides advice to the Secretary of State and to ministers on policy development for the NHS. Second, he is responsible for the management and overall performance of the NHS; as Accounting Officer for the NHS he is directly accountable to Parliament for the effective stewardship of NHS revenue and capital resources. The third role is handling questions of internal and headquarters organization.

Chief executives of the various Health Trusts do not have a line management responsibility to Alan Langlands. Established by 1994, there are 433 of them and Alan Langlands could not have a relationship with them all. He explains that he works through eight regional directors and that the main line management relationship is with health authorities. The Trusts are monitored by the regional offices and have to cooperate within the NHS regulatory framework – particularly on issues of public accountability. It is complicated and essentially a federal structure.

Alan Langlands' background is in health service management. Seconded from the NHS i... may transfer over as a subst... the civil service and the re... is now not unusual that pe... have not been civil servant...

His is a high profile acti... in the management organi... changes – the ageing popul... ing ongoing attention and... sent 16 per cent of the... resources spent on them,' ... is an organization that mai... There isn't all that much i... ture, although everyone in... from time to time. So dem...

Changing social expect... ways. Alan Langlands says, 'Quite rightly, people are demanding much more from the NHS, they want to influence the shape of

Health Services in regard to what happens to them as individuals and what happens to their family.' People know their rights, and that has been encouraged, of course, with the Government's Citizens' and Patients' Charters. The Patients' Charter is an explicit statement of patients' rights, extending choice, accountability and quality in public service. It gives the right to choose a GP, receive emergency treatment at any time, receive detailed information of local services, guaranteed admission times and waiting times for an ambulance, immediate assessment in Accident and Emergency and improved outpatient care. The government is extending this initiative.

All health systems have to absorb advances in science and technology – this can't be a casual relationship. There has been a breathtaking speed of change in science and technology; advances in basic science (genetics and molecular biology) are feeding very quickly into new screening and diagnostic techniques, improved procedures and treatments that people want because they think they are going to make them better. 'That transfer from basic science into practice is happening a lot faster than it used to,' says Alan Langlands. 'There are changes at the interface between biology and engineering, advances in genetics and in transplantation biology; these are all major issues for us. The NHS will become ever more sophisticated as we move towards the next century. There is pressure for staff on the front line who have to keep up with a very complex set of technical developments. Yet another issue facing every health service in the world, is the whole question of finance. If you link advances in technology with population changes and all these other factors, it raises questions of the availability of money to meet these demands.'

The overall NHS budget is negotiated with the Treasury in the public expenditure round, in competition with Defence and Education and all the other departments. The big change that has taken place over the past couple of years is that in the UK money to institutions is no longer allocated on an historical basis. As Langlands explains, 'We don't say, for example, Hospital X in Leeds spent £96 million last year and needs £97 million this year. We allocate money to populations; the Leeds Health Authority acts as the agents of the population. We assess the position in every health authority. For example, we now take account of factors relating to social deprivation and the age structure of the population.'

He confesses that no financial allocation formula covering the whole population of England is ever going to be accurate. His

Executive do try to sensitize the figures as far as possible to population need: 'They have spent years searching for the Holy Grail.'

With just over one million people working in the NHS it is a labour-intensive organization. About 73 per cent of its costs are tied up in staff, and that is a major issue into and beyond the year 2000. 'We envisage a very different mix of skills over the next ten years,' says Langlands. 'The need is for ever increasing technical skills and for highly qualified nurses, paramedical and medical staff who have these sophisticated skills. We also need people with caring skills, looking after older people, looking after more people in the community who suffer from mental illness or learning disabilities.'

Planning the workforce for now and into the millennium is a difficult balancing act. Just take the medical side. 'The lead time,' says Alan Langlands, 'in training a consultant anaesthetist is something like twelve to fourteen years. When you are planning the medical workforce of the future you have to influence the tap that controls the number of medical students entering into the system; the NHS is pretty well the monopoly employer of doctors in this country. Sometimes we've had the foresight to predict technological and scientific change or changes in clinical practice. When we get it wrong we get shortages, and we have to retain or develop faster streams. We have to be a good deal more sophisticated in the future and we have to allow the Trusts to influence the course of events.'

In the UK we depend on overseas doctors coming to work in this country. Many of them like to do this to gain training experience anyway. However, Alan Langlands believes: 'Over the next ten years or so we will probably grow more of our own. I think there will need to be an increase in the number of fully trained doctors in the country, and that requires increased students, increased numbers in training. When looking at the international comparisons, we are not over-doctored by any means. We certainly have shortages in some specialities, but there is more of a balance than in many other countries.'

In the mid-nineties there has been media attention on the distribution of staffing, the proportion of managers to folk who are hands-on carers and medically qualified, with a suggestion that there has been a massive increase in managers and accountants. Langlands says the reality is that you could cut the headline figures by 75 per cent, and that would be about the right increase! 'There certainly has been an investment in professional managers at a local level. All Trusts have better accounting staff than they used to have. We didn't know the cost of anything in the NHS. They also have better personnel management than they used to have. Local pay means you have to employ skilled people at local level; you need to take an integrated approach to workforce planning, employee relations and pay and reward systems. A lot of the changes that are hyped in the media are changes in the classification of staff. Many of the so-called managers are actually nurses who have been put on to management pay scales, and who do management jobs. Go into any Trust in the country and there are directors of nursing on every Trust board. They are classified as a management cost, whereas five years ago they were classified as a nursing cost. That's been translated by the political mischief-makers into a big story.'

Alan Langlands admits there have been some increases. What his Executive is now doing at a local level, having established better – though still patchy – management, is stripping out the bureaucracy at the top. For example, it is currently going for an approximate 20 per cent cut in its headquarters in Leeds. The DofH in London is having the same reductions. The number of people working at regional level has reduced in the past few years from a figure of nearly 4,000 down to around 1,000. Regional Health Authorities are to be abolished, thus flattening the hierarchy. 'We are taking out £200 million over the next two years at the top of the organization. That £200 million in staff savings goes straight into the NHS kitty. There should be better patient services as a result. That is offset against the investment. There have been costs associated with the changes, transaction costs have increased, but over the past ten years, year on year, the NHS has become more efficient in terms of the work it does for the money available, and better, according to the OECD, than any of their other member countries.

One of the paradoxes of the Health Service, I have discovered, is that we actually have a much better reputation internationally than in the UK. There is this peculiarly British phenomenon wherein a lot of the people who work in the NHS criticize it. Alan Langlands agrees. He says it is 'partly because they think by so doing they will maintain pressure on the Government to increase the resources available. We don't really know what a change of government would mean. British politics is converging on the centre ground and there should not be the huge swings of policy that we have seen in the past such as when Labour's Barbara Castle took over from Conservative

Keith Joseph as Secretary of State nearly two decades ago. Joseph had moved in one direction – the process of establishing a planned NHS – and Barbara Castle then promoted ideas of democracy and worker participation in the Health Service. I do not think we are going to see such extremes of change in the future. Looking at what is happening round the world, any government would find a compelling case for a managed Health Service. You cannot just let it flow free. It is necessary to be able to cap the resources and manage them effectively. Most governments would recognize that allocating the money to people rather than to institutions is a good idea, because it creates a dynamic in the system, which keeps everyone on their toes.'

He is convinced that the NHS is on the right track. 'We provide at the moment what is still, compared to most countries, a comprehensive health service for £678 per person in the British population. I know of no better way of doing it than that.' However, he accepts there is scope for partnership with the private sector. 'We already have a tremendous influence there. We train most of the nurses that are working in the private sector, and we train and employ most of the doctors who practise in the private sector. Despite people's concerns about the Health Service, the uptake of private health insurance in this country has drifted between 11 and 15 per cent for the last eight or nine years. Where there are opportunities for partnership we will take them – the biggest number of private beds in this country are in the NHS and some NHS hospitals run very good private services as a means of generating additional revenue.'

That dichotomy no longer disturbs him as it used to because today standards are a lot closer. Parts of the NHS now feel no different from those within a private hospital. He admits there are still large parts of the NHS with old buildings and equipment that need to be greatly improved, but the gap is closing. 'I believe the creation of the NHS was an important and ultimately sustainable concept of social legislation, the most important thing that has happened in this country this century. But I am not ideologically driven to the point where I would ever refuse to work with the private sector. There are a lot of very able people supplying good services, and we are working increasingly in partnership with them to finance big projects. However, privatization of the NHS is not remotely on the agenda for any government, certainly not in the timescale of the year 2000 and beyond: it will remain firmly in the public sector.'

There has been a significant growth in private nursing homes for the elderly over the past ten years. The difference between health and social care has existed since 1948. However, the boundary between the two has been questioned, and is there not an argument which says the Health Service has drawn back rather too far from its responsibilities in relation to these services? 'I think that probably is right in some parts of the country,' responds Alan Langlands. 'We are about to start reinvesting and expect to see shifts in emphasis over the next year or two.'

He also has strong views on consultants in the NHS and their new management roles as a result of NHS reforms. 'The days of standing at the head of the patient's bed and shouting about the patient without actually talking to them, are gone. Usually the people who are good doctors also make good managers. We do not want to create an environment where being the clinical director or taking over some (as their colleagues would perceive it) administrative responsibilities, is a way of keeping someone out of the clinic. It is the reverse. We want the brightest people, the real leaders, to take part in managing the Health Service in which they work. I think that involvement has progressed well in some parts of the UK, but there are other parts of the country where it has been eclipsed by wider changes in the Health Service. Every Trust has its own medical director. Usually these are very able people who enhance the decision-making process. There is now a body called the British Association of Medical Managers, born from nothing, putting a lot of effort into developing that professional management in the Health Service, and we work a lot with them.'

He admits that the attitudes of the younger consultants coming through the system are very different, as are the attitudes of younger GPs. Alan Langlands says they understand their traditional roles are changing. 'There has got to be a much closer relationship on three fronts. First, between patient and doctor – and the patient must have some choice in that. Second, there is a recognition that doctors should not just be concerned with the people sitting across the table from them, that they have a wider responsibility to the population. Third, the recognition that the specialists, the consultants, cannot operate in a vacuum. They need a team, and they are part of a team – they need people to clean the theatres, they need technicians to programme their equipment, they need nurses to support their clinical practice. They are and must be *team* leaders.' He feels therefore that the popular view of the 'Consultant as God' is going but he has no difficulty with the idea of a consultant-based service, where the consultant is leader of the team, conductor of the orchestra.

He is also trying to address the relationship between the NHS and the media. 'The Health Service does not get a good national press, but we do get quite good local press publicity. You cannot control an organization of this size sitting in a building in Leeds or Whitehall. You *can* offer some direction, and we try to do that. Good relationships, good communications, must be built from the ground up. When you go out and about as I do, and ask people in the NHS what they think, you discover they are hugely committed. They strongly support their local hospital or their local Trust. The idea that there are millions of disenchanted people in the Health Service is rubbish, but many people do work under great pressure. There is a lot of balanced press coverage of the NHS at local level. That reflects the true Health Service, a local service.'

Alan Langlands knows that customer service issues require more attention. 'We have to concentrate our effort on our people who have the front line contact with the public. People want safe services in pleasant surroundings, and they want the sensitivity of a one-to-one relationship.'

He confesses to there being some vitally important service issues to be tackled. 'Services for people who are mentally ill in this country are not as good as they could be. We have got some very good, sound policies and ideas but we have not implemented them properly. We need to do that, we need to plug that gap urgently and improve things. The NHS cannot take the commitment of its staff for granted. The four or five hundred Trusts around the country each have to be regarded as good employers.'

Langlands feels the NHS needs in the future a much better developed relationship with the public over the issues, problems and constraints. It is actually *their* Health Service, and they make choices when they vote the government in, and they pay taxes. They have views, and we need to listen more.'

The NHS is a labour intensive service. When you get a million people providing a service to 56 million people, by definition things are going to go wrong every day, just by sheer law of averages and human error. Alan Langlands feels the NHS could afford to be less defensive about that. 'Of course there are risks. For example, if you're providing services to people who are mentally ill. Society has got to decide whether these people spend more time in hospital and have a say in shaping the pattern of community-based provision. These are difficult decisions; they should not be performance scored for NHS managers, nor are they for politicians to make the final judgement on.'

There is, he believes, good progress in discussing health care issues more widely, but it tends to be selective and must be improved. 'There is often good dialogue with voluntary organizations, such as Mind, Age Concern or the British Diabetic Association, people that we have constant communication with at all levels in the NHS. It is constructive and helpful, but that dialogue does not always reach the wider population. That is more difficult – a lot of people do not particularly want to think about the Health Service, or these issues, if it is not touching their own lives. You think about the NHS only when one of the kids, your partner or your granny is unwell.'

The Health Service, he says, has to be a lot better at opening its doors, at welcoming people to come and see what we are doing and trying to achieve. Many large hospitals, for example, are the largest employers in their community. They cannot be insular.

His wish for the millennium would be for improved services in some areas that he knows to be deficient at the moment. Mental health is his prime example, but there are more: 'better strategy for developing primary care services, better approaches to harnessing the commitment and the contribution of the staff, and a much more open and easier relationship with the public aimed at maintaining and building public confidence in their Health Service.'

Alan Langlands admits with honesty that the NHS is an organization that needs much clearer direction than it has. 'That means foresight, understanding all these trends that we have been talking about, harnessing them and being innovative in the way that we come to terms with them. It means clear objectives and good management at every level.'

He is often asked about control of the monster monolithic NHS. 'It is not about control,' he states, 'it is about setting a framework in which highly professional, highly competent experts can work together to meet the needs of the people in their community. The results of that will be manifest, I think, in the views of staff and the perceptions of the public and of our partners. I understand the importance of working across boundaries with the scientific and academic communities, with social services, the housing organizations, the police, the criminal justice system and all the other caring professions. That is the real issue towards the year 2000 and beyond. We have to build public confidence, and we have to play off the front foot about the successes of the NHS.'

QUANTUM INTERNATIONAL LTD

Turnover (1994)	US $80 million
Employees	42

World-wide leader in entertaining home shopping infomercials. Owns 400 hours of infomercial air time per week across five continents and 53 countries on satellite, cable and terrestrial television in 12 languages.

David J.Carman – President and Chief Operating Officer

Appointed as President in 1991 and Chief Operating Officer in 1995.
International and Executive Vice-President of National Media Corporation.
Past Managing Director of the Franklin Mint.
Past President of the International Division of the Franklin Mint Europe.

The Company

Quantum International is the wholly owned subsidiary of National Media Corporation, the largest publicly quoted infomercial producer in the world.

It has developed five internationally recognized branded channels: Sell-A-Vision, Quantum Channel, Super Shop, What's In Store and Novedades Increibles.

288

Quantum International Ltd
David Carman, President and
Chief Executive Officer

New technology is having an enormous impact upon the buying habits of people around the globe, cutting out any kind of distribution in between the manufacturer and the consumer.

Quantum is the fastest growing international television direct marketing company in the world, broadcasting in twelve languages, on five internationally recognized branded channels reaching over 200 million households worldwide. How it identified and then capitalized on the opportunities is an interesting story.

Quantum was originally known as Quantum Television Marketing and had been operating before David Carman and his team arrived. It was the brainchild of an entrepreneur in the USA who had already had some success in the 'infomercials' business in the mid-eighties. Some of those infomercials that Quantum inherited are still being broadcast around the world: the oldest one was launched in Japan in 1995 and is shown every night to over 44 million homes.

For the uninitiated, an infomercial is a twenty-five minute programme extolling the virtues of one product or service, often filmed before an audience. During those twenty-five minutes it demonstrates and entertains, explains the product and gives people three opportunities, during that time to purchase. Quantum, however, is not just in the business of broadcasting infomercials. It also produces them, owns the TV time, develops branded products, innovates specific home shopping infomercial-style channels, attracts an audience, creates buyers, takes the orders and handles the fulfilment and all the customer service thereafter. It is a vertically integrated operation that's being pushed out around the world.

The foresight of National Media in the United States was

establishing a beachhead in Europe, well before anybody else. Today that decision has resulted in Quantum having no effective competition in the European market. 'Not that others could not have come,' says David Carman. 'However, the disciplines and the manner in which you run an international organization are very complex, even at the small end of the company size frame – that is to say, with sales that are about to break US$100 million for this company, which is relatively small if you compare it with other organizations in your book. For American companies, in particular, the prospect of operating in other countries is a dire one because you not only have risk of personnel, you have very long communication lines and there is an often a lack of understanding of language, culture, people and regulations, and a complete belief that if it works in the US it must be steamrollered around the world.'

David Carman, however, is convinced that if you attempt to run a company in the same way as you do in the United States, it cannot work. 'The only principle that actually works is the principle of leverage. That is to say, how do I leverage my investments and my methodology in the US into other countries? That means you have got to tailor those offers, you have got to understand the differences, the different nature of doing business everywhere.'

As far as Quantum is concerned, is that you must have personnel who understand how to run businesses at a local level. 'That may sound simple,' he says, 'but negotiating in France or Germany, Israel, India or Japan is completely different. If you can find the key to leveraging your business, then, leveraging within the confines of the culture, the way that business is done, is very important.'

To achieve this Quantum has a staff that is drawn from throughout the world. They have people from Australia, New Zealand, the UK, who have lived and worked overseas. David Carman's executive assistant is fluent in Japanese (incidentally a trend he sees becoming a norm into the millennium). Quantum has all the major languages covered, and a core team of people who have experience in building and developing global companies with the key connections in media distribution fulfilment and telemarketing. This is why it has been able to establish a differential edge in the marketplace – it can offer a one-stop shop.

Looking at the next five years of Quantum in Europe, where is it going and what are its potential problems? Quantum is a British company, but because there are few cable homes here at the moment, the

UK represents less than 5 per cent of its business, most of which comes from Europe, Asia and South America.

To explain what Quantum is going to do in the next five years, let's review what it has done in the past three.

The company existed when David Carman arrived in London in 1991 but it was a small organization, with ten employees: three directors – managing, finance and operations – and seven others. The company was doing around US$10 million dollars, and had consistently lost money for the two years it had been in the UK. It had to stem that loss. David Carman discovered that the television time was under-utilized. The company had two contracts that the former management had negotiated, but it didn't know what to do with them.

One view was: Quantum had to develop the largest bank of media time that was available in new commercial business. This has now been established, with over 400 hours of programme throughout the world excluding America and Canada – that is 800 infomercials per week.

Secondly, Quantum said it wanted to leverage its programmes developed and tested in the US. As David Carman says, 'Immediately your strike rate increases from three out of ten to ten out of ten, because the correlation is such that if the programme works in the US, nine times out of ten it will work everywhere around the world providing it's tailored.' The capital investment into programming at the start was therefore very low.

A third principle was that of leverage of personnel. What did that mean? Explains David Carman, 'Most companies are lured and tempted into owning everything around the world. Setting up, fixed capital costs, warehouses, staff, a general manager. They are going to work as integral operating units.' Quantum, however, decided to joint venture everything – with one exception; it would own the business if it was within one or two hours' flying time of London. If it was farther afield, they decided to license it like a franchise: that is, license the name and take royalties. Quantum would not own the business in the traditional sense that it would own the capital or the people; it would license the parts of the income statement that could be turned into variable costs. Carman says, 'For our fulfilment, our telemarketing and everything to do with licensing and operating the business in Europe, we would pay a fee only when we transacted an order. In that way we could control our income statement. We could develop an organization that was focused on control and statement.

291

So, after these three successful years, we will be somewhere between $150m and $175m next financial year, and we still only have forty-two people on the staff. Our bankers tell us that our profitability per head makes us their most profitable client company. In fact, they tell us we have the highest profitability per head of any company in one of the five major trading banks in the UK. That's because we have the exploited leverage concept.

'As indicated, however, one cannot simply take any product or business system which works in the USA and assume it will work around the globe. Obviously, we do make changes to our programmes. We dub into the languages of the countries targeted, but more than that, we look at every programme and make subtle changes: we change the statements that are made, and take out things that are culturally insensitive. In the USA it is acceptable to have a doctor on a programme that is selling something that has a medical significance. We don't do that globally. We also change the offer. Generally speaking, we increase the value added that's offered to a European customer. We improve the packaging. We offer more products in the package.'

He believes that the European customer is more sophisticated, and has higher standards. 'They expect, when they open the box to have a pleasurable experience. In the US, customers look for something different out of a mail-order or a home shopping company. We also brand our channels. That was another key strategic difference. In the USA people buy and sell time. But in taking the high ground, in developing our media time, it wasn't just a case of getting large blocks of time over several years, it was developing a strategic partnership with the vendor, with the media. We do business with people who see home shopping as a strategic point of difference that their channel offers. We brand the channel. When you view in Europe, you see after EuroSport, which is the leading sporting channel in Europe, "Welcome to the Quantum channel. It's great to have you with us. You're going to be seeing a terrific range of products over the next six or seven hours." It is a stand-alone channel. When you switch on to Quantum, you switch on to the channel.

'In the USA, if you see an infomercial selling an item on Saturday morning at 7am, you won't see that again, because when you switch on the next day, there will not be a channel or a home shopping programme there from the same producer. It will be from someone else, who decided to pay more for the time. We took a strategic view that said we want to be in business with media companies over the long term. We want to develop a business alongside theirs, or within theirs, so that with NBC Superchannel, we've got a business running within a business. We have one hour a day. It is only one hour, but it has been strategically placed and is branded Supershop. People become Supershop viewers. That's the key point of difference in our approach to business.'

In Europe Quantum has set up its own competition, because as well as the Quantum channel, there is Sell-A-Vision on another transponder, and 'What's In Store', broadcast after UK Gold closes. There is also a deal with TVI in Portugal, on a national terrestrial channel, to present two hours a day. It is taking the best of both worlds, mounting its own programmes and channels, plus mounting channels within channels. 'Europe has 350 million people,' reminds David Carman. 'Our channels just scratch the surface. We enter countries not generally perceived as mainstream TV markets, because we are a satellite broadcaster. We are probably one of the few licensed UK satellite broadcasters who are actually profitable on a pan-European basis.'

Quantum has to buy the time, or get a lease, to 'own' a channel. It sub-leases its time from people who actually own the twenty-four hours, taking up time they don't want. 'If you take, for example, EuroSport,' says David Carman, 'we lease all of their night-time hours, on a long-term lease which goes for several years into the millennium. We are paying them according to a specific business formula. It costs millions of pounds but we are able to cover that cost and make a very respectable profit.'

In Europe, Quantum started out principally as a pan-European satellite broadcaster, which is why it is in Poland and other places such as Hungary, Greece and Israel. David Carman illustrates another point and principle of leverage: 'If you are already paying for the time on the satellite collecting orders across the European Union, why wouldn't you accept orders elsewhere by putting up the flag on the screen? There is no extra cost involved. We're now dubbing in twelve languages. Every language and every country you add is free. It doesn't cost any more in terms of media cost, and it expands the marketing opportunities.'

Quantum programmes that are produced in America are not always added to its UK schedule. This is because of European legislation regulations. There are seven or eight separate pieces of legislation Quantum operates under, all governed by a separate part of the EU: distance selling, broadcasting directive, packaging, cosmetics, for example. Carman believes that you must have a team that knows how to work within the confines of the legislation. He had been running international companies for about ten years and he brought three key employees with him to Quantum: his chief financial officer, who at the time was twenty-eight, his marketing director who had worked with him for many years, who was thirty-six, and his market development and control director who at the time was thirty-three. They each had six or seven years' experience with international business.

Says David Carman, 'Over the past ten years I have only worked for American companies who have been global and in the consumer area. I have learnt a great deal from being in the UK. My management style has changed significantly. I've learnt a lot here in terms of patience and persistence. I have learnt to listen more than I used to. My negotiating style is now a lot more measured and paced, and flexible in the sense that I understand that there is just a different way of doing business in Europe.'

He admits, 'UK companies have tended to be very inward looking, and too highly structured.' This adds to his problems of finding the right team. 'Initiative and entrepreneurship do not seem to be concentrated upon, highlighted, nourished or nurtured within the British companies that I have dealt with. Sights are often set lower, in terms of international expansion. British companies seem to be hesitant and have not been working to develop teams of people have have been intellectually inclined and targeted to take the companies global. More often than not, the international development directors are executives who have been home-grown in the organization, which means their extremely active years were fifteen to twenty years ago, when Britain was not a world-player, particularly in our field of media. It is only now that Britain is taking an international role in media. For example, I admire Greg Dyke's appointment to the Pearson Group. Greg is a go-getter. He came from TV, he has vision, and he has the energy to be able to do it.'

So there is an issue of energy, too, in business? 'Yes,' enthuses Carman. 'You have to have the energy and the ability to get out and make it happen. You have got to be prepared to take risks, and sometimes those risks cannot be measured, cannot be calculated, you have just got to do it.'

How have Quantum been able to do it? Says David Carman, 'We had some talented young people here when we arrived, but they did not understand the business, did not know what to do with it. So we had to train them. Now the average age of the people in this company is about twenty-six. I am the oldest person, at forty-four. All my colleagues have been trained by us in international business. We put an enormous amount of time, money and cost into training and developing these people.'

David Carman came from an academic background, having spent five years at university, teaching, and also had a consultancy practice which, amongst other things, had a training function. 'I have an inherent interest in training,' he says, 'and whilst a proportion of the training at Quantum is done by me personally, my associates are also committed to training, so there is a lot of coaching and counselling going on. We have restructured the company twice to take account of the growth. It is like riding a tiger. One minute we are doing thirty-five million, then we're doing forty-five, then we're doing seventy-five million. Now we're going to do a hundred and something million – all with the same group of people. How do we improve their productivity, how do we get them to be superior decision-makers? How do we get them to cope? Recently we held our first non-internal training programme. I flew a consultant in from Australia with whom I have worked for a number of years. We took our people away for three days, and did the classic bonding session to try to help them understand the process they're in. We will do that every three months. We might spend $150,000 on that each year. But through that we gain a more loyal and trained people. We have had negligible staff turnover in the time I have been here. We have made all the changes, achieved increased output and huge growth with not a single resignation.'

Quantum has taken recruits straight from university, or from their first job, training them how to run a global business, to negotiate, to achieve the very tough objectives the company sets, to manage their people and to manage their time. 'For example,' says David Carman, 'people now going out to be trained in finance are people that you wouldn't even think would train in finance. I'm training my executive assistant in finance, who came from a non-business background. I don't need an MBA telling me how to run my business. Instead I have taken someone who is young, who has been tested, who has great interpersonal skills, great personality, clearly demonstrated intelligence, whom I'm going to train in all aspects of our business.

'When we started our organization structure it was like a cart-wheel, with me as the axle. A year ago, I realized that I did not have the time to run everything single-handedly. We restructured the company.'

Even if you are a big operation, David Carman insists you must send empowerment down the line; a much flatter and more flexible organization is the way forward to the year 2000. He will divisional-ize, and is already forming an Asian and European division.

'The challenges are in how to build the culture and in deciding the kind of culture I want to create, that is right for our business into the millennium. In two years or three years, I'll move on, or move to chairman and not be so involved. But into the twenty-first century we will continue to rationalize and leverage our operation.

'We are now at a critical mass where we *can* own it, because we have got a structure in place. But we're not doing it alone. Out in Asia, for example, we spent a lot of time developing a joint venture with the Mitsui Corporation. We don't license any more. 'Mitsui is a $173 billion operation, one of the largest in the world. Every time we need something, we call our partner and say, "We've got a prob-lem." "Fine, we'll get back to you." They find somebody in their structure who will help us. But we don't own anything. We control the programmes, we jointly control the time, we sub-contract out everything else and we solve problems together. So even though we might grow to a $400–500m business in three years time, you will not see a thousand people. You will continue to see less than 100 people in the company.'

Towards the millennium Quantum's original licensee strategy is now changing. It is less likely to license because licensees give income, never equity. The other principle Quantum has built its business on is to maintain a lack of bad debt. 'We never do business with anybody unless we get paid before we do it.'

David Carman goes on, 'Let me make one point about people. We cannot turn everybody into a millionaire, but we want to make sure our people make a lot of money. We have an incentive programme which enables people to double their salary on the achievement of their objectives. Obviously the company has to make money. But these young people will have the ability to buy a home, we hope, before they get to thirty. We are not concerned about directors and others receiving large payments because they will ensure that share-holders make a handsome return on their investment. We are like a structured group of entrepreneurs.'

Quantum will certainly use innovative marketing methods to their customers into the twenty-first century. Carman is not concerned with jumping on to the bandwagon that he believes everybody's on. 'The digital revolution is here. And we will decide carefully what we are going to do. But will we be using CD ROMs instead of television stations? Maybe. Will we be using Internet? Maybe. Will we be using some other means of distribution and mechanisms? Maybe. We are just flexible, and we are waiting to see. We probably will not know till the year 2000 really what the strategy is going to be or the particular channels that we will use to distribute our product until we are into the next century.'

Then, as now, there will be no doubt that Quantum will be a global operation. It is already in five continents, and sees major expansion in Asia, which is already an influential part of its business. It is a little hesitant about China. 'It is not that China is not an attractive market to us,' says Carman, 'it is just that we are really trying to understand how to do business in China. We are not rushing there. Other countries were able to get in more rapidly, and quickly set up a business, but I would expect that in the next two years we will be in at least eight or ten Asian countries by terrestrial and satellite TV. We are currently in Singapore, Japan, the Philippines, Malaysia and New Zealand. Competition will grow. It will be a lot tougher, and principally in Europe it will grow through terrestrial TV on a country by country basis. In France we've already started giving licences for three 24-hour home shopping networks. In Germany, a competitor already has a lease on a transponder where he wants to start some shopping.'

Quantum will have more competition, but feels that it has several advantages. Carman suggests some: 'One, we've got a huge library of programmes. Number two, we are not a live home shopping company. We are not another retail store − most of the home shopping companies are another way of selling retail. We offer unique products and we do not offer the same products that customers can get in the store. One other thing I should say is, that whilst competition will grow, we are not a threat to the retail industry.

'In the US today the total of the entire home shopping business is about \$4 billion. Recent reviews predicted that it would go to \$10 billion by the end of this decade. In the USA, one retail chain alone does in excess of $50 billion. So when you put it into perspective, in a country that's got full cable distribution and full retail distribution, you can see that far from bringing competition, it can augment and help retail sales, because what happens is that television drives customers into the stores.'

He believes that what retailers should concentrate on is how to improve their bottom line. How to improve their margins. How to improve their customer service. 'One thing that I can do better than anybody, is demonstrate my product in my half-hour better than any retailer can, because their staff aren't trained, they're not focused on customer service, even though they say they are. We have millions of customers as a result.'

His views on leadership and teamwork are potent. 'Success and service are to do with the quality of management, and of leadership. I don't think it can be taught. Every managing director, or head of company, has their own style or technique. I hear people who talk about turf. You know, "We should all be a team, there should be no turf." I'm the opposite. I am saying great to have the team, let's work on it, but *I want you to have turf*. Turf means you're going to fight for what *you* believe in. My three bywords therefore are not teamwork and all of that stuff. They are *leadership, discipline*, and *detail*.'

His first speech to any company that he has ever taken over is about leadership. 'You can't train people to lead. It is in them. My first job at twenty-three was running a factory with a hundred and five people working for me. I'd never done it before. I believe it is something that we try to seek out, that we try to identify in people. Natural born leaders. We can help them understand how to harness their leadership, and what to do. We can help them in their decision-making. We can help them explain when they made a poor decision versus a good one, but it's natural.'

He doesn't believe you can teach leadership. 'You can take a person who is a leader, who you believe is going to be a leader and train them up. And get them into this mind-set of how they are going to run their business. I believe it is as appropriate to a 40,000 employee company as it is to a 100 employee company. You can do it. It is just the way you do it that is different.'

What does discipline mean? 'Discipline is not discipline with a big D,' explains Carman. 'We don't wield a stick. It's self-discipline. It's the discipline to do what you said you were going to do, and if you don't, the discipline to make sure people understood why not. It's the discipline of managing your time effectively.'

And what about detail as the last of his bywords? 'Detail is what you have to have to stay on top of the business. I'm not saying that a manager has to cross every "t" and dot every "i", but you had better know what is going on in your business. Be like somebody who owns the business. My people have got to consider that every time they do something, they are risking their own money. So stay in touch with the detail like an entrepreneur does. Like an owner of capital does.'

He puts earnest emphasis on Europe. 'We are quite comfortable working in Europe. We do not have a problem with the legislation. The European community has recently reviewed our broadcasting directive and the result of that is likely to be an opening of time for Quantum and other people. The issue in Europe is where national legislation and national attitudes conflict with what European legislation is trying to do on a pan-European basis.'

As the new millennium approaches, he would like Quantum to be either part of another large company that has strategic value to the shareholders and management, or to take Quantum, which is a division of the parent company, public, to allow UK citizens and other European citizens to buy into it. It could be a combination of both of these things.

'We can still remain small. What we're talking about is an involvement by a large company in our register, which will give us access through them to their relationship and power.'

His personal ambition is to lessen the amount of travel that he does. 'I've been travelling 140 or 150 days of the year. I don't think that's good for my health and it's not good for the company. I can't make every deal. Helping people under me to take the deal-making is a positive way forward. Number two ambition is to hand over the management of this company to the next level. To step back and to be involved either as a full-time chairman or as non-executive chairman. I would say, by the millennium, I will be doing the thing I do best, which is helping companies develop their structure and strategy. I may not live in the UK, I'll probably move somewhere where the sun shines! These are my personal objectives by fifty, and that's what I'm going to do, with six years to do it.'

SCOTRAIL

Turnover (1994–95)	£320 million
Income:	
Revenue	£95 million
Government Support Grant	£225 million
and Strathclyde Passenger	
Transport Executive	
Employees	4,000

A train operating unit (TOU), running 97 per cent of all rail services in Scotland, including sleeper services to and from London.

John Ellis – Director

John Ellis joined British Rail Western Region as a graduate management trainee in 1962. Since then he has held posts in South Wales, Southern and Eastern Regions, Network SouthEast, InterCity and Railtrack as well as Scotland. He was appointed Director, ScotRail, in 1995.

Graham Smith – Customer Services Director

Graham Smith joins the new company from InterCity, which recruited him in 1992 after a 20-year career with British Airways. At InterCity he led initiatives to improve facilities for customers and to focus efforts on quality of service.

Operations

ScotRail operates around 1,900 services a day between 332 stations. More than 170,000 passenger journeys are made per day, totalling over 50 million annually. A fleet of over 600 trains operates over 1,500 route miles, and overnight sleeper services run six nights a week (Saturdays excepted), connecting Scotland's major cities to London.

ScotRail leases its stations, depots and trains, and pays Railtrack for access to the track. ScotRail is funded by the Office of Passenger Rail Franchising (OPRAF) to operate the comprehensive range of passenger services specified in OPRAF's Passenger Service Requirement.

ScotRail operations are divided into four service groups:

Express	–	Links Scotland's major cities, including Aberdeen, Inverness, Glasgow and Edinburgh;
Rural	–	Links communities all over Scotland, and includes the West and North Highland lines
Urban	–	Links towns in Fife, Lothian and Central Region
Strathclyde PTE	–	The largest UK commuter operation outside London, covering the whole Strathclyde Region

Scotrail
John Ellis, Director
Graham Smith, Customer Services Director

The government's rail privatization plan, the Railways Act, 1993, created a radical restructuring of the UK rail industry, with the underlying aim of bringing the operators closer to their customers. All of a sudden, what most people saw as one complete industrially integrated body has been atomized. Out of it came twenty-five individual passenger train-operating companies (TOCs). The intention is that each of these will be offered as a franchise operation.

The Act also created Railtrack, which comprises the track on which the trains run, all the signalling that controls the movement of the trains, and the stations (3,000 throughout the UK). The property and the infrastructure of the track belong to Railtrack, which currently remains government owned, but is no longer part of British Rail [BR]. It sells track space to TOCs on which they run their trains. Lots of ancillary companies are also being created, like the rolling stock leasing companies, Roscos, from which the train-operating companies lease the rolling stock. They are still government owned but the intention is to float them into the private sector as well. In addition there is British Railways Infrastructure Services [BRIS], which comprises a series of companies formed in support of Railtrack, maintaining the track, and so on. All the freight side, too, is being separated. Apart from the twenty-five new companies there are at least that number, if not more, of other subsidiaries of BR or different organizations being set up, most of which are going to be privatized. That's what I call atomization!

The Labour Party's deputy leader has said that, if the railways were privatized by the time they return to power, he would want to return them to greater public accountability, although Labour will recognize franchise contracts and allow them to continue. Whether that

means a restoration of public ownership or a mixed enterprise culture it is difficult to tell, and frankly, at the moment, they don't have
to spell it out. I think what they are currently saying is that the
processes by which railways are being privatized are highly complex,
highly destructive, and not conducive to customer service. That is
their perception. The present Tory government, however, is saying,
from its point of view, 'Hang on a second, this is a way of liberating
the train companies to concentrate exclusively on giving the customers what they want. Let's free them from owning stations, maintaining track, operating signal boxes, those heavy engineering
production-based activities, and make the train companies concentrate on giving good customer service.'

In a nutshell, there are two conflicting views, both of which have
some attractions and downsides.

The ScotRail train company operates over 97 per cent of all rail
services in Scotland. It was born out of the reorganization and is one
of Scotland's largest businesses. According to John Ellis, the director
with full responsibility for ScotRail, 'The general economic climate
in Scotland continues to look like steady growth, with a real chance
of not being as seriously affected by any future economic recession as
other parts of the UK. The business climate for ScotRail remains in
a process of change, with some evidence that the political and public climate is moving in favour of rail development. However, the
uncertainties over future privatization and ownership of Railtrack,
place some inhibition on our long-term planning.'

The policy of ScotRail is quite clear: as a train company it will be
seeking with all the power it possesses to attain the franchise. The
government timetable suggests it should be on offer in 1996. Says
John Ellis, 'We will be doing all we can to persuade the Franchising
Director, who ultimately awards the franchises, that we are the fit
and proper management and staff team to be awarded that franchise,
irrespective of the politics. There is no doubt in my mind, everyone
at ScotRail wants the railway to stay in hands which *we* would say are
competent to run it. The really key jobs – train driving, running safe
practices on the railway, conducting, selling tickets, maintaining your
assets at the depots – those things should be in the hands of people
who have a competence and an affinity with the railway and know
its customers well. I want to see those front line activities left in the
hands of competent people.'

Where there is scope for enterprise is in marketing, customer service, the financial way in which the company is run. For ScotRail this has encouraged the introduction of fresh blood. It has a new commercial director who joined from the private sector, bringing with him a new team and fresh thinking into the marketing. Says Graham Smith, director of customer services, 'I am hardly from a railway culture! I'm ex-British Airways, with a particular focus on the customer service side. We have brought in people from the outside who have buying and contract supply skills. Towards 2000 you need a fusion of both the long-serving, experienced people who have always run the railways and people who will challenge that, who will bring an outside and reflective view into it. It is a creative partnership.'

Essentially, the objectives of Railtrack and any of the train-operating companies should be the same – maximizing the number of people using the trains because the more business they generate, the more they both profit and increase wealth. Where John Ellis thinks in the short term, there is potential for conflict is that both Railtrack and the train-operating companies are very new at this coexistence. 'It used to be an integrated organization, with a single command structure, a single government set of objectives, a board structure, all that you would associate with a homogenous organization. If there is conflict it is because, suddenly last year, the two organizations were separated. Sometimes they have different visions of where they should be going. We are having to catch up fast in learning what private industry has learned over many years, and that is a contractor-supplier relationship that is new to us. *We* would see Railtrack essentially as our supplier, and therefore they should be responsive to us as their biggest customer in Scotland. Currently *they* still see themselves as the landlords, and to a certain extent us as the tenants, therefore we should to a certain extent jump to their whim. Both of us have to work out this new culture and environment we are in. We have only been doing it for a year, most of which was devilled by strike. We have got off to the worst of all starts. No one blames anyone for that. It's a fact of life, we got off to a rotten start. Now we have to reinforce public confidence in delivering the system and service.'

The reality is that since 1948 the railways have been public sector, and have largely put public service above commercial considerations. Graham Smith agrees: 'Nowadays, what is good about public service, in my opinion, is there is a huge degree of loyalty among the staff.

You probably find this in the NHS and police force as well. When people have been in public service a long time, they have an ethical commitment to that service, which is a huge asset. Secondly, the railway people in public service tend to stay a long time, so you can benefit from a huge amount of experience. On the whole, you get a dedication and a practical expertise that is useful. Thirdly, the public service ethos is in itself quite a virtuous thing, as long as it doesn't cloud some of the other disciplines of commercialism in progress and modernization. The private sector is very good at innovation, at challenging, at changing, at keeping up with customer receptiveness. Sometimes out of that comes some conflict, but there is no organization I know that is not at some stage in conflict with itself about the way forward, and reconciling it can be very healthy.'

What ScotRail must do is keep the best of the public service virtues they have, and the history, but build on to that some of the modern, private sector thinking. Can it achieve the best of both worlds? Can that be done?

Says John Ellis, 'Historically, we have been losing market share in what is a consistently growing transport sector. Although, relative to other parts of the UK, road congestion is at present limited in Scotland, car ownership is increasing at a much faster rate, giving rise to concerns. This could adversely affect the quality of life, environment and Scotland's appeal to tourists. Competitive pressure continues to be severe, partly due to the high quality of the road network in Scotland, but also due to the continuing development of various forms of telecommunication which can reduce the potential demand for physical travel. In addition, customer and public expectations continue to rise both in terms of basic product quality and in customer service aspects.

'Success has been achieved to date in ScotRail by focusing on total quality management and the customer. Consistently reliable delivery of the product is essential in going forward. Looking more widely at resources, obviously the quality of the infrastructure on which we operate, and the rolling stock equipment which we use to provide our service are vitally important. Our key resource is our people (in the case of the ScotRail franchise they will represent almost literally the only asset!). Our primary aim is to widen and deepen the commitment and motivation of all our customer service employees to delivering high quality customer service.'

The potential for throwing up bigger customer service benefits is there, no question of it. When ScotRail was an integrated company with rolling stock to look after, stations and bridges to build, 3,500 miles of track to maintain, and 360-odd stations, a lot of its preoccupation was with production matters. It spent much time on areas like capital investment, replacing rolling stock, maintaining the track, electrification, all those issues which indirectly have customer benefits, but not obviously so. As ScotRail no longer has those obligations, its sole responsibility now is to concentrate on running dependable services day in and day out, for the customer. Says Graham Smith, 'Concentrating on things such as marketing, the product, punctuality, cleanliness of trains, ease of ticket purchase, looking after the disabled – I'm not saying we neglected those aspects in the past, but I think they were to a certain extent overshadowed by the "bigger" issues.'

Historically, ScotRail has been used to having the whole infrastructure under its wing. Now it has to adjust to this contractor-supplier arrangement. Says Graham Smith, 'If you look at most organizations, particularly in the private sector, they cope with that, day in and day out. If you are a Marks & Spencer, you are reliant on the contractor who brings all your food in high quality condition. We have to learn to co-operate as contractor and supplier in a way the private sector has been doing in the past. In essence, our objectives should be convergent. It is in Railtrack's interest and our interest to run an efficient railway that looks after customers and gives them punctual departures, with trains that work. I don't think anyone is under any illusion that we have to forge this partnership. We have a lot of responsibility, having said that, for the way our own trains run. OK, we rely on decent signalling from Railtrack etc. But we maintain our trains, we look after them ourselves. If a train does not work well, we have only ourselves to blame. What we cannot start with Railtrack is a blame culture – we really have to avoid that.'

ScotRail runs 1,900 trains a day from Wick to Stranraer, Mallaig to North Berwick. Its aim is to create a commercially successful train company, dedicated to giving their customers value for money, and becoming the most dependable and friendly way to travel in Scotland. 'That word *dependable*,' says John Ellis, 'underpins everything. We must have continuous heightening of product delivery levels and improved customer service. The train must be there, its seats and toilets must be clean, the information must be helpful and audible. Unless we have a basic product, we won't stay in business.'

'When you go into a dark house and switch on a light switch, you get light. You don't applaud it. You don't say this is a wonderful Thomas Edison invention. You just expect electricity to come flooding through your house. The ambition of any train company must be, at the very least, to say, that 95 to 98 per cent of the time, a customer should be getting on a clean train, on time, in comfort. They must just expect that to be a basic delivery. When we can do that routinely, day in, day out, we move to the more exciting detail and the finesse of that. We are judged through the Passengers' Charter. I have some reservations about the Charter, but at least it is a measurable series of performances, that say to our customers, if ScotRail doesn't get you to your destination within an hour of its published time of arrival you will be compensated. It's a fairly minimal set of standards, but nevertheless it is published, and we are accountable for it.'

What are Graham Smith's reservations? 'My criticism of the Charter is that by dint of being so all-embracing it does not target its customers in a way they would see was relevant. It was invented with good intentions, but, like most things, when you start applying it into detailed practice it has limitations. What we are doing in terms of our satisfaction criteria is to say we will go way beyond what the Charter described as minimalist and will be far more responsive to putting things right if they go wrong.'

ScotRail is an organization of 4,000 people, and for most it has been drilled into them over the years that operations, production and engineering are the pinnacles on which the business survives or falls. Graham Smith says, 'What ScotRail must do now is excite staff about the marketing offer, the product, the way it is delivered, the way it is served, so the customers feel they are getting value for money over and above their expectations.'

Will some staff say the change is all about abandoning the past for pastures new? 'It's not,' says John Ellis. 'It is actually about maintaining the high ground of the past and going to even higher ground in the future. We started as a group of directors by saying, "This is a new company in a new environment. In order to lead our workforce towards this higher ground, we need to establish a set of vision and values." We involved, over a period of time, 200 of the other managers, and said, "This is what we think we need to lead this company in terms of our vision, values and core strategies. Do you agree with us?" They refined them. We half baked the cake and they finished off its baking. Our job was then to say, "Right, we at least have a management vision of how we need to change. How do we bring the 4,000 people we manage on board with us on this journey?" We launched a communication roadshow and began the "Friendly ScotRail Programme" [FSP], part of which is talking through with people what we mean by change, new values, customer service, by marketing. You can only change a company from where it has been to where you want it to go by a very assiduous, consistent process of communication, and demonstrating through management that changes are desirable. The way we are doing it is, I hope, by example, but certainly by a massive amount of communication, and by trying to keep the message fairly simple but very consistent.

There is always going to be some caution in ScotRail. Anything new and promoting change invites a degree of resistance in whatever quarter. But more than resistance, there is curiosity. Graham Smith explains: 'From all the contact I had with the staff through the roadshows and the FSP, I'm very impressed by their open-mindedness. That doesn't mean acceptance of change, but they will listen to what change means in the global sense of ScotRail, and also what it might mean to them as individuals. The resistance I have encountered so far is they sense the change is politically motivated, rather than "best-business" motivated. A lot of them like the idea of looking after customers better, earning greater revenue, better marketing, better product. It makes sense to them. They know that nowadays, no business has a right to survive. Business has got to earn the right to survive. They are under no illusion: womb-to-tomb employment in the railways, or any other industry, is dead. They know that. A lot of the staff now are willing to accept change, as long as there is a lucid reason for it and it's something they can see themselves influencing. If there is resistance, it is to ask, are we being pushed down a path, rather than volunteering to go down it? All of us want to have some degree of control over our destiny, and if we feel that destiny is being manipulated, we tend to be concerned and resistant.'

If anyone is resistant, no one believes that would delay the inevitability of change and franchise. Ellis agrees. 'They couldn't delay the totality of what we are trying to do. It's like putting bumps in a road. It can slow down your progress, but it doesn't stop or divert you from the objective. But people do need to be won over. There is no point, me and my other directors sitting in our offices, pontificating and preaching. We really have to get out and about. It's a cliché, but we are managing by walkabout and talking. We are out there getting as many staff aware of what we are trying to do as possible. It is quite difficult with 4,000 people spread over the whole of Scotland, and now we have sleeper trains it also means staff down in London; but if we are serious about change, it's their hearts and minds we have to get to.'

Staff I met in ScotRail were willing to accept that unless they change, they will get left behind. That does not mean they are lying down and saying, run all over me. It certainly means people are more attuned to change, as long as the reasons for that change are lucidly spelt out. Says Ellis, 'There are no doubt a number of my colleagues in the company who feel, because we have to win the franchise at all costs, that if we don't win it a Sword of Damocles will fall, and undoubtedly, some people will be decapitated. I don't think at the moment it is demotivating people, but we'd be foolhardy to ignore it.'

ScotRail have staff who can no longer expect jobs for life, because a franchise is going to be for only seven years. Anyone who is in the franchise may have to think in terms of medium-term contracts, certainly at the management level, of five to seven years. John Ellis says the ScotRail organization model will inevitably become flatter, and less rigid over time. 'We shall be looking for greater flexibility and reduction of job demarcation wherever possible, and the use of information technology will reduce the staffing required for managing and administering ScotRail.

'Also, self-empowerment and self-management will become a progressively greater feature. It follows that leadership will inevitably have to be open, team-based, and consultative. It will also be actively looking for ideas to flow from employees and for a high degree of self-induced development and improvement and sharing of good practice. Managing the people will become in some ways more demanding as self-empowerment develops, but also easier in the sense that self-empowerment creates self-management and will lead to simpler organization structures. Staff training is, of course, vital. We'll need to refresh and tighten the quality of our customer service performance continually and that can only be done by continuous retraining.'

Part of this training has been the two-day residential FSP programme, which marries with ScotRail's mission statement on becoming the most friendly way to travel in Scotland. 'The intention,' says Graham Smith, 'is all 4,000 of us in the company go through this over an eighteen month period. It is an intensive two-day workshop, facilitated by ScotRail people who have been specially chosen, tailor-trained to help deliver this programme. We cover a vast array of subjects, including the mission statement, values and teamwork. We look at ourselves as others see us. You get some stark images when you ask sixteen people in a room, who are a cross-section of the railway. "How do you think your customer sees you? How would you like your customer to see you?" We look at the service chain and how one job can have an impact on another. The drivers who come on this say, "Why am I going on a course about customer service?" As they didn't normally see many customers, or have contact with them, they didn't think they had a customer service role – but the whole essence of their job is providing service. Just that in itself is making people think afresh about where they fit in ScotRail. What is the company trying to do for the future? Where do they fit in, in terms of the team? On every course a director comes for a good couple of hours at the end, and will answer any questions that the staff have to ask.

'On the second day of the programme, the group works with their area or depot manager, problem-solving. What they problem-solve are real issues. So the person who says, "Why don't we ever have timetables in this particular booking office?" gets an opportunity to work at solving that kind of nitty-gritty problem which is the very basis on which our business rises or falls. The director tends to get the more strategic questions on the first day. But the second day is about how to solve the problems.'

ScotRail in the year 2000 will be more different internally than externally, foresees Ellis. 'I see a radical internal shake-up. We as managers will have become far more contractually streetwise because we will be dealing with a lot of suppliers where real money will be changing hands. Under the previous BR organization, money changed hands. It was real money but it was all flushing around within BR. Come the year 2000, we will have had five years where we will have paid real pounds, from ScotRail to Railtrack; to the rolling stock companies; to the British Transport Police for their services. We will have a whole new set of suppliers with whom we have legally and commercially binding agreements.'

The extent to which ScotRail manages those contracts will determine two things: the quality of service it gives its customers, and the wealth that flows into or out of the company. If it generates wealth, the more it can afford to look at specific price targeting. There are times of the day, peak hours, when it would not suit its marketing to cut fares. However, Sunday is a huge opportunity for ScotRail. It has reviewed the things it is poor at, and Sunday is a market it has traditionally failed to exploit. I discovered that myself, trying to get out of Oban for Glasgow/London. Graham Smith apologizes! 'Also our trains in the evenings could be such a good way of coming into town, for theatre, night-clubbing, and getting back again – all those opportunities we have not traditionally worked as hard on expanding, and we must in the future. We have a business plan 1995 to 2000. Part of it is to identify a new range of markets we should be getting into, new products that actually unfold like a fan over the five years, so we can keep adding interest and value to the company.'

There are two really powerful people in the new scheme of things. One is the franchising director for the privatization programme and the whole of the railway industry who is a government appointee, directly accountable to the Secretary of State for Transport. He will ultimately be the authority which awards the franchises to anyone who is a contender. The other is the regulator who is accountable ultimately to Parliament. He will oversee all that ScotRail do, from services to safety, regulation and pricing – a very significant, potent force.

The franchising director issues the 'passenger service requirement' for all train-operating companies. It varies, but he is saying to any potential bidder for a franchise such as the ScotRail team: 'Here is a minimum level of service you will operate if you are to be awarded the franchise.' From the consultative document more than 90 per cent of the services ScotRail currently run must be run in the future. ScotRail are not actually allowed to dispose of railway or train services as they see fit, as proved by the attempted removal by BRB in 1995 of the Fort William sleeper service to the Highlands. In the future, the franchising director's passenger service requirement will probably tie operators to a high minimum standard of timetabling service for the period of the franchise.

John Ellis doesn't see the railway network being revolutionized in five years. 'I think elements of the service will be better. The method of delivery may be far crisper and sharper, but the core of the business will still be commuter, rural, inter-urban trains, running a service that we hope meets more and more of the passenger needs. I do not see that changing dramatically in the next five or seven years.'

What will change dramatically is the method by which ScotRail manage that. Ellis knows that they will be far more contract-based, more financially prudent, taking ScotRail from a 'transport' to a 'service' organization. 'We will be as hot as mustard on service, and I think customer service issues will dominate board meetings. At the moment they are on the agenda, but they have to fight for their space. I think you will find that service issues will really dominate the board agendas. The customer will continue to be a major influence on our organization. It is difficult to see direct stakeholding or partnership, although it is possible to see customer representation at board level. Certainly there will be increased seeking of customer views on the organization and the service it provides.'

John Ellis says ScotRail will probably have more outsiders coming in, some on short-term contracts to help act as catalyst for change at the management level. 'We will have a younger group of staff, and encourage a more rapid turnover of people. We will certainly encourage people to move between jobs within the company more rapidly. I hope the unions will allow that. I think there will be a lessening of power exercised by the unions, but I would like to think they will still be interested in working with us influentially, in changing things. I don't think to be successful you need to expunge the unions, you just need to have them working far more with you. The trade unions think and act differently from ten or twelve years ago. They are becoming quite modern business units in themselves. They have research and development departments, bring in graduates and are interested in the business profitability. So I would believe, provided they feel we are treating the people they represent well and with dignity, we can work with the unions very happily.'

Historically, for ScotRail, there has not been much impact from, or interference by, a regulatory authority outside the UK. John Ellis says, 'While some aspects of the influence of national government will be reduced by privatization, it will not be eliminated and the influence of European government will inevitably increase. Some of that will be beneficial in terms of strengthening our competitive position. We are more likely to be influenced by Europe at the margin of the business, in terms of safety regulations, employment conditions, rather than the core business. The core business is sufficiently regulated by existing UK legislation and control authorities, but how we treat people in the future towards 2000 could well be more influenced by Europe.

ScotRail doesn't think it needs to be meaner to be better, but it admits it needs to be leaner. Says John Ellis, 'I think we have to encourage people to say we can do more, better, with fewer of us. it may mean we pay better, which is good for productivity, flexibility and accountability, but we are certainly going to need fewer people to do more work better. As I've indicated, we are going to be a flatter organization, and hallelujah to that, because the flatter we are the easier it is to communicate, to empower, to delegate, the easier it is to get things done. Probably at the moment we are still too hierarchical, too over-structured. So leaner, certainly flatter, certainly happier will be the ScotRail of the future. If we can get all those other things working, the people who are left should feel more accountable and more involved in the running of their business.'

ScotRail uses a fairly sturdy infrastructure at present and it doesn't see the need for Railtrack to build many new bridges, much more track or massive new stations. The kind of stations opened nowadays are quite small and commuter-based. As long as the infrastructure is maintained well, Ellis doesn't see a huge amount of extra capital investment required. 'The responsibility of an organization is to achieve its business objectives and to do this without adversely affecting the wider community and the environment. It is evident that by providing an important element in the transport infrastructure, ScotRail is contributing to the growth of the Scottish economy and to its future prosperity.'

The very nature of its business is likely to contain ScotRail within the UK. 'It is feasible to consider selling our expertise to other countries but our resources are always likely to be limited and to remain focused on our core activity. Core business development will be predominantly through greater use of the existing service. In the longer term however, there will inevitably be some consolidation within the industry by acquisition, merger or major stake holding.'

Running the business in the next millennium, John Ellis believes there will be far more emphasis on the exploitation of information technology in delivering high quality performance and particularly in providing customer information at all stages of the journey. 'The use of electronic remote monitoring of critical equipment will be an essential part of that process and will require new forms of high quality telecommunications. Technical skills in pro-active diagnostic monitoring and preventive maintenance will also require continuous heightening of skills in our existing workforce.'

In Scotland the press is largely sympathetic to ScotRail, which bodes well for the future. As Graham Smith says, 'That is quite a difference from down south, where everything is tarred with the BR brush. Our media up here is a bit more selective, so I don't think we start with a negative image. If our customers have a bad impression of ScotRail, it is because *we* have let them down, not because they've read about us in the newspaper. If we have let them down, the chance is we can recover their loyalty to the train company more quickly. It is very difficult to change perceptions, but if somebody is unsympathetic because they have actually experienced something bad, then we can put that right.'

Is ScotRail not worried that complaints have risen in the last year? Graham Smith says, 'Terrific. Every comment or complaint is a free bit of feedback which enables me to take action and put matters right. We are encouraging more people to talk back. We are currently getting 1,000 letters a month. We have one-to-one sessions at stations, making ourselves available for several hours with a whole group of staff, including managers and directors. At a central station we see some 300 customers. We are seeking their advice and their comments. Managers go up and down the trains at busy periods of the day with notepads, sitting down and talking to commuters. The directors write in our house magazine and say, "We want to hear from you Mr, Mrs and Miss Customer. We have actively gone out saying we are in pursuit of your experience on our trains, and we want to hear." Unless we hear, we must assume, as any company does, that the customer is at least relatively satisfied. We think by asking them to contact us more frequently we will find out whether or not they are satisfied with our service. If passengers tell us they are dissatisfied then we have some chance of putting that right. If we are not told, we can't do nearly enough.'

ScotRail have to do these things quickly. In an ideal world they would pace themselves getting internal mechanisms right. Admits John Ellis, 'We have not got time.' We want to win the franchise, and if we win the franchise we then have seven years. We are running a 100-metre sprint, not a mile. We would not have opened the flood gates on customer comment and criticism if we did not think we were going to do something about it fast. I certainly would not have encouraged my colleagues to take such a high profile if I didn't feel we were worthy of receiving comments and doing something about them. I think we have got better systems now for responding and tracking, using trends and customer satisfaction surveys. We have a lot of our own in-house infrastructure in place, not all of it yet, but sufficient that says we can make a go now of a better customer response.'

In the year 2000 John Ellis and his team hope they will be managing a ScotRail private franchise: 'One where we have our staff buying into the business as well. 'By "buying" I mean not only literally but also metaphorically, buying in emotionally. We hope we will have a Management Employee Buyout [MEBO], so the staff who are still with us by the year 2000 will feel they are part of the company more than just by being on the payroll. They should themselves be shareholders, and to a certain extent own the company in which they are employed.

'Ideally, if we have 4,000 people in the company, we want all to have at least one share each, and possibly to own a lot more in a perfect MEBO. That means they are not only employees, they are owners. The National Freight Corporation are fantastic people for that concept: they have so many of their staff involved in the business that of course it took off. Not only did it make the employees wealthier, it made them happier in their job, more productive. And the share price went through the roof. Even if the share itself doesn't accumulate in value, I think owning the company that you work for is what most of us dream about, isn't it?'

Two years on, ScotRail will be thinking about consolidating all the gains it has made, in the hope that, once the franchises are re-let at the end of seven years, it is again the obvious candidate. 'Maybe not the only one, but the obvious one to re-win it,' says John Ellis. 'Everything we will have done in terms of customer service, efficiency, safety, good product, imagination and contribution to Scotland's economy – all those things that would matter in terms of how well we have managed the business – will, I hope, make people say, "These guys, on their track record, deserve the next seven years."'

There are two key reasons for wanting to win the franchise: one is that ScotRail believes it has something to contribute to running the railway. Second, and less nobly, more selfishly, ScotRail wants the franchise because it is a way of making money for all the people who buy into it. 'Let's not be coy about this,' admits John Ellis. 'This is a downright commercial proposition. Unless we add wealth to the business, the government will get to a point where it will freeze the subsidy, and what we do not want to be is entirely dependent on government subsidy, we want a bit of growth in our own business.'

Getting all ScotRail's people interested in creating wealth is a big challenge. The virtues of public service are about getting value for money and being efficient. They are not about generating money. As Graham Smith says, 'We have to try and take people with us in believing that creating wealth is not dirty, it is not unhelpful. It actually can be damn good for business if we take public service into that new area that I call customer service, where we have lost nothing of the good of public service, but we ratchet it up to a level that says customer service is every bit as good as public service, and better! Because we are adding wealth to the business and turning it back into customer benefits.'

Privatization opens up new challenges and new opportunities, particularly in Scotland, for all ScotRail. John Ellis has achieved a number of ambitions within the railway industry. 'My ambition now is to lead a successful bid for the ScotRail franchise, to realize the opportunities which flow from being masters of our own destiny, and to see ScotRail fulfilling an increasingly important role in the economic and social development of Scotland.'

SECURICOR GROUP PLC

Turnover (1994)	£800.3 million
Profit before tax	£80.6 million
Net assets	£294.1 million
Employees	43,508
UK	23,447
Overseas	20,061

Securicor operates in the UK and overseas with a structured portfolio of complementary business to business services.

Roger Wiggs – Group Chief Executive

A solicitor, Roger Wiggs was appointed to the Board in 1977. He is a director of Cellnet Group Ltd and a non-executive director of BSM Group PLC.

Sir Peter Imbert, QPM, DL – Non-Executive Director

Sir Peter Imbert joined the Metropolitan Police in 1953. He transferred to CID in 1956 and served for many years in Special Branch. After senior appointments with Surrey Constabulary he became Chief Constable of Thames Valley Police in 1979. In 1985 he was appointed Deputy Commissioner of Metropolitan Police and then served as Commissioner from 1987-93. In 1993 he was appointed to the board of Securicor Group PLC. He is a non-executive director of Camelot Group PLC and of Help the Aged.

Business is in the following divisions:

Security Services – transportation, counting and redistribution of cash and valuables, guarding, alarms and custodial services.

Distribution Services – domestic and international delivery services, from urgent to heavyweight consignments, by road, sea or air. Integrated logistic solutions.

Communications – cellular products and service provision, radio systems and Linear Modulation Technology, telecoms equipment and technology, Datatrak vehicle location and data communications, electronic engineering and design.

Business Services – Vehicle services and bodywork conversion, hotels, recruitment and computer services.

Securicor Group PLC
Roger Wiggs, Chief Executive
Sir Peter Imbert QPM,
Non-Executive Director

Securicor began life in 1935 as a small group of guards in the West End of London, and continued after the war guarding properties in Mayfair. The business was acquired in 1960 by a small hotel chain, Associated Hotels Ltd, who found Securicor to be an exciting business. It grew from there. Securicor became involved in the secure transportation of cash, which led to an involvement carrying bank data and related documents. As it already possessed an extensive fleet of vehicles which were carrying all types of valuable goods, it was a natural progression to move into the transportation of parcels. The postal strike in the seventies gave Securicor the opportunity to expand.

Explains Roger Wiggs, Chief Executive, 'Whilst the distribution of letters was a Post Office monopoly, it did not extend to the movement of parcels. Our distribution network was well suited to pick up a lot of parcels and distribution business during that strike, which we subsequently retained. The majority of the Securicor businesses as they are today have grown out of, or are complementary to, our two original core businesses, i.e. parcels and security services.'

Today, the group's business is worldwide and includes freight haulage, mail and express parcel services, document delivery, transportation and processing of cash and valuables – it is the UK's largest carrier – hotels, recruitment services, telecommunications and more recently custodial services. Securicor provides security guards for premises from docks and harbours to airports to industrial estates, together with electronic surveillance and alarm systems – monitoring some 50,000 systems worldwide – a spread of security services demanding high standards of personnel integrity throughout their businesses.

'The recent diversification of our Security Services Division into another growth area – custodial services – was in response to the Government's privatization programme for prisons and prisoner escorting,' says Wiggs. 'There is no reason why prisons cannot be managed by the private sector, and Securicor has the base skills and management abilities to do this, although clearly there are some extra skills that needed to be brought in.'

Today, Securicor Custodial Services is responsible for 200,000 prisoner movements each year in the London area, covering eight prisons, 82 police stations and 60 courts. A major decision had to be made when Securicor decided to go into the movement of prisoners, as opposed to the movement of cash. 'This was largely because of the financial investment we would have to make, plus the additional resources, premises, vehicles, personnel etc. to ensure it was successful. It wasn't a monumental decision in principle. We have three-quarters of the expertise in-house anyway. Securicor already transports high value loads across the country, whether it is gold, cash or valuable securities. Our job is to ensure customers' cash and valuables are carried safely. The secure and humane transporting of prisoners was accordingly well within our ability. The question was how to marshal the resources, how to recognize what else was needed to be put in place to obtain that contract, and then consistently to provide a first class service.'

Sir Peter Imbert, a non-executive director, was formerly a Commissioner of the Metropolitan Police. He believes Securicor are the natural deliverers and lookers-after of these prisoners. 'I have never considered the police as being the right people to do that task. The police are too highly trained. They should be concentrating on what the police ought to be doing, patrolling our streets, investigating crimes, preventing crime, talking to the community. Forging that partnership. They shouldn't be driving prison vans. That is such a waste of enormously valuable resources.'

Sir Peter agrees that initially there was a certain amount of opposition from some police areas to this contracting-out policy, generally from those who were actually involved in transporting the prisoners. 'Of course, there are also those who would be politically opposed, because they question whether the transportation of prisoners should be done by private enterprise. However, when we look back from the year 2000, I believe we will find the task has been performed much more economically. Not just financially, but economical as far as expertise is concerned. Securicor can provide a dedicated workforce to do that. They have to be properly trained, and they have to learn the "language". In policing terms, it was a demand on the police they couldn't afford to satisfy, with all the other purely policing services they have to provide.'

The development of Securicor from 1935 onward has been a natural progression. Because of the secure nature of its base business it has developed many of its own support services rather than buy these in, and over time many of these have been made available to external customers. For example, as well as managing its own fleet of over 7,500 vehicles, Securicor Vehicle Services maintains and manages 3,000 vehicles for third parties. Their bodyworks business manufactures vehicle bodies for Securicor's own cash-in-transit and custodial vehicles. Why not also for the emergency services and local authorities? Datatrak, a vehicle protection, tracking and recovery system, not only protects Securicor's own vehicles but became a business in its own right, tailored for the private motorist, plant and food markets, alerting the authorities as soon as a theft attempt is made and guiding the police to the stolen property.

As expected in this type of industry. Securicor must have sophisticated recruitment policies and training arrangements. On the security side, they have to ensure all their guards and drivers, for example, are properly vetted. As Roger Wiggs confirms, these front-line staff are subjected to a very strict training régime, in order to know what to do if a problem occurs in the line of duty. 'We have extensive recruitment and ongoing training requirements, bearing in mind within the UK we now have over 23,000 employees.' This is one of the reasons why Securicor entered the recruitment business and acquired hotels in Richmond and Coventry to provide training and conference facilities. Both now obtain over 90 per cent of their business from external customers, at the same time as fulfilling Securicor's internal needs.

Communications, now Securicor's third core business, is another area of business that grew out of the original base business of security and parcels. It is today one of the UK's top service providers on the Cellnet network, with over 320,000 subscribers offering a range of mobile phones, tariffs and value-added services through high street dealers and a national sales force. Securicor has 40 per cent stake in Cellnet with its majority partner British Telecom. It may at first appear unusual to the reader that a business in the context of security and parcels is also involved with a high-tech industry and mobile phones. Roger Wiggs explains, 'The fact is that we had the largest private radio network in the UK and were the first to have a facility to connect to the public telephone network. We had to have radio communications with our cash and parcels vehicles and because it had to be a very secure communications network, we had to control it ourselves. It was natural development to take that further and allow our control rooms to act as message passing operations for third parties and ultimately to provide them with full systems of their own.

'At that point, in the early eighties, we had the opportunity of bidding for the Cellnet licence. We were able to negotiate a mutually satisfactory joint venture with British Telecom [BT], to which one of the two cellular licences was granted by the Government. The Cellnet success has spread from there.'

Securicor is today at the forefront of the mobile communications revolution, not just in the form of Cellnet and cellular voice communications, but in private mobile radio, vehicle location and data communication, and, indeed has recently been awarded the fifth mobile data licence in the UK. It has also developed new technologies and products such as Linear Modulation Technology [LMT] which is unique. LMT products offer high quality voice and high speed data capabilities whilst occupying less than half the current channel spacing within the limited radio spectrum where channels are in heavy demand.

Securicor has also entered mainstream telecommunications, both in developing and marketing telephone exchanges and in developing ISDN software equipment. The ISDN revolution allows networks to carry digital voice, data, image and video information across the world. With substantial orders from North America and world-wide interest in LMT and ISDN there is no doubt that these are areas of future growth for the group that excite Roger Wiggs and Securicor.

Another example of development from the original businesses is Datatrak, another part of the Communications Division. If there were a raid, there was a need for some means of tracking the cash-in-transit vehicles. Roger Wiggs explains, 'We came across a technology which was in the process of being developed by Wimpey, and being used to position oil platforms. The technology was developed and Datatrak was born and a nationwide vehicle tracking system established. For the first two or three years we were content merely to use that tracking system for our own vehicles. Then it became clear there was a demand for application of this network from outside, both for fleet management as well as security purposes. One such application was the development of TrakBak stolen vehicle tracking system for use by the private motorist as well as business users. The potential for developing these markets and further applications in the future both here and overseas is very encouraging.'

Over the years the growth of Securicor was so rapid that focus was being lost and it was necessary to separate the businesses into more clearly managed entities. Roger Wiggs explains: 'We identified the three main business sectors in the group and decided that these three core business sectors would be divisionalized, each with a Divisional Chief Executive in charge. The grouping gives us balance from an economic point of view, since each is reasonably self-sufficient in its own right and it is unlikely that any economic downturn would affect all at the same time, given that we are also operating internationally in 33 other countries. Of particular importance was the clarity of reporting lines, areas of responsibility and ownership which the new structure gave to management and much improved financial information.'

As mentioned previously, recruitment and training in Securicor's business are vital. To run a parcels network you must have sophisticated procedures, to make sure you actually do get to B at the right time, at the right place, with the right load. Similarly, a team running a cash-in-transit vehicle must live and breathe the strictest of procedures so that their training will enable them to act automatically should an attack take place, with the safety of their customers, the public and themselves paramount.

'There is another dimension to it,' adds Sir Peter, 'which is selection. In the police service people are selected to be officers on the beat. Through that system the detectives and senior officers emerge. Here, within Securicor, we know what we want the people for, whether it is for custodial services, cash in transit, patrol guards, alarms guarding, communications or hotels. The selection procedures, the background enquiries all have to be good. I probably see it clearer than somebody who is actually working here full time. I'm very impressed with the way in which they check on an applicant's background and qualifications. Later on in one's career there may be opportunities to move across from one area to another, but first of all, personnel are selected for a particular area. So selection procedures, deciding on the job description, the level of intelligence, the aptitude the person is going to need, directing the advertising in the right area, doing a proper selection, doing absolutely first-class background checks, are absolutely vital in a security organization. Any talk of reducing the period of background checks to ten or five years will be resisted by Securicor. They believe that one has to go back a long way, but once that has been done and selection procedures completed, once you have them all on board, then thorough training becomes the cornerstone, the first building block of this organization.'

Securicor would like to see all other parts of the industry carrying out their selection and training as rigorously as they do. It is a constant in excellent organizations, that they innovate standards for the rest of the industry to follow.

Says Roger Wiggs, 'Securicor was instrumental in setting up the BSIA (the British Security Industry Association). We are anxious that standards should be raised in the industry. Additionally, like other majors in the industry, we very much support the idea of compulsory regulation from the Government to keep cowboys out of the business.'

However, the Police Federation has voiced its concern along with the Association of Chief Police Officers, that for budgetary reasons a growing area of the UK could be policed by private security guards well before the year 2000. There is anxiety that security guards are being brought in to replace police as a cut-price alternative service. As a result, they feel that beat patrolling by private security guards and companies may lead to an overall decline in policing standards. The concern is that a layer of private security guards inserted between the regular police and their customers might deny many opportunities to build up the public goodwill and acquire information on which much police success relies.

Sir Peter responds, 'The police do want to divest themselves of some of the mundane areas which they have been called upon to guard. Take, for example, shopping malls. The police cannot afford, nor do they want, to have to provide manpower to go into those all the time. After all, they are private areas. Even though their numbers are increasing, there does not seem to be an increasing number of personnel being used to guard them. Technology is taking over. The surveillance in a large shopping mall used to require half a dozen people at any one time round the clock. Now it can be done with one or two people watching television cameras. Television cameras can be used to watch the main street. Securicor is involved in helping to man those. Police officers do not have the time to sit down and watch those cameras all the time. We are able to provide the personnel to do that for them. Once we see there is a need for the police, we alert them immediately. It is definitely a partnership business. Not only with our customers who might be the owners of the shopping mall: we are in a partnership also with the police, who must undertake responsibility ultimately for applying the criminal law.'

In the cash services business there is a question as to whether or not the market as a whole is going to decline as more credit cards and systems like Mondex gain hold, and to what degree cash handling, in its widest context, is going to continue as a major market. Says Roger Wiggs, 'Certainly, we are the dominant force in the market now, and we would expect to remain so. What that will look like in 25 years time, is difficult to say. I suspect we will still be the dominant force, but the breadth of services will be very different from the ones we see today. We already move credit cards around. It may well be we will get into maintenance or the provision of front line EPOS (electronic point of sale machinery). There will always be need for cash. There will always be a requirement for ATM machines for somebody wanting cash at short notice, and it follows therefore that there will always be a need to refill those machines. Securicor's job is to satisfy the market it is in, but also to anticipate five or ten years on what is going to happen. That is why we have a very close partnership arrangement with the banks and all involved in that market. As trends emerge, we anticipate what the opportunities might be.'

Towards 2000 Securicor is already spreading its security services extensively throughout the world, largely through partnership arrangements. It is the dominant force in the UK parcels distribution business, and is spreading that business into Europe and into warehousing, logistics etc. 'We are,' says Roger Wiggs, 'in a very prominent position throughout Europe. We will continue to build on that, and would expect 25 years on to be a major player in the parcel distribution business within Europe, with links throughout the world.'

Securicor's declared mission is to ensure that the distinctive 'Securicor' brand remains synonymous with the qualities and reputation it has earned for itself over the years for 'integrity, reliability and security'. A new millennium wish for Roger Wiggs, would be to maintain and improve these standards in order to satisfy, not just the customer, but all stakeholders. 'The world-wide nature of

Securicor will become more apparent as it moves towards the millennium, with wholly owned operations as well as joint ventures along the lines of those it has in the Far East, the Americas, the Caribbean, Europe and South Africa. Historically, our security businesses were the first to be established overseas. Now, however, both the Distribution Services and Communications Divisions are following suit. The predominant drive is to provide a quality service to customers both at home and overseas (often the same companies). There is competition in this business, and that is good because it stimulates the market. However, Securicor would never abdicate its standards by giving a lower service for a lower price. We are not prepared to compromise on our hard-won reputation for integrity, reliability and security.'

One of the hopes for the next millennium for Securicor is to bring on new managers throughout the organization as good as, if not better than, they have today. 'That is not easy,' admits Roger Wiggs. 'We have put a lot of time and effort into identifying and training up young and middle-aged potential managers, as fast as we possibly can, and have given them all the equipment they need to be a good manager into the future. That is critical, not just for Securicor but for most organizations. Some people will inevitably be headhunted. What we need is sufficient stock of good people, who are really high quality managers, who will enrich our businesses and make them work and work well.'

This is one of the reasons behind the acquisition and use of the new Securicor management training centre at Hartsfield Manor: to uncover latent talent within the organization and give it the advantage of better training, looking at the future, discussing strategy and the organization, and giving it the opportunity to mature in a vibrant and thriving group.

Says Roger Wiggs, 'I am confident that within Securicor we have some very bright people who will come through. But they have to be given the opportunity, the training and the encouragement, and get real experience. Mistakes will be made, but they will be monitored. We have the great opportunity of being able to cross-fertilize talent by giving our people opportunities to work in different divisions and through different businesses.'

In the UK, Roger Wiggs points to the fact that Securicor has a number of well proven, experienced and exceptional managers, many of whom are now in the 50 plus age range. 'What we now

324

need to do is grow and train more rapidly the next generations of management and to give them the hands-on experience they need. At the same time we need to identify the bright people with potential in their 20s and 30s to ensure that they are encouraged, trained and most important of all imbued with the Securicor qualities and culture. No business, whatever it produces, is successful without people. Securicor is no exception. It is the people who make it, first, foremost, and last. It is they who will take us into the next millennium.'

WHITBREAD PLC

Turnover (1995)	£2,471.8 million
Operating profit	£264.6 million
Profit before tax	£255.1 million
Total fixed assets (inc. investments)	£2,629.6 million
Employees	65,238
Full-time	33,374
Part-time	31,864

Leading UK food, drinks and leisure company.

Sir Michael Angus – Chairman

Appointed a non-executive director in 1986, deputy chairman in January 1992, and chairman of Whitbread PLC on 1 August 1992.

Other appointments:
   President of the Confederation of British Industry, May 1992 to May 1994.
   Past chairman of Unilever.
   Non-executive Chairman of The Boots Company PLC.
   Non-executive Deputy Chairman of British Airways PLC
   Non-executive Director of National Westminster Bank PLC.

The business is in four divisions:

Whitbread Inns

Operates 1,600 pubs and pub restaurants. Includes Brewers Fayre and Wayside Inns.

Restaurants and Leisure

Restaurants, shops, hotels, including Beefeater, Threshers, Pizza Hut, T.G.I. Friday's, Country Club Hotel Group. Overseas restaurants in Germany, Canada, USA.

Beer

Integrated brewing, distribution, sales and marketing includes Heineken, Stella Artois, Murphy's, Boddingtons brands.

Pub Partnerships

Leased pub operations: includes 2,300 pubs mainly on 20-year leases to individual business people.

Whitbread PLC
Sir Michael Angus, Chairman

When Samuel Whitbread died in 1796 he was the sole owner of the largest and most famous brewery in the world. Two hundred and fifty years later his company has not just survived but has become one of the top 100 in Britain. It has the largest group of off-licence chains in the UK, exclusive hotels and high street restaurants throughout the country and overseas, with names as familiar as Beefeater and Pizza Hut – and it still brews beer.

Members of the Whitbread family have always played a significant part in the business. Today Sam Whitbread is a non-executive director. He admits that Whitbread is often seen as a rather traditional business. 'This does not mean, however, we are an old-fashioned company. What will, I hope, keep Whitbread at the forefront into the next century are our traditions of financial prudence, social responsibility and, above all, innovation.'

Innovation is certainly one of the common threads woven through the 250 years of Whitbread. 'It's no exaggeration,' says Sam Whitbread, 'to claim that Whitbread has been innovating for two-and-a-half centuries, from brewery design and the mass production of porter through the development of bottled beer in the 1860s to the introduction of lager, wine boxes and food retailing in modern times.' Whitbread was one of the first brewers to spot the changing UK demographics that would witness the slow death of the traditional blue-collar boozer. Today its businesses are focused on large consumer markets and its future depends on its continuing ability to anticipate the changing lifestyles and tastes of its customers. Its intention is to expand further by developing its existing businesses and constantly seeking new ways of applying its operating skills in food, drinks and leisure.

Whitbread has the strongest balance sheet in the business and is ambitious. Although the mid-1990s have been marked by increasingly competitive trading conditions, it has maintained its strong market position by not only anticipating the changes in customer tastes and lifestyles but also recognizing the emergence, post recession, of a more value-conscious consumer.

Sir Michael Angus became chairman of Whitbread in 1992. He says, 'The business climate is at present healthy. Inflation is under control, and, so far as we can see, there is growth in the economy even though it may not be totally reflected in consumer confidence. Add to that a competitive exchange rate, helping our export markets. We have comparatively healthy labour costs as we don't have many of the social costs associated with Europe, and we are very well poised in Britain to have the makings of an industrial renaissance. As far as the rest of the world goes – and something like 55 per cent of our exports go to continental Europe – it does look as though they're coming out of the doldrums as well. That is good for us because we trade there. Yes, I'm fairly positive about the future for industry in general.'

Despite the subdued economy and the highly competitive market Whitbread has been able to record increasing profits before tax and positive cash inflows as a result of operating efficiencies, cost controls and careful management of capital expenditure in all parts of the business. As Sam Whitbread says, 'Generating enough money to fund our expansion plans emerges as a perennial challenge for all our partners and directors – a difficulty perhaps eased by Whitbread's proximity, both physical and personal, to the City of London and its financial markets.' I suspect its success is also consummated through marriage between anticipating changing consumer concerns and innovative, imaginative ideas. I hasten to add that my colleagues suggest the real secret of Whitbread's success is quite simply it brews good beer, producing a long list of famous names in bitter, lager and stout – such as Boddingtons, Heineken, Murphy's Irish, Mackeson, Stella Artois and Flowers.

According to Sir Michael, 'There is a fundamental change in the way business operations are run in the western world. The old pattern of organizational command really stemmed from military theory. This has been found less effective today, and there's much more scope for networking, consultative opportunities, the involvement and empowerment of people down the line. What we are

328

seeing in company structures today are flatter organizations. We've devolved responsibility as far as is practical and encouraged people to be more involved in their total job – not looking for instructions from on high (military-wise) but very much wanting to be involved in the decision making.' Sir Michael says that this enriches business today, and particularly in the area of customer service. 'Customer service opportunities are very often seen at the bottom of the business before they're seen at the top. Therefore, if one's got a constant information stream going in both directions, this can only be beneficial.'

Sir Michael is adamant that Whitbread's future depends on its determination to provide products and services which 'exceed customer expectation'. 'In the case of Whitbread, customer service is really what makes this place tick, and what gives us a competitive edge. We need to be giving people who visit our establishments – pubs, hotels, restaurants, T.G.I. Friday's, Beefeaters and so on – we need to give them a good time. Part of giving people a good time is to look after them – otherwise they'll go elsewhere. Of course that's not just being nice to people. Without any doubt, customer service comes from very structured training, understanding what people are looking for and why they choose one establishment over another.'

Too many companies make the mistake of launching a customer service initiative with all the glitz of a new Ford model. A big session with everybody, and they are suddenly supposed to be switched-on staff. Says Sir Michael, 'One has got to be building and setting the criteria you wish for the company, that you wish to get close to. You then need to do measurement to see if you've got near to your objective, continued measurement – market research, interviewing customers, and so on. You must have a reinforced training schedule that's continuous. Staff have to return and be reminded what we've found about customers, their preferences and so on.'

As Sir Michael has indicated, Whitbread monitors and measures customers' perceptions of service and they are reviewed by the executive committee of the company alongside financial performance. The outcome is that it is better able to demonstrate a direct correlation between standards of service and the successful growth of its concepts. For example, with its off-licence chain, Thresher, it monitors the quality of customer care throughout its approximately 1,600-strong chain of shops. The company measures customer care trends and sales growth and notes the direct correlation between improving standards and its sales and operating growth. Retailers like Whitbread know today's customer demands a high-quality product with outstanding service and a value-for-money price. The recessionary pressures have had an enduring effect and consumers remain highly value-conscious. This means Whitbread has to compete on both price and quality if it wants customers to choose its establishment ahead of its competitors.

For Whitbread to meet the challenge of more cost-efficient ways to run their business and make assets work harder, a flatter and more responsive management structure is considered essential. As modern effective organizations have developed they have removed layers of supervision and management. Sir Michael uses a military analogy, 'What one's trying to avoid in business is: you tell your officer, who tells his major, who tells the colonel of the regiment, who asks the general. That is changing – in fact, it doesn't really go on in the military any more either. It's the fellow out in the field who has to take initiatives. In commercial organizations, layers have grown in the past that need challenging now if British industry is to thrive into the next century.'

Sir Michael recalls that when he was chairman at Unilever, in a company with sales of £30 billion and 300,000 employees only four layers existed between him and a first line manager: 'I agree there would be functions undertaken in a non-operating sense all over the place, but the actual layers in the command part of the business were four. Whitbread is of the same order. That means the chap who is managing a shop for Thresher, has a Beefeater to look after, or is in charge of one of our hotels, has got total responsibility. He is individually allowed a considerable amount of initiative for which he has to account. If there's somebody in a Threshers' shop who's complaining about something, we look to the manager of that shop to put it right. Afterwards, there may be something for us all to learn from that incident, but we *don't* want him to say, "Well, I'll let head office know, and they'll come back to you." The manager on the spot has to put it right. Layers in a command sense – and you must have some command over a profit-making enterprise – are one thing, because you had better know where profit responsibility lies, and where financial limits are exercised. However, you don't want all these command layers. What really is the point of layers? I think people can take broad responsibilities very much more than was accepted in the past. If people are empowered, they break the organizational diagram. They go across boundaries, particularly if you have companies with great geographical spread. Layers produce more work, more correspondence, and more personnel reviews. Layers need to be limited as much as possible.

Sir Michael endorses the need to encourage problem-solving. The need to consult, gain ideas, spin off initiatives and be in an innovation mode, for which Whitbread has always been a model. This requires much investment in training. Whitbread spends some two million pounds each year, and rising, and has won a number of awards for its training programmes. Its overall staff training programme is seen as a leader in its industry. To encourage staff to acquire even better marketing and customer care skills, training is now linked to Whitbread's pay structures in a scheme that has become known as 'earning for learning'. In addition, each member of staff participates in an incentive scheme called Share Inn Success. Staff accrue credit points – according to how well their pub or regional company is performing – which can be traded for goods ranging from electrical equipment to holidays. This scheme, coupled with the staff training programme, has helped to reduce staff turnover by 30 per cent in an industry which has a history of high labour turnover and a traditional reliance on part-timers.

Sir Michael believes fervently that for a company to grow successfully into the millennium there must be a priority emphasis on training, training and yet more training. The importance of training is increasingly being seen as a competitive advantage. In the end businesses aren't going to train for the good of the British economy; they are going to train to gain a competitive knowledge. I've never looked at the training of the medium-sized brewer, but my bet would be they know customer satisfaction is as important to them as it is to us. Training tends to be neglected when the fruits of it are not totally evident. We are in a good position, because when we train people we can see the results. We train people in a unit, the people in that unit become more effective, and we can measure that effectiveness. Training pays. It is as clear as that. It's like asking us why we advertise? We advertise because advertising pays. It gives us business in commercial terms. Likewise with training.'

Businesses grow in a variety of ways, and towards 2000 Whitbread will certainly swallow smaller rivals. In 1995 they made two acquisitions in one week – the £180m purchase of sixteen UK Marriott hotels and the recommended £201m takeover of David Lloyd

Leisure (whose story is also in this book). Whitbread paid top dollar for the chance to expand its transformation from just another brewer and pub operator into a more broadly-based leisure group for the millennium.

Whitbread's main vehicle for growth at present, however, although it may seem dull to the City compared to those 'big deals', is investment in its own current businesses, where Sir Michael believes there are great opportunities. 'We are investing some £350 million a year, of that order, in building new Beefeaters, hotels and so on. I suppose it's around 10 per cent of our net worth we are putting into capital invested in our current operations. That is a lot of growth.' As far as acquisitions are concerned, Sir Michael indicates that they often have the advantage of being quicker in growth terms. However, they also cost a lot of money. Whitbread has been selective in the acquisitions it has made throughout the nineties and will continue to be so. In recent years there have been four acquisitions which have had a major effect.

It took over the Peter Dominic wine chain which, put together with its own Thresher operation, gave it the biggest off-licence chain in the country – 1,600 stores. It also took over Berni Inns which it was able to marry into its Beefeater enterprises. 'Both of those acquisitions have been extremely successful,' says Sir Michael, 'and they've been "natural" really. They've used our skills. Beefeater had better skills than Berni. It was as simple as that. Our team has managed to take the Berni enterprise and make it far more effective as part of the Beefeater chain. It has merged with our core business. There's no diversification and, of course, the synergistic benefits in taking on businesses that are similar to the ones that one already has can be quite major.'

A third example would be the acquisition of the Boddingtons beer brand where Whitbread was able to take a brand which was essentially regional – Manchester was very much its home – and distribute it widely, making it a national brand. When the company bought it some five years ago it sold 300,000 barrels of Boddingtons per annum. This year it will sell around a million barrels. It grew because Whitbread was able to offer a distributional and support mechanism that the original Boddingtons company did or could not have. The Boddingtons company still exists as an entity and the beer brand and brewery, clearly, have been a very successful buy.

The fourth acquisition was the Maredo purchase. This was a chain of steak-house type restaurants in Germany, which Whitbread was able to add to the chain of restaurants it already had in that country. That, again, is typical of an acquisition which it can bolt on to existing proven skills. Says Sir Michael: 'Looking towards the millennium, we're always interested in monitoring opportunities that are round the edge but we are never going to go into making custard pie, custard powder, or something like that; it isn't our skill. In this total area of restaurants, pubs, hotels and so on, there are always opportunities to add on new concepts that draw upon existing skills, but perhaps also involve taking on some new ones.'

There are different ways of growing, and Whitbread's intention is to become more leisure-based, as progress in brewing and selling beer towards 2000 will be tough. They have a keen appetite for food, drink, and for acquisitions, clearly demonstrated by their 1995 purchases, which will cannon them to the forefront of the beer and leisure industries for the millennium. 'Clearly we are a British company with a British heritage,' say Sir Michael. 'We're in the beer business, part of which, up to now, Europe hasn't actually come to terms with. For example, the pub is a very British institution. The reality of Europe is around us and Maredo has been an example of our being more conscious of us being more in Europe than a mere British niche player, but there are some areas where it is difficult to think of us going over and changing the European culture. The pub remains a British concept, and just to pick up British pubs and put them down anywhere will not work, although you'll always get the odd one in the Champs Elysées. However, for Whitbread it makes more sense to expand in keeping with local European concepts. For example, Maredo is a concept more easily in keeping within a European context than a John Bull pub. Another area where we are conscious of European opportunities is the Boddingtons brand. Through tripling the barrelage over the few years we've had it in this country, it illustrates it is a product that has some innovative properties. We believe there are opportunities to export that to Europe. Although we are indeed a company that is UK based and our heritage is British, and we don't have many foreign managers, except in Germany, we recognize the reality of Europe and will use whatever properties we have to adapt and grow into 2000 and beyond.'

All of this Whitbread progress and success takes leadership skill. Are Whitbread leaders born or made? Sir Michael admits he doesn't know! However, he thinks there are certain characteristics which people need to have if they are going to make a career in industrial management. 'Take one rather obvious example,' he says. 'Numeracy. Today, if people aren't numerate they are going to have a problem in industrial management because it is becoming more and more qualified. Management in the broadest sense of the word, of being an executive, is something which can be taught, given some basic individual skills. Clearly, potential managers need a fairly high level of intelligence, but we are talking about the top 5 per cent perhaps, not the top 0.1 per cent which the Civil Service, for example, often say they are going for. So there is a filter. Numeracy, ability to deal with people, a decent balance between being an introvert and an extrovert, are all essential characteristics for business leadership.' Sir Michael says that once you have got those abilities, it's amazing the effect training can produce. 'The biggest companies grow their own timber, even if they don't always keep the trees.'

There have been many studies to find the characteristics of people who go to the top, and Sir Michael feels such research has all been unsuccessful. There are characteristics which he concurs could eliminate people from an industrial career, but good experience on the job, combined with training, can turn a lot of potential industrial careerists into decent managers. As he says, 'People go to the top for different reasons. If I were to pick out a few characteristics, apart from the obvious ones such as intelligence, there are people who have a state of mind which enables them to get to the essential of a problem. A sense of the essential is, I think, terribly important for leaders in industry, otherwise you just get buried under a mass of data. You have to have the mental equipment that cuts through to seize the essential need, or point or whatever it is the problem involves. I believe it is a characteristic most great businessmen have. Secondly, there is something to do with people. I think it is very hard to generalize because "people-business" leaders have got different styles. Even some of the leaders we still have around today with an autocratic style, which people would normally say is not really the way to do it, have produced some pretty successful businesses. But there has to be a *consistent* way of dealing with people, and the word consistent is important. If your style starts to change and if your values keep changing and people are worried about the direction you're going in, then I think leadership falls away.'

According to Sir Michael the third characteristic effective business leaders require for the millennium is a broad approach to innovation.

'Businesses can't stand still. Leaders have to have the ability to encourage innovation, and sometimes themselves participate in it. I have found that great business leaders are not afraid of their intuition. Intuition comes from many sorts of internal characteristics and experiences. Business leaders that I know and respect have never been afraid of intuition. To some extent, I suppose, this is associated with problem-solving. What I like, once you have identified a problem – particularly one that seems intractable – is trying to push back the boundaries to find some new way in which the problem can be expressed. It is an innate human characteristic that some people have and others do not. You must allow yourself to free think, and that essentially is calling upon your intuition.'

As we move towards the millennium, what attributes does Sir Michael believe a good business leader must possess? Immediately he restates, 'Consistency, particularly in dealing with people. Innovation and intuition.' And integrity? 'Yes, but integrity in a very broad way. It's self-evident that one should have integrity in a material way. If not, you turn into a crook – and normally are found out. I'm not really talking about people with their hand in the till, which is clearly a bad thing. I'm talking about intellectual integrity.' By this Sir Michael means thinking a problem through with the emphasis on logic and evidence, rather than letting prejudice and preconceived notions come in and deform the thinking. As he says, 'If you are not careful, the thinking can start with prejudice and preconceived notions. I was trained as a mathematician and I suppose that's why I enjoy this feeling of almost abstract thought.'

What can deform thinking? 'It can be,' says Sir Michael, 'good things, such as concern for people. You say, "Well we ought to be . . . but, you know, we cannot really . . . Poor old Jim. I mean – that community, the village, it depends on us." That stops the thought process as to what actually *ought* to be done. I've always remembered a wise piece of advice: "*Ruthlessly make up your mind as to what you have to do, and then do it as compassionately as possible.*" There's a lot in that. If you let the compassion come into the job or problem analysis first, you are not, if you like, approaching the problem with total intellectual integrity. It could well be that you do the analysis and you say we cannot do it because of this or that event: the government has said that it will nationalize us if we close that plant, or something like that. These are events or situations which one just has to take account of. But once people let the emotional or prejudicial thoughts obstruct the analysis of problems, that is when a business starts, I think, to decline.'

Sir Michael selects three principles which he insists should lie behind one's approach to continuing corporate success towards 2000. The first is a 'continuing restless dissatisfaction with the status quo. You know, there is never a time when you say in a business, "Right we're OK; we've achieved it, we've got the organization right, we've got the growth factors in and so on." At whatever level you are in the business you have got to challenge the status quo all the time. You have constantly to be saying, "Are there ways in which we can do this better?" The chairman or managing director of the business, and indeed all line managers, have to be continually saying, "What in the status quo can we be dissatisfied with today?" Businesses don't have a choice. Businesses can't stand still. I know of no business that stood still. They either grow or they decline. That is a reality. Things will ensure you do decline if you're not seeking growth. You could be seeking growth like hell and thrusting and pushing, and you stand still. That's OK, because it's the belief in growth that has to be right through a business. Everybody wants to be in a growth business. Growing businesses are not just for the shareholders' benefit – if a business is growing, staff feel happier because they see more opportunity, feel more stability, they feel greater job security. The continuing involvement of people is an organic process which doesn't stand still.' I am reminded of the wise saying of my Highland gran on that point: quite simply, if you are coasting you are going downhill!

The second principle Sir Michael highlights for millennium success is 'your success depends upon *people*. The motivation, organization and training of people. These are going to be consistent things for the future. The days of the old mill manager who would come out in the morning and tell you what you've got to do for the week, are over.' Sir Michael's own personal preference for the future style of management for corporate success is that it be non–authoritarian. He has always found 'this approach easier to deal with.' Generalizations can be rather dangerous, but he says there do remain UK businesses which are run on a basis of a boss with the old mill manager mentality: sadly, some family businesses are still a bit like that. However, he insists this has not been the case with the family businesses he has been associated with – Whitbread, Boots and Unilever.

336

This brings him to his third principle for corporate success in the year 2000. He believes a continuous theme running through the organizations he has been involved with, including Whitbread, is the conviction that social and commercial benefits go hand in hand. Sam Whitbread always believed that 'what is good for society as a whole is of benefit for the company. It is as true today as it was 250 years ago that our business can only thrive if the communities in which we trade are also flourishing.' It is a sentiment – or, more than that, a philosophy – Sir Michael totally endorses. A distinctive feature of Whitbread is its Community Investment Programme. Most decisions on projects it supports are made locally by people in direct touch with the specific needs of their area. By working in partnership with local authorities, schools, colleges and voluntary organizations the company is able to ensure that maximum benefit is achieved. Whitbread invested some £1.8 million last year in such activities and a further £2 million was raised for charitable activities in its businesses. In addition, the company has been at the forefront of the employee volunteering movement in the UK and actively encourages Whitbread people to become involved in their local community through fundraising and practical support. Organized through twenty-four site committees, thousands of its employees contributed their time and energy. As a result, Whitbread last year was named overall winner of the Employees in the Community Award.

'There has been a culture that is perhaps difficult to define but concerns community responsibility.' says Sir Michael. 'It is about ensuring the community you operate in is being treated responsibly by everybody, including yourself. I see that characteristic strongly here in Whitbread, where we have the most amazing amount of voluntary community service.'

Sir Michael remains a bit sceptical about all this millennium stuff. 'I'm not sure a bell is going to ring and suddenly things will change. I don't see businesses in those dramatic terms. I see business as being a continual hard slog on a number of important fronts. The millennium, of course, is getting close. Most businesses with five-year plans must be embracing it. I suppose it's rather banal to say that I just hope it's a continuing progress in the directions that we forecast, but I can't think of any significant sudden change in business direction that I would be talking about simply because it's the end of the millennium. I just hope we go into the next one as strong a business as we are today; that our strategy is paying off. I believe in cash, rather than

337

profit. I therefore hope our bank account is extremely healthy as we pass through into the year 2000!'

Sir Michael has been a European manager all of his life. He has run companies throughout Europe and categorically states Europe and the single market are a reality. 'As a president of the CBI I got very involved with Europe then, and I'm Britain's representative on the deregulation committee over there, which is great fun! I believe firmly in a Europe of nation states. I am bound to say, every time I go to Brussels, it bruises my belief a little bit. We need to do something about Brussels.'

What of his personal ambitions? 'You know, at sixty-five ambitions for the future are difficult. Immortality is one that occurs to me! No, I think my ambitions are for as long as possible to make a contribution to industry. I don't want to go and play golf. The number of top executives who retire and die quite quickly afterwards is worrying. I believe in run-downs rather than retirement. Ambition — well I haven't really got any major ambitions now. I suppose I'd like to be in the House of Lords where I could preach industrial needs. I'd like some platform, because I believe I have something to say.'

Sir Michael would like to be remembered as a successful industrialist, and I would enjoy hearing him in the House of Lords. As a millennium wish for Whitbread I can think of none better than the words of the first Samuel Whitbread two centuries ago: 'Your family has raised it from a very small beginning, by great assiduity in a very long course of years and with the highest credit in every view by honest and fair dealings. And the beer universally approved and the quantity brewed annually great indeed.'

Index